Introduction to Political Science

An Anthology

FIRST EDITION

EDITED BY John P. Miglietta

Tennessee State University

SAN DIEGO

Bassim Hamadeh, CEO and Publisher
Jennifer Codner, Senior Field Acquisitions Editor
Michelle Piehl, Senior Project Editor
Alia Bales, Production Editor
Emely Villavicencio, Senior Graphic Designer
Greg Isales, Licensing Associate
Natalie Piccotti, Director of Marketing
Kassie Graves, Vice President of Editorial
Jamie Giganti, Director of Academic Publishing

cognella® | ACADEMIC PUBLISHING
3970 Sorrento Valley Blvd., Ste. 500, San Diego, CA 92121

CONTENTS

CHAPTER 1

The Study of Politics

KEY TERMS

Qualitative	State
Quantitative	Political Behavior Approach
Theory	Structural Functional Approach
Independent Variable	Philosophical Approach
Dependent Variable	Rational Choice Theory
Nation	Political Systems Analysis
Legitimacy	French Revolution
Failed States	

DISCUSSION QUESTIONS

1. What is the definition of nation? Discuss some specific examples of national identity and why they are important.

2. What is the definition of a state? What are the components of statehood?

3. What is the significance of theory in political science?

4. Discuss the importance of the different types of variables in developing a social science theory.

5. Relate nationality and political legitimacy.

6. Define and address the significance of the concept of responsibility to protect.

7. What is a failed state? Discuss an example.

8. Address the economic and political significance of the enclosure movement.

POLITICS

What is politics? The political scientist Harold Lasswell has defined politics as "who gets what, when, and how." Politics is often understood as the allocation of resources by the government to satisfy some goal(s). Government establishes policy priorities, takes in resources though taxes, and redistributes across society. The redistribution process is determined by the interaction of political institutions, political parties, interest groups, the media, and public opinion. This is referred to as politics. The goals of government can vary over time and given the type of government. Democracies are accountable to the people because of elections. Some government systems want to increase the power of the state (i.e., fascism) and focus on policies that promote heavy industry and the military. Other governments want to redistribute wealth to their citizens and provide education, health care, and relatively high standards of living. An example of this would be countries that have a social democratic ideology.

POLITICAL SCIENCE

Political science is an academic discipline that attempts to predict political behavior. It is divided into various subfields. The major ones are American politics, comparative politics, international relations, and research methods. Each of these fields can be divided into numerous other subfields. For example, in international relations, scholars can focus on international security, political economy, and international organizations to name a few.

Qualitative versus Quantitative Approaches

There is a major debate in the field between qualitative and quantitative approaches. **Qualitative** analysis looks at political science as more of an art. It focuses a great deal on studying aspects of culture, history, geography, religion, and sociology in an effort to explain political behavior. **Quantitative** proponents emphasize the "science" part of political science. They focus on data and trying to explain political behavior by using hard numbers.

WHAT IS A THEORY?

Political scientists attempt to gather specific evidence and generalize why, when, and under what conditions a certain type of behavior is likely to happen. An example of this is revolutions. Political scientists who study this attempt to isolate under what conditions revolutions are likely to happen. Researchers start out with a hypothesis, which is what they are trying to prove. At the beginning of a research project, the researcher identifies variables. Variables are factors that affect the research question. The **independent variable** is something that is constant and affects the **dependent variable**, which is essentially the hypothesis that is trying to be proved. There could also be a countervailing variable, which is between the independent and dependent variables. It acts as both a dependent and an independent variable.

For example, when attempting to research why the Russian Revolution of October 1917 occurred, researchers have argued that the strain the state was under because of World War I weakened it and allowed the revolution to occur:
- Independent Variable: World War I
- Countervailing Variable: The toll World War I took on the Russian state, especially the military and security services.
- Dependent Variable: This weakening of the state led to the revolution of October 1917.

NATION VERSUS STATE

Nation is an abstract concept in which people are united based on a common language, history, culture, and/or religion. Most nations have one or more of these factors present. Nationalism is the passionate identification people have for a nation-state. This process started with the American and

French Revolutions when people began to think of themselves as citizens of a state as opposed to subjects of a ruler. For example, in France, the links that bind the country are a strong identification with the French language and culture. This is also a way that immigrants to the country can become integrated.

State is a political unit with a defined territory, population, and government that can make and enforce laws, and it has the ability to conduct relations with other states. Symbols of statehood include a flag, national anthem, and government institutions, as well as representation in international organizations. Some states have the symbols of statehood but a very weak sense of nationhood. An example is Afghanistan. It is made up of diverse ethnic groups. Its geography is very mountainous; a large percentage of the population lives in rural mountainous areas that are very remote from large population centers. As a result, the authority of the government is very limited in these areas, even in the best of times. Likewise, there are some groups that have a strong sense of national identity, such as the Kurds of the Middle East. The Kurds are a separate and distinct ethnic group. They occupy significant portions of Iran, Iraq, Syria, and Turkey. They speak a distinct language and have a strong sense of history. However, for the Kurds to achieve their national aspirations, several countries would have to lose territory. In addition, an independent Kurdistan could also upset the balance of power in the Middle East, which draws the interest of regional and international powers. As a result, Kurdish attempts at national independence have been limited. Currently, only the Kurds in Iraq enjoy a type of autonomy. Traditionally, various countries have sought to use the Kurds against their rivals. During the Iran-Iraq War, the Iranian government assisted the Iraqi Kurds against the Baghdad government. Iraq, at the same time as they were oppressing their own Kurds, aided the Iranian Kurds.

Failed States: Some established states have disintegrated as their governments have collapsed due to a crisis of political **legitimacy**. Examples of this include Yugoslavia and East Germany as their governments collapsed with the fall of communism in 1989. Six new states were created out of the former Yugoslavia. The former German Democratic Republic (East Germany) was incorporated into the Federal Republic of Germany (West Germany) forming a united Germany.

MAJOR APPROACHES IN POLITICAL SCIENCE

- **Political Behavior Approach**: Focuses on how individuals act politically and seeks explanations for the behavior of individuals. How do human beings act politically?
- **Structural Functional Approach**: Identifies important political roles in society. What roles are performed politically, and how does this affect the governance of society?
- **Philosophical Approach**: Attempts to look at the meaning of political life. Looks at larger questions of justice and what the ideal state should be.
- **Rational Choice Theory**: Attempts to model political behavior by analyzing verbal and mathematical data to anticipate political outcomes.
- **Political Systems Analysis**: This approach studies an entire nation attempting to look at the institutions and processes of a political system in an effort to explain political behavior.

ENLIGHTENMENT ECONOMICS AND THE FRAMING OF THE U.S. CONSTITUTION

Renée Lettow Lerner

Did the Framers have an economic theory in mind when they wrote and ratified the U.S. Constitution? Some say the principal Framers did not have a common, cohesive set of views on economics.[1] Others consider the question to be irrelevant. Society and constitutional interpretation have moved on, these commentators argue, so what the Framers thought or whether they embedded economic views in the Constitution has about as much relevance today as a typewriter. Another possible position is that the Framers might have had common understandings about economics but largely left them out of the Constitution, except in odd bits like the Contracts Clause or the Takings Clause.

The principal Framers did, in fact, share a basic set of economic views, though they did not agree on all economic questions. These economic views permeate the Constitution and are not manifest only in odd clauses. Many structural features of the Constitution are designed to further desirable economic ends, as the Framers envisioned them.

Economic Principles of the Enlightenment

What was the content of the Framers' economic beliefs, and where did those beliefs come from? These economic beliefs were shared throughout Europe in the late eighteenth century, although events in America helped to reinforce them.

Historians and students of philosophy have long explored the political thought of the Enlightenment: the contractual theories of Locke, the checks and balances of Montesquieu, and so forth. This political thought, however, went hand in hand with Enlightenment economic thought.

To understand the Enlightenment economic thought that the Framers shared with many in Europe, it is necessary to understand the workings of the old regime. Guilds, monopolies, and mercantilism characterized that regime. The guilds formed an elaborate regulatory apparatus. To have a dress made in France, for example, one had to buy cloth from a draper, get accessories or ornaments from the mercer, and bring it all to a tailor, who then set to work according to the rules established by his guild for cutting cloth.[2] The tailor was forbidden to stock or sell cloth.[3] If these practices resemble union work rules today, that is not an accident. Governments sold monopolies, or patents as they were known, on the manufacture, exportation, or importation of coal, soap, starch, iron, leather, books, wine, and fruit—in short, on almost everything imaginable—to raise revenue.[4] Colonial Americans resented English mercantilism in the form of the Navigation Acts, which required colonists to export certain goods only to

---

1   *See, e.g.,* Charles A. Beard, An Economic Interpretation of the Constitution of the United States 189–216 (1913) (describing the differing economic views of the Framers).

2   Philippe Perrot, Fashioning the Bourgeoisie: A History of Clothing in the nineteenth Century 36 (Richard Bienvenu trans., Princeton Univ. Press 1994) (1981) (describing ancient régime practices for the making and selling of clothing in the eighteenth century).

3   *Id.*

4   *See* P.J. Federico, *Origin and Early History of Patents,* 11 J. Pat. Off. Soc'y 292, 292–95 (1929).

Renée Lettow Lerner, "Enlightenment Economics and the Framing of the U.S. Constitution," Harvard Journal of Law and Public Policy; vol. 35, no. 1, pp. 37–46. Copyright © 2012 by Harvard Society for Law and Public Policy. Reprinted with permission. Provided by ProQuest LLC. All rights reserved.

England or its colonies and to conduct their trade entirely on English or colonial vessels.[5]

These old-regime economic ideas dominated thought and policy throughout Europe in the first half of the eighteenth century. Commerce was viewed as a "kind of warfare";[6] mercantilism was widespread. Gradually, in the second half of the eighteenth century, different economic ideas took hold. Thinkers praised free trade as leading to economic growth for all participants; trade was seen less and less as a zero-sum game. Rent-seeking (the transfer of wealth from producers to non-producers through political power) and monopolies came under increasing attack. Most prominent among Enlightenment economists was Adam Smith at the University of Edinburgh. Smith's arguments in favor of free trade are well-known. In *The Wealth of Nations,* published in 1776, he called monopolies the "great enemy of good management."[7] Other thinkers also praised free trade and condemned monopolies, even before publication of *The Wealth of Nations.* Montesquieu, in the first edition of *The Spirit of the Laws,* published in 1748, discussed how trade brought prosperity to all participants and declared: "The natural effect of commerce is to lead to peace."[8]

In Britain, these ideas had political consequences. The old economic regime was passing away, despite the restrictions on the colonies. As historian Joel Mokyr puts it, Britain by the mid-eighteenth century had "free internal trade, weak guilds, a relatively effective fiscal system, and a state that was firmly committed to protection of property."[9] This relative economic freedom encouraged the gradual improvements in technology that drove the industrial revolution. In continental countries, the old economic regime lasted longer. France struggled free from it in a bloody revolution and aftermath from which it took decades to recover. Eventually, however, the countries of Western Europe instituted Enlightenment economic principles to one degree or another and experienced their own industrial and agricultural revolutions accordingly.

Enlightenment Economics and the U.S. Constitution

Fortunately for the new Republic, two of the most important Founders least affected by Adam Smith's thought were not at the convention in Philadelphia. John Adams was a Malthusian pessimist,[10] Thomas Jefferson an idealistic agrarian,[11] and both were busy in Europe during the summer of 1787. Benjamin Franklin, another agrarian, was at Philadelphia but in his dotage. At center stage in the Constitutional Convention were those who had studied *The Wealth of Nations* carefully and had absorbed its principles. These delegates included James Madison and Alexander Hamilton.[12]

If the most important Framers in Philadelphia largely shared the economic views of prominent Enlightenment thinkers such as Adam Smith and Montesquieu, why do we see so few direct traces in the Constitution? To be sure, there are the Contracts Clause[13] and the Takings Clause,[14] evidence

---

5   *See* Second Navigation Act, 12 Car. 2, c. 18 (1663) (Eng.).

6   JOEL MOKYR, THE ENLIGHTENED ECONOMY: AN ECONOMIC HISTORY OF BRITAIN 1700–1850, at 64 (2009) (quoting Josiah Child, seventeenth-century mercantilist and economist).

7   ADAM SMITH, AN INQUIRY INTO THE NATURE AND CAUSES OF THE WEALTH OF NATIONS 149 (Kathryn Sutherland ed., Oxford Univ. Press reissue 2008) (1776).

8   CHARLES DE SECONDAT, BARON DE MONTESQUIEU, THE SPIRIT OF THE LAWS 338 (Ann M. Cohler et al. eds., Cambridge Univ. Press 1989) (1748).

9   MOKYR, *supra* note 6, at 65.

10   *See* FORREST MCDONALD, NOVUS ORDO SECLORUM: THE INTELLECTUAL ORIGINS OF THE CONSTITUTION 99 (1985).

11   *Id.* at 106–108 (arguing that agrarian French physiocrats, including François Quesnay, significantly influenced both Jefferson and Franklin).

12   *See id.* at 128; RON CHERNOW, ALEXANDER HAMILTON 347, 376–77 (2004); ROBERT ALLEN RUTLAND, JAMES MADISON: THE FOUNDING FATHER 54 (1987).

13   U.S. CONST. art. I, § 10, cl. 1.

14   U.S. CONST. amend. V.

of the importance to the Framers of upholding contracts and protecting private property from government interference. Many of the broad principles of Enlightenment economics, however, such as promoting free trade and preventing monopolies and rent-seeking, would have been difficult to enact directly. One could imagine a variety of exceptions under different circumstances that would make it hard to draft a general rule. In the area of patents for intellectual property, the Framers actually sanctioned monopolies in the Constitution itself,[15] though not without controversy. We therefore, for the most part, should not expect to find direct enactment of these ideas.

Nonetheless, the Framers crafted numerous parts of the Constitution to further these principles indirectly. I will discuss four of them here: (1) the Commerce Clause;[16] (2) the interstate and alien diversity clauses;[17] (3) the elaborate procedures of bicameralism and presentment for enacting bills (and the provision allowing the Senate to amend financial bills);[18] and (4) the enumerated limitations on legislative power.[19]

The clause giving Congress the power to regulate interstate and foreign commerce was intended to prevent the States from restricting trade. This purpose can be difficult to remember in our post-New Deal era, when the clause is used to justify congressional regulation of almost every conceivable action, including the growing of marijuana for one's own consumption.[20] Concern that the States would restrict trade was not merely hypothetical. The States were imposing tolls and tariffs on each other and attempting to do the same with foreign commerce, as well as creating monopolies that restricted trade.[21]

The case of *Gibbons v. Ogden*[22] perfectly illustrates how the Commerce Clause was intended to operate. The state of New York, in unenlightened old-regime fashion, granted a monopoly on steamship travel in New York waters to two investors.[23] Congress had enacted its own, non-monopoly licensing scheme governing ships. The Supreme Court invalidated New York's monopoly, citing Congress's power under the Commerce Clause.[24] In one blow, the Court, applying the Commerce Clause, simultaneously struck down one of the most despised features of the old economic regime—the monopoly—and furthered one of the Enlightenment economists' chief goals: free trade.

The interstate and alien diversity clauses concerning federal jurisdiction in Article III also were based on a desire to increase trade. The Framers realized that trade could not flourish if out-of-state and foreign merchants suffered from bias against them in state courts. During the Virginia ratifying convention, in June 1788, James Madison argued in favor of federal diversity jurisdiction for this reason: "We well know, Sir, that foreigners cannot get justice done them in these [state] Courts, and this has prevented many wealthy Gentlemen from trading or residing among us."[25] The same difficulty applied to out-of-state merchants. To this day, a number of businesses fear bias in state courts, and make litigation and commercial

---

15   U.S. Const. art. I, § 8, cl. 8.

16   U.S. Const. art. I, § 8, cl. 3.

17   U.S. Const. art. III, § 2.

18   U.S. Const. art. I, § 7.

19   *See* U.S. Const. art. I, §§ 8–9.

20   *See* Gonzales v. Raich, 545 U.S. 1, 28 (2005) (holding that under the Commerce Clause, Congress may regulate the growing of marijuana for the grower's consumption).

21   *See* McDonald, *supra* note 10, 102–106.

22   Gibbons v. Ogden, 22 U.S. (9 Wheat.) 1 (1824).

23   *Id.* at 2.

24   *Id.* at 186.

25   Anthony J. Bellia, Jr. & Bradford R. Clark, *The Federal Common Law of Nations,* 109 Colum. L. Rev. 1, 38–39 n.187 (2009) (quoting 10 The Documentary History of the Ratification of the Constitution 1469 (John P. Kaminski & Gaspere J. Saladino eds., 1993)); *see also* Bradford R. Clark, *Federal Common Law: A Structural Reinterpretation,* 144 U. Pa. L. Rev. 1245, 1348 n.507 (1996) (noting Madison's support for diversity jurisdiction).

decisions accordingly.[26] The continuing perception of bias in state courts suggests problems with many limitations on diversity jurisdiction, including the requirement of complete diversity.[27]

The Framers also designed the legislative process to further commerce and to prevent rent-seeking indirectly. They viewed faction as one of the greatest dangers to a republic. Madison defined a faction in *Federalist* No. 10 as a "number of citizens, whether amounting to a majority or minority of the whole, who are united and actuated by some common impulse of passion, or of interest, adverse to the rights of other citizens, or to the permanent and aggregate interests of the community."[28] One form of faction is the modern, rent-seeking interest group. In *Federalist* No. 10, Madison confidently declared that factions would not easily be able to attain their ends under the Constitution because of the diversity of interests in a large republic.[29] He referred to the difficulty of a faction getting its program through "the national council."[30] He and his fellow Framers had carefully designed the federal legislative process as a system of checks and balances to thwart faction. Through bicameralism and presentment, each chamber could check the other, and the President could check both.[31] The Framers believed that this elaborate process would help to weed out faction-inspired measures that were rent-seeking.

The Framers also were alert to the dangers of "tacking." Tacking is a procedure in which an unrelated measure is "tacked" to, for example, an appropriations bill to encourage legislators who would not otherwise vote for either measure to do so. Tacking can be a form of logrolling. The members of the Philadelphia convention discussed the problem of legislative tacking in detail at several different points.[32] The convention concluded that the President's veto and each chamber's power to amend the other's bills to strip out extraneous provisions were sufficient safeguards against tacking. This is why Article I, Section 7, which sets out the House's power to originate bills for raising revenue, carefully preserves the Senate's power to amend those bills.[33] This analysis has interesting implications for reconciliation procedure, earmarks, and other notable features of the legislative process today.

Finally, the Framers intended the enumerated powers of Congress to limit the subjects the national legislature could address. This limitation served not only to preserve powers in the States, but also to control the possibilities for national rent-seeking and congressional interference in the economy. An exchange between Nancy Pelosi and a CNSNews.com reporter in October 2009 illustrates the modern fate of the idea of enumerated powers in Congress:

---

26   *See* Jerry Goldman & Kenneth S. Marks, *Diversity Jurisdiction and Local Bias: A Preliminary Empirical Inquiry,* 9 J. LEGAL STUD. 93, 104 (1980) ("Both survey groups have acknowledged that fear of local bias enters the calculus of decision in selecting a judicial forum."); *see also* Neal Miller, *An Empirical Study of Forum Choices in Removal Cases Under Diversity and Federal Question Jurisdiction,* 41 AM. U. L. REV. 369, 408–409 (1992) ("The bases of client-related bias that defense counsel reported to be the most common were out-of-state status (50.7%) and business/corporation status (44.8%).").

27   *See* Strawbridge v. Curtiss, 7 U.S. (3 Cranch) 267 (1806); *see also* Tammy A. Sarver, *Resolution of Bias: Tort Diversity Cases in the United States Courts of Appeals,* 28 JUST. SYS. J. 183, 194 (2007) ("The finding that federal court judges do not tend to favor non-diverse (in-state) litigants over the diverse party suggests that the prerogative of invoking diversity jurisdiction goes a considerable way to eliminate the potential for state court bias, real or perceived.").

28   THE FEDERALIST NO. 10, at 78 (James Madison) (Clinton Rossiter ed., 1961).

29   *See id.* at 83–84; *see also* THE FEDERALIST NO. 51, *supra* note 28, at 323 (James Madison).

30   THE FEDERALIST NO. 16, *supra* note 28, at 115 (Alexander Hamilton).

31   *See* Michael Rappaport, *The President's Veto and the Constitution,* 87 Nw. U. L. REV. 735, 742 n.16 (1993) (citing 2 JONATHAN ELLIOT, THE DEBATES IN THE SEVERAL STATE CONVENTIONS ON THE ADOPTION OF THE FEDERAL CONSTITUTION 86 (1937) and JAMES MADISON, NOTES OF DEBATES IN THE FEDERAL CONVENTION OF 1787, at 385–86 (1987 edition) (original year)).

32   *Id.* at 746 n.33–34 (citing 2 MAX FARRAND, THE RECORDS OF THE FEDERAL CONVENTION OF 1787, at 233, 263, 273, 275–76, 545–46 (1966)).

33   U.S. CONST. art I, § 7. "[B]ut the Senate may propose or concur with Amendments as on other Bills." *Id.*

CNSNews.com: "Madam Speaker, where specifically does the Constitution grant Congress the authority to enact an individual health insurance mandate?"

Mrs. Pelosi: "Are you serious? Are you serious?"

CNSNews.com: "Yes, yes I am."[34]

Mrs. Pelosi then shook her head before taking a question from another reporter.[35] Her press spokesman later clarified the Speaker's meaning: "You can put this on the record. That is not a serious question. That is not a serious question."[36] There is a stylistic similarity between Mrs. Pelosi and her spokesman. Alas, terse repetitions do not substitute for reasoned debate about constitutionality of the sort that used to go on regularly in both chambers of Congress and that fill up pages of the old *Congressional Record*.[37]

Legislators are not the only officials with a lax sense of their constitutional responsibilities. Recent presidents have failed to exercise their veto power as earlier ones did, instead contenting themselves with issuing signing statements that object to the constitutionality of particular provisions. Past presidents vetoed bills containing provisions they deemed unconstitutional, including, occasionally, bills they otherwise thought good policy. President Washington explained that his first veto was based on constitutional grounds[38]

and his successors through Andrew Jackson similarly explained the vast majority of their vetoes.[39] In vetoing the Internal Improvements Bill in 1817, President Madison delivered a message that included the following:

> I am not unaware of the great importance of roads and canals and the improved navigation of water courses, and that a power in the National Legislature to provide for them might be exercised with signal advantage to the general prosperity. But seeing that such a power is not expressly given by the Constitution, and believing that it can not be deduced from any part of it without an inadmissible latitude of construction and a reliance on insufficient precedents; believing also that the permanent success of the Constitution depends on a definite partition of powers between the General and the State Governments, and that no adequate landmarks would be left by the constructive extension of the powers of Congress as proposed in the bill, I have no option but to withhold my signature from it.[40]

There are recent glimmers that some citizens and officials are paying more attention to the enumerated powers set out in the Constitution. In each Congress since the 104th (January 1995 to January 1997), a bill known as the Enumerated Powers Act has been introduced in the House of Representatives. The bill would require that every bill specify the constitutional

---

34   Matt Cover, *When Asked Where the Constitution Authorizes Congress to Order Americans to Buy Health Insurance, Pelosi Says: "Are You Serious?"*, CNSNEWS.COM (Oct. 22, 2009), http://www.cnsnews.com/node/55971.

35   *Id.*

36   *Id.*

37   On November 14, 2011, the U.S. Supreme Court granted certiorari to consider several questions relating to the constitutionality of the Patient Protection and Affordable Care Act, Pub. L. No. 111–148, 124 Stat. 119 (2010), as amended by the Health Care and Education Reconciliation Act of 2010, Pub. L. No. 111–152, 124 Stat. 109 (2010). *See* Florida *ex rel.* Atty. Gen. v. HHS, 648 F.3d 1235, 1241 (11th Cir. 2011) *cert. granted,* 11-393, 2011 WL 5515162 (U.S. Nov. 14, 2011) and *cert. granted,* 11-398, 2011 WL 5515164 (U.S. Nov. 14, 2011) and *cert. granted in part,* 11-400, 2011 WL 5515165 (U.S. Nov. 14, 2011). The Eleventh Circuit held that the Act's individual mandate to buy health insurance was unconstitutional; the Sixth Circuit and the D.C. Circuit held that it was within Congress's power under the Commerce Clause. *See id.; see also* Seven-Sky v. Holder, No. 11-5047, 2011 WL 5378319 (D.C. Cir. Nov. 8, 2011); Thomas More Law Ctr. v. Obama, 651 F.3d 529, 534 (6th Cir. 2011).

38   *See* ROBERT SPITZER, THE PRESIDENTIAL VETO 27–28 (1988).

39   *See* EDWARD CAMPBELL MASON, THE VETO POWER: ITS ORIGIN, DEVELOPMENT AND FUNCTION IN THE GOVERNMENT OF THE UNITED STATES 129 (Albert Bushnell Hart ed., 1890).

40   James Madison, Veto Message on the Internal Improvements Bill (Mar. 3, 1817) (transcript available at http://millercenter.org/scripps/archives/speeches/detail/3630).

provision giving Congress the power to enact it.[41] At the beginning of the 112th Congress, in January 2011, the House adopted a new part of a House Rule requiring the sponsor of a bill or resolution to submit a statement "citing as specifically as practicable the power or powers under the Constitution authorizing the enactment of that bill or joint resolution."[42] The new House leadership organized briefings for House staff and circulated a memo to members on how to comply with the new requirement.[43]

If the enumerated powers set out in the Constitution are thought to be too restrictive, the proper solution is to amend the Constitution, not to distort certain provisions beyond recognition. Although amendments to the Constitution have become very rare, in earlier times—when judges and other officials and citizens took the language of the Constitution more seriously—amendments were more frequent.[44] They might become so again. There is nothing radical about the idea of a constitutional amendment to give Congress the power to regulate environmental pollution, for example. Such an amendment might well garner the necessary political support to be ratified.

If constitutional language is not taken seriously and regularly amended, a dangerous vision of the Constitution arises: the constitutional text as a fossil, an outdated relic that must have life breathed into it by "creative" interpretations. This is the current notion of a "living Constitution." This vision invites much mischief. Among other things, Congress sinks into sloppy practices leading to economic favoritism and massive intrusions into the economy, the President

becomes a party to these practices and fails to protect the common good of the entire nation, and judges— particularly Supreme Court justices—alternately ignore their proper constitutional responsibilities and award enormous political power to themselves to act like unelected and unreviewable legislators. Of course the Constitution should be "living," in the sense of having meaning relevant to current activities. Few would want an irrelevant Constitution. The question is "living" by what means?

The Framers designed the Constitution to further certain core principles of Enlightenment economic thought: protecting private property, enforcing contracts, preventing monopolies, and encouraging free trade among states and nations. In some clauses these principles are explicit.[45] In others, the Framers allocated powers and arranged procedures to further these principles indirectly. Interpreting these clauses according to their animating economic principles enriches our understanding of constitutional meaning and guards against judges' fancies or political fads. Such interpretation might well be more practicable than some think and might have the added benefit of salutary economic effects. Just as deviation from this animating understanding occurred in different branches of government and the electorate over time, a return to this understanding might require broad encouragement. Support and, indeed, virtue among legislators, government officers, judges, and ultimately, voters are important to maintain the economic principles the Founders sought to encourage through the framing of the Constitution.

---

41 *See* John Shadegg, *Enumerated Powers Act*, John Shadegg Congress, http://www.johnshadegg.com/issues/enumerated.aspx (last visited Nov. 1, 2011). The Tea Party movement has been calling attention to this proposal. *See, e.g., HR 450 Enumerated Powers Act*, Tea Party News Watch (Nov. 8, 2009), http://teapartynewswatch.com/hr-450-enumerated-powers-act/. *See* The Enumerated Powers Act of 2011, H.R. 125, 112th Cong. (2011); *see also* 157 Cong. Rec. 1, H37 (daily ed. Jan. 5, 2011). In January 2011, the House Judiciary Committee referred the most recent version of the Enumerated Powers Act to the Subcommittee on the Constitution. *H.R. 125: Enumerated Powers Act*, Govtrack.us, http://www.govtrack.us/congress/bill.xpd?bill=h112-125 (last visited Nov. 1, 2011).

42 H.R. Res. 5, 112th Cong. (2011) (enacted).

43 *See* Richard E. Cohen, *House GOP: Bills Will Have to Cite Constitution*, Politico (Dec. 20, 2010, 10:01 AM), http://politico.com/news/stories/1210/46565.html.

44 *See* Janice C. May, *Constitutional Amendment and Revision Revisited*, 17 Publius 153, 162–68 (1987).

45 *E.g.*, U.S. Const. amend. V (Takings Clause).

CHAPTER 2

Ideology

KEY TERMS

Anarchism

Habeas Corpus Act

Lumpenproletariat

Imperialism

Natural Rights

Karl Marx

Liberalism

John Locke

Common Law

Mikhail Bakunin

Nationalism

Glorious Revolution

Communism

Nihilism

Classical Conservatism

Edmund Burke

Fascism

DISCUSSION QUESTIONS

1. Identify the five stages of human history as defined by Karl Marx.

2. Address the values of classical conservatism.

3. What was the significance of the Glorious Revolution?

4. Compare and contrast anarchism and socialism.

5. Identify and discuss the significance of three qualities of fascism.

6. Address the significance of John Locke's idea of natural rights.

7. Define nationalism and discuss its impact.

THE DEVELOPMENT OF IDEOLOGY

Ideology is an important component in the study of politics. It provides individuals with a value system of how the world does or should work. Many political movements are characterized by a distinct ideology that guides their political behavior. Ideology is an important component of the modern political world. It is action oriented and future focused.

The development of ideology can be traced to the challenges against monarchy and the evolution of political institutions. Ideologies tend to be labeled left, center, and right. Typically, ideologies such as Marxism and socialism are on the left, while liberalism and conservatism tend to cluster around the center, with monarchism and fascism on the right. The development of the political spectrum began as a result of the French Revolution. In the seating of the national assembly, those who supported the king sat on the right of the chamber while those who were against the king sat on the left.

GENERAL IDEOLOGICAL PERSPECTIVES

Anarchism

Anarchism developed as a reaction against large bureaucratic monarchies. Many of the early anarchists were pacifists who believed that government oppressed people and that people would do better if they governed their own affairs. It is a common misconception that anarchists believe in no government, but, actually, anarchists believe in a very limited form of government. Many anarchists were also against the institutions that propped up the state, such as organized religion.

Anarchism was divided into several tendencies. The earliest manifestations of anarchism were pacifists. Pacifists are people who do not believe in any forms of violence. They argued that people were naturally good, and it was the state that was an instrument of violence.

Anarchism also had a radical stage in which people challenged the state by attacking its symbols and institutions. This was especially true in Russia in the latter portion of the nineteenth century. Among the officials that were assassinated was Tsar Alexander II, who was known as the tsar liberator because he emancipated the serfs.

One of the more famous of the anarchists was **Mikhail Bakunin**, who was the "father" of **nihilism**. The nihilists believed in violence and the smashing of the state. Bakunin talked about arming the underclass, "the lumpenproletariat." The **lumpenproletariat** was defined as criminals, the homeless, etc.

Communism

Communism is the belief developed by the political thinker **Karl Marx** that focused on looking at how society is organized based on social class and the control of the means of production. Marx looked at human history as a struggle between social classes. Essentially, those who controlled the means of production and those who did not. The following are the five stages of human society as discussed by Marx.

Communal Society

This was precivilization. There were no private property goods and tools were held in common.

Human beings were hunters and gathers following the herds and cooperating to gather food, hunt, find shelter, and for defense.

Slave Society

As human beings developed agriculture and domesticated animals, they began to settle down and develop communities, which led to civilizations. These civilizations needed a governing structure, which usually centered on a monarchy. In addition to monarchs having political power, they also had a central position in the religion. Often, they were viewed as gods. Virtually everything was owned by the ruler who often based political legitimacy on religion. An example of this was the pharaohs of ancient Egypt.

Feudalism
Eventually, society evolved into two social classes: the aristocracy who controlled the agricultural land, which was the principal means of production in an agrarian society, and the peasants who worked the land. An example of this was medieval Europe roughly between 500 and 1500 CE. The nobility owned the land and controlled society economically, politically, and socially. Peasants worked the land and may have had a few rights, but by and large, they were dependent on the nobility.

Capitalism
With the development of industry and a money economy with an emphasis on trade as well as industrial development, the principal social classes changed. Two major social classes are the bourgeoisie who own the means of production (i.e., factories and machinery) and the members of the industrial working class who worked in the factories. They were referred to as the urban proletariat. This period also saw the growth of cities, a direct consequence of industrialization, and the development of centralized nation-states.

Socialism
Because of the contradictions of capitalism, emphasis on profits and limiting costs, competition would force more and more people into the ranks of the proletariat. As a result, resources would be concentrated in fewer and fewer hands, prices would go up, and living conditions would continue to deteriorate. Eventually, the working class would rise up and establish a dictatorship of the proletariat.

Communism
According to Marx, the final stage of human history is the withering away of the state as society reverts to a communal nature.

Socialism
As was the case with most ideologies, Marxism split into a number of different branches. The orthodox Marxists worked for revolution and followed Marxist thought rigidly. However, most socialists were revisionist socialists who thought that socialists could come to power peacefully. They were encouraged by the reforms that were established during the nineteenth century, which included broadening the voting franchise by ending restrictions based on property. This allowed working-class men the right to vote. By the end of the nineteenth century, social democratic parties were represented in most European parliaments.

Liberalism
Liberalism arose in opposition to the growth of strong centralized states. Strong monarchies dominated society and controlled its resources. The dominant economic system was mercantilism in which a state attempted to provide economic incentives to increase its power. This meant promoting military industries and trade. Governments encouraged state-sponsored monopolies. Often the upper classes and the clergy were not taxed, and the tax burden fell disproportionately on the lower and middle classes.

Modern liberalism had its origins in Britain. Unlike other monarchs, the British monarchy had checks on it as a result of several factors:

Common Law

Common law is law based on precedents, previous court decisions. This makes it very difficult for the king to change laws quickly.

Habeas Corpus Act 1679

Habeas corpus is a legal concept that means defendants must be informed of the charges against them. This allows defendants to prepare a defense. It also places limitations on state authorities, as they cannot hold people indefinitely.

Glorious Revolution 1688

The **Glorious Revolution** saw the overthrow of James II. James II was an autocrat who sought to rule without Parliament and ended up angering many constituency groups, with the exception of the Catholics. The overthrow of James II led to greater independence and power for the British House of Commons. John Locke was involved in this event. This led to the adoption of the English Bill of Rights and greater limitations on the monarchy.

John Locke

John Locke developed the idea of natural rights. **Natural rights** are rights people have because they are human beings. They are not given by the government nor can they be taken away unless the government goes through a due process. The three concepts of natural rights are life, liberty, and property. Property is a general term; it does not necessarily mean land but your goods and the tools of your trade. Locke was the philosopher of the middle class who challenged the authority of centralized monarchies. The values of Lockean liberalism are limited government, capitalism, and individual rights.

CONCLUSION: LOCKE AND LIBERAL THEORY
Ruth W. Grant

The general presupposition of Locke's political theory is that demonstrative normative theory is possible. Locke's *Second Treatise* deduces a theory of rights and duties from a clearly stated premise, and the argument proceeds logically to conclusions that are meant to be as certain as conclusions of a mathematical proof. The particular presupposition of Locke's political theory is the premise that men are by nature free. On the basis of this premise, Locke seeks to establish standards that distinguish legitimate political power from illegitimate despotism.[1] The general framework for his argument is set by the question of legitimacy. The primary task of any political theory is to identify the criteria by which legitimate and illegitimate power may be distinguished. The argument is further shaped by the need to show that these normative criteria are applicable in practice, and especially that the criteria elaborated by

---

1   "For example, if it be demanded, whether the grand seignoir can lawfully take what he will from any of his people? This question cannot be resolved without coming to a certainty, whether all men are naturally equal; for upon that it turns, and that truth, well settled in the understanding and carried in the mind through the various debates concerning the various rights of men in society, will go a great way in putting an end to them and shewing on which side the truth is" (CU.44).

liberal theorists on the basis of the premise of natural freedom can be defended against the charges made by those who criticize such theories as impracticable. Locke proceeds to show that, on the basis of liberal principles, legitimate governments can be stable and continuous over time in many different communities, each with its own territorial jurisdiction. Moreover, one can clearly know who ought to be obeyed and to what extent. Locke responds to the critics by showing that liberal theory can provide a justification for the duty to obey legitimate authorities while allowing for a right to resist illegitimate power.

It is in Locke's *Essay* that his argument for the possibility of his theoretical enterprise can be found. There he attempts to establish that the truths of morality, personal and political, are available to unaided human reason. Beginning with self-evident propositions, men can link these propositions into demonstrations that will lead to sound conclusions about the moral basis and moral limits of political relations. The certainty of this sort of reasoning follows from the fact that the ideas that are its elements are mixed modes, ideas that men create as models by which to order and understand experience rather than ideas meant to serve as copies of things in our experience. Abstract reasoning affords access to truths of which we can be certain, particularly in the area of ethics. In political theory, such reasoning can provide us with knowledge of the rights and duties of men in society.

Moreover, sound theoretical knowledge of political right, of political legitimacy, has important practical consequences. If the distinction between legitimate authority and power simply is not established theoretically, political authority is undermined, tyrants and usurpers are encouraged, and civil peace is threatened. This is the central failure of theorists of absolute monarchy. By teaching subjects that they have an absolute duty of obedience to whoever is in power, they justify the rule of the strongest and support challengers to established rulers who think they might succeed in establishing a new order. They fail to understand that a duty to obey rightful authority is inseparable from a right to resist the wrongful use of force, and that both are necessary to secure the peace. Political theory, by defining the distinction

between legitimate and illegitimate power, supports both a duty of obedience and a right of resistance. In doing so, successful political theory serves the cause of peace as well as the cause of truth.

Political theory, then, can discover the standards by which governments are to be judged, and it should direct itself to that task above all. But the abstract theoretical argument will be successful only if it can be demonstrated that the standards are applicable to political reality. One must know what the standards are, and also how to recognize when they have been met. For example, whether the right to rule is based on divine gift, consent, or heredity, the legitimate claimant of that divine grant, consent, or hereditary position must be clearly identifiable. The right to rule must also be a right that can be legitimately exercised simultaneously by different men in different political communities but cannot be legitimately claimed simultaneously by many men within the same political community. Moreover, it must be possible to distinguish in practice not only between legitimate government and tyranny, but also between legitimate resistance and anarchy. With these requirements met, a political theorist could claim to have contributed to just and peaceful political life.

Locke's is a liberal political theory. He attempts to meet these requirements for political theory with an argument that begins with the premise that men are by nature equal. The premise of natural equality is identical to the premise of natural freedom. Both can be negatively stated in the same way: there is no natural political authority. Locke's argument proceeds from its premise with the additional understanding that there can be no political authority without a reason for it. Power can be rightfully exercised only as a means to legitimate ends. These ends also are to be inferred from man's natural condition. Men have an equal natural right of preservation, and political authority must consequently be directed toward the preservation of the members of the political community.

These two principles, freedom and preservation, drawn from the natural law, are the touchstones for distinguishing legitimate and illegitimate exercises of power in all social relationships, including political relationships. Any government that sacrifices the safety and prosperity of its citizens for the benefit of its rulers is a tyranny. Any government that operates without the consent of the people is equally illegitimate, a usurpation. The requirement of consent follows directly from the principle of freedom, since with no natural basis for authority, authority can arise only from agreement among equals. In no case can a government be considered legitimate unless it fulfills both requirements. It must be based on consent and serve the public good.

Although Locke recommends a certain sort of government with separated powers and an elected representative assembly, a wide variety of institutional arrangements could meet these requirements for legitimate government. Locke seeks to identify not the best political order, but the basic minimal conditions that every political society must satisfy if it is to have legitimate rule. And there can be legitimate rule in democracies, aristocracies, hereditary monarchies, and tribal kingdoms. But in any form of legitimate government it must be understood that political power is a trust from the community as a whole and that all members of the community, including those in authority, are subject to its laws.

These two ideas taken together are the essential components of the constitutionalist conception that Locke adopts to replace more traditional conceptions of sovereignty. Once it is understood that the law is supreme over any private will and that the people are supreme in the sense that they determine when their trust has been violated, the central issue for political theory no longer is to identify whose will is sovereign.

This dual supremacy is related to Locke's distinction between society and government, and that distinction is the basis for his solution to the practical problem posed by liberal theory. To say that the people are supreme as final judge of the fulfillment of their trust is to say that political authority reverts to the society as a whole when the government is dissolved by a violation of its trust. The supremacy of the law follows from the notion that all members of the society without exception, by consenting to membership in it, obligate themselves to the government of that society so long as the government operates according to its trust.

The distinction between political society and the government created by it permits Locke to argue that a theory based on natural equality can nonetheless justify true political obligation. It is also the basis for his solution to the practical problem of justifying a right of resistance without at the same time justifying anarchy. Because men are by nature equals, political societies can be formed only by unanimous consent of their members. But neither the decision to form a particular sort of government nor the actual legislative decisions of the community need be unanimous. The agreement of each member to join the society entails an agreement to abide by the decisions of the government. Such obligation is necessary to maintain the society, and it can be assumed that no rational man would seek to establish a political unit without the conditions necessary for its continuation. An individual's natural right is exercised not by participation in government, but by the decision to become a member of society. Consent can provide a practical means of determining who is to rule and of establishing lasting obligation to the authorized government without any abridgment of natural freedom. But when the government is dissolved, either through actions harmful to the public good for which there is no legal redress or through alterations of the authorized form of government itself, then all obligation to the government ceases. Yet each individual member remains obligated to the society, if the society remains and can act as a functioning unit to halt the subversion of the government or to establish a new one. A situation of anarchy arises only in the case where government and society have both dissolved and all return to a state of nature. A right of resistance can be exercised by the people in circumstances of clear abuse and before the authorities have been completely transformed without immediately introducing a condition of anarchy.

In making this case, Locke offers his solution to the theoretical problem confronting theorists of his time. One alternative had been to defend a right in Parliament to act on behalf of the people in resisting abuses of the king. But this alternative was incompatible with a defense of mixed and balanced government where king and Parliament were independent and coequal. It tended to undermine the ordinary authority of the king. It also left unanswered the question of a right to resist parliamentary abuses. The second alternative was to locate the right of resistance with the people, keeping the balance within government intact but running the risk of justifying frequent rebellions or anarchy without the possibility of distinguishing between justified resistance to oppression and simple criminal disobedience.

Locke tries to show that mixed and balanced government is compatible with a popular right of resistance. The law rules while the government stands, and society can act to prevent its own dissolution once the government has dissolved. Neither legislative nor executive is given sovereign authority within the government, and the obligation to obedience is not undermined by the right to resist. The right of resistance is exercised by the people acting as a political unit, and it is a carefully limited right. Resistance is justified only when the basic minimal standards for legitimacy are being threatened. Revolution is described not as a step toward realizing an ideal of justice, but as resistance to political degeneration.

But Locke is not entirely successful in his resolution of this problem. The theoretical framework for its solution is in place in the form of a distinction between the dissolution of society and the dissolution of government, but Locke does not resolve all the difficulties presented by the practical application of his principles. Ultimately, each individual must judge for himself whether conditions are such that the government or the society has dissolved, and his obligations with them. This is the radical political individualism characteristic of liberal thought. Each individual is the final judge of his community and its government. And there can be no assurance that these judgments will be made correctly.

But there can be both clearly articulated standards of right and aids to correct judgment as to their applicability in the circumstances. For example, when a conquered people participates in the legislative assembly of a new government, this can be taken as an indication that they consent to the government. When rulers operate in violation of established legal procedures, this can be taken as an indication that they may be overstepping their bounds. Established conventions and institutionalized procedures serve as indicators of legitimate and illegitimate action. They also serve as barriers against the degeneration of a political situation to the point where each individual is left to his own judgment. Resistance is not justified so long as there are legal channels for resolving a dispute. The characteristically liberal emphasis on the legal order is a response to the problems posed by liberal individualism. Or in Locke's terms, an authorized common judge is the solution to the problems posed by the condition where each is his own judge—the condition of natural freedom.

It is a solution in the sense that it is a means of managing the problem, but it cannot do away with the problem once and for all. Locke cannot guarantee that there will never be unjust resistance, just as he cannot assure that there will never be tyrants who manage to secure the allegiance of their subjects. But these are fatal shortcomings only if political theory is expected to provide perfect solutions or guarantees.

It is important to maintain a clear understanding of what political theory and political practice can and cannot do. Locke keeps the reader constantly aware of the gravity of the political problem and of the fragility of human solutions to it. The political problem arises because there is no natural political order. All men are free and equal, and some men are always willing to use force to impose their will on others. There is no natural common authority to ensure that force is always coupled with right. The establishment of such an authority according to principles of right that can be clearly demonstrated goes a long way toward solving the problem. But men strong enough to impose their will in violation of the rights of others always will be tempted to do so, and there will not always be a common authority able to peacefully settle the dispute. We cannot finally overcome our problematic situation.

So Locke does not provide techniques for ensuring that correct political judgments will always be made and enforced; that would be beyond the scope of any political theory. Theory cannot simply secure peace and justice. What it can do—its most important task—is to let men know what political evil is. Or to put it positively, political theory defines political justice, and this is itself the most important prerequisite for keeping the peace.

Locke's attitude toward the political problem is the same as his attitude toward the problem of human understanding. Men cannot know everything, but they can know enough to govern their conduct rationally. Action need not be arbitrary; it can be guided by rational principles of conduct. But the application of those principles to practice will always involve an element of judgment and uncertainty. And some men will simply fail to submit themselves to the guidance of their rational faculties. Government is necessary because of these limits of reason. But government according to reason is possible. The premise of Locke's political argument, that men are naturally free, depends on his view of men as uniquely capable of governing their actions according to reason. His view of legitimate government is of free government understood as government where reason rules according to general laws. Liberal government, with the particular role of the law within it, is an attempt to provide the conditions for impartial, rational, and therefore free government. But Locke, always aware of the limits of human capacities, does not claim to provide a perfect solution. His liberal politics are supported by his estimation, positive and negative, of the extent of human understanding.

Locke's is a cautious liberalism. Unlike some more modern versions, it has not been coupled with a faith in the inevitable progress of human communities. There is instead a constant anxiety about the possibility of political degeneration. Consequently Locke's political theory contains two tendencies that are not entirely harmonious. On the one hand, there is what could be called Locke's conservative side. Locke recognizes that political order is precarious and that change might be for the worse. This is ground for caution concerning change in forms of government and tolerance of less than perfect justice if abuses have not grown general and severe. On the other hand, Locke appears as a radical, urging citizens to be ever watchful for abuses and ready to act before it is too late. Moreover, he chooses justice over the kind of peace that can be found under tyrannies, defining tyranny as a state of war.

This ambivalent attitude is an expression of the central axis of conflict within liberal theory generally. Every liberal theory must find some more or less uneasy reconciliation of the claims of order and revolution, society and the individual. Any theory whose premise is the equal individual rights of each, or natural freedom, must confront the difficulty of justifying stable and effective political authority without violating that premise. Although Locke argues that justification of political authority is the central task of political theory generally, it is clearly a task confronting liberal theory. If the starting point is natural freedom, the question is bound to be the grounds and extent of political obligation—of legitimate authority.

That Locke defines the political question as the question of legitimacy is also one indication of his generally moderate attitude. In both his epistemological and his political investigations, he seems to think it is dangerous both to expect too much and to aim for too little. Utopian expectations and a political theory that concentrates on perfect justice make every real political order appear unjust. This is not a perspective that can provide useful guidance for men who need to know whom to obey and to what extent. Moreover, when expectations are unrealistically high, inevitable disappointment produces nihilistic reactions. And if you simply expect the worst from men, the worst is what you will get. A political theory that finds it necessary to justify the absolute right to the use of force in the hands of one man will provoke in the end "perpetual Disorder and Mischief, Tumult, Sedition and Rebellion" (2T.1).

Locke's attitude, in contrast, gives men their due while recognizing their limitations. A just estimation of men's capacities must be the foundation for any theoretical effort that hopes to offer men practical guidance in managing the political problem and in avoiding the worst that can befall them. Locke demonstrates the necessity for limited horizons, but he also offers the possibility of limited success.

> When we know our own *Strength,* we shall the better know what to undertake with hopes of Success. ... 'Tis of great use to the Sailor to know the length of his Line, though he cannot with it fathom all the depths of the Ocean. 'Tis well he knows, that it is long enough to reach the bottom, at such Places, as are necessary to direct his Voyage, and caution him against running upon Shoals, that may ruin him. (Essay I.1.6)

Bibliography

Locke, John. *Conduct of the Understanding.* 2d ed. Edited by Thomas Fowler. New York: Lenox Hill/Burt Franklin, 1971.
———. *An Essay Concerning Human Understanding.* Edited by Peter H. Nidditch. Oxford: Clarendon Press, 1975; reprinted with corrections, 1979.
———. *Two Treatises of Government.* Edited by Peter Laslett. New York: New American Library, 1960; revised ed., Cambridge: Cambridge University Press, 1963.

Conservatism

Traditional conservatives believed in the importance of a centralized state and traditional institutions, such as the aristocracy and the established church. One of the main proponents of **classical conservativism** was the British statesmen **Edmund Burke**. Burke valued traditional institutions, such as monarchy, the aristocracy, and the established church. He believed that change was good if it developed and strengthened institutions. He detested the French revolution; however, he was supportive of the American Revolution because, he argued, it developed political institutions. He also believed that society should be based on social class. He argued that even though the members of the aristocracy dominated society, they needed to make decisions with the long-term interests of the entire society in mind.

Contemporary Conservativism emphasizes policies of law and order; a unilateralist foreign policy; and economic policies of tax cuts; and the deregulation of business by government. In more recent times conservatives in the United States have become more socially conservative supporting issues such as school prayer, and limitations on abortion. During the first half of the 20th century the Republican Party emphasized economic deregulation. In the second half of the 20th century the Republican Party became much more socially conservative. Social conservatives gained ascendancy in the party with the nomination of Barry Goldwater (R-AZ) for president in 1964. While Goldwater lost by a wide margin social conservatives gained control of the Republican Party. This made possible the elections of Ronald Reagan in 1980 and George W. Bush in 2000. Both these administrations emphasized government deregulation and a favorable business climate, along with a pronounced socially conservative agenda.

WHAT WOULD BURKE DO?

The Neglected Tradition of High Church Conservatism
Daniel McCarthy

Edmund Burke might not like what American conservatism has become. With its devotion to abstract rights, democracy, and perpetual growth, the American Right today looks more like a stepchild of Thomas Paine than an heir to the author of *Reflections on the Revolution in France.* But Burke would recognize the conservative movement's rhetoric of liberty, its anti-elitism, and its alienation from institutions of authority. Those are the hallmarks of a disposition Burke described as "the dissidence of dissent, and the protestantism of the Protestant religion." In 1775, that was how he characterized the creed of Britain's rebellious New England colonies. Today, those words apply to the faith of many in the Republican Party's base.

Burke was no Protestant, though he was not Catholic either. (His mother, wife, and sister were.) He was an Anglican who defended the establishment of the Church of England, even as he eloquently argued for toleration of Dissenters—that is, Protestants—and Catholics. Indeed, he wrote to his friend Thomas Erskine, "I would give a full civil protection ... to Jews, Mahometans, and even pagans." Burke was, in the words of scholar Peter Stanlis, a "High Church Anglican" for whom "the Church of England was Protestant in her national sovereignty, but essentially Catholic in her inherited doctrines and forms of worship."

His attitude toward Dissenters—who sought to disestablish the national church or separate themselves from it—was ambivalent. In the case of the American colonists, he sympathized with their Whiggish political principles (he was a Whig himself, after all), but the philosophy he espoused, most famously in *Reflections,* was a high church conservatism to match his High Church Anglicanism. His understanding of the proper relationship between faith, culture, and politics was very different from that of the radical Protestants, whose antiestablishment views held revolutionary implications for the social order.

High church conservatism may seem odd to Americans accustomed to the culturally Protestant and politically populist low church variety. But Burke was just the first in a long tradition. "A considerable amount of English conservatism," sociologist Robert Nisbet noted, "beginning with Burke and extending to such minds as Coleridge, Newman, Disraeli and Matthew Arnold, was activated and shaped by the religious revolution ... that paralleled the democratic and industrial revolutions."

Not all high church conservatives are Anglican; some are not even religious. Similarly, not all right-wing Anglicans or Catholics are politically high church. Perhaps the majority of Catholic conservatives today, swayed by Republican propaganda, have assimilated downward to the low church conservatism of their allies. The distinction arises not from doctrine but from one's overall approach to politics.

Low church conservatism, more familiar, is readily described. It has five common characteristics. First, it values faith over works—what counts is the character of a politician and the intentions behind his actions, not the outcome of his policies. No man, of course, can read another's soul, thus in practice the low church conservative places great value on professions of ideological purity. Sinning politicians like Newt Gingrich and David Vitter may be forgiven, so long as they say the right things. Disastrous policies—wars gone awry, for example—may be pardoned on account of righteous aims. Conversely, good works count for naught without profession of the right political faith.

Second, low church conservatism retains the anti-clericalism of its religious counterpart. This entails a pervasive anti-elitism. For the low church conservative, a popular broadcaster such as Rush Limbaugh possesses greater authority than a scholar such as Russell Kirk. The former derives his position from (or has it affirmed by) the congregation—his listeners. A Kirk, on the other hand, appears all too priestly. To be right requires no special learning, only acceptance of a basic creed.

A third trait is a tendency toward cultural separatism. The low church conservative prefers building parallel institutions to compromising with existing centers of authority. Sometimes this is commendable. More often, it is not. The proliferation of "conservative" movies, "conservative" dating services, "conservative" universities, and a "conservative" counter-counterculture—complete with "conservative" Che T-shirts—is emblematic. The low church conservative abhors the mainstream; the word itself is a pejorative.

Fourth is a belief that the eschaton is imminent (if not immanent). Every political battle is a clash of titanic principle, a skirmish in the final conflict between light and darkness. Every bellicose dwarf in command of a developing nation is a potential Antichrist, or the geostrategic equivalent, a Hitler. No Saddam or Chavez is merely a tin-pot dictator.

Fifth, and most important, right makes might. Moral truth is easily known, and nothing should stand in the way of its application in policy. The goal of politics is to enact what is right and true. When a Bush administration official told Ron Suskind, "We're an empire now, and when we act, we create our own reality," he was not being cynical. He was naïve: for how could righteous men possessed of great power fail to achieve whatever they set out to do? From this logic, it follows that abortion can be ended and the sexual revolution repealed, if only we elect enough Republicans.

Not all of these convictions are blameworthy. Some are justified. Much of the mainstream culture is irredeemable, even if conservative alternatives are lousy. Truth should prevail in politics: the high church conservative simply pursues this end in a different way, working through customs and institutions rather than against them. There lies a crucial distinction: low church politics dissolves hierarchies and structures. And it proceeds with the self-assurance of the elect, in contrast to the circumspection of high church conservatism.

For the low church conservative, politics is teleocratic—a purpose-driven activity. In the language of British philosopher Michael Oakeshott (very much a high church type), the low church conservative views the state—and perhaps his church, too—as an "enterprise association." The high church conservative, on the other hand, considers the state to be a "civil association," whose enjoyment is its own reward. He believes politics should be nomocratic—a matter of upholding a constitutional framework within which diverse ends can be pursued. As Oakeshott says, "the intimations of government are to be found in ritual, not in religion or philosophy; in the enjoyment of orderly and peaceable behaviour, not in the search for truth or perfection."

Critics of the high church disposition in religion contend that it reduces faith to pure ritual—"bells and smells." A critic of high church conservatism might see in Oakeshott a correspondingly substance-free politics. Irving Kristol, for example, thought Oakeshott's philosophy "irredeemably secular" and "impossible for any religious person."

Yet Oakeshott is exceptional. For Burke and other high church conservatives such as Samuel Taylor Coleridge or Russell Kirk, politics does have limited substantial ends. But those ends are more open than liberal or libertarian critics of conservatism deign to acknowledge. There is a strong inclination among high church conservatives against interfering in the social order except to preserve its constitutional architectonics.

High church conservatism is the opposite of low church. It privileges works over faith, being more concerned with prudent policy than with the inner moral character of politicians or what they profess. It is deferential (sometimes to a fault) to hierarchy and suspicious (also sometimes to a fault) of popular movements and enthusiasm. It is leery of eschatological passions. And above all it works to avoid schism—the high church conservative's objective is to preserve the fabric of society and, so far as possible, elevate its culture. This, he believes, can only be done within the mainstream of national life. For Coleridge and the 19th-century poet and literary critic Matthew Arnold, the function of an established church is less religious than cultural. As Coleridge writes, "Christianity, and *a fortiori* any particular scheme of Theology derived and supposed (by its partizans) to be *deduced* from Christianity, [is] no essential part of the *Being* of the *National* Church, however conducive or even indispensable it may be to its wellbeing ..." Its being, or essence, is in the preservation of culture.

For his part, Matthew Arnold in *Culture and Anarchy* proposed a dramatic solution for low church Protestantism's culturally schismatic tendencies—establish the Presbyterian and Congregational churches alongside the Church of England. That would inject "popular church discipline" into the establishment, while immersing the Protestants in the mainstream of the nation's culture. "Being in contact with the main stream of human life," he writes, "is of more moment for a man's total spiritual growth ... than any speculative opinion which he may hold or think he holds."

Some variation on this principle is an indispensable tenet of any high church conservatism, except perhaps Oakeshott's variety. And it is, of course, completely inapplicable to the American circumstance, where the First Amendment—to say nothing of public opinion—precludes the establishment of any religion. Nor are the federal government's cultural organs, such the National Endowment for the Humanities and the National Endowment for the Arts, sufficient to fulfill the mission that high church conservatives ascribe to a national church. On this rock, the prospects for such conservatism in America might flounder.

But not necessarily. High church conservatism has had a surprisingly robust history in the United States—a country born in a Whiggish and Protestant revolt. There may be less cause for astonishment than one might think. Before the Revolution, and for a while afterward, many of the colonies-cum-states had established churches, either Anglican or Dissenting. Though the Revolution was in no way high church and hastened disestablishment, the Constitutional Convention was another matter. After all, it produced a nomocratic charter, sought to integrate potentially schismatic factions (big states, small states; slave states, free states), and was infused with a spirit skeptical of democracy (inspired in part by Shays's Rebellion). It is even tempting to suggest that the Constitution serves for Americans the same function that the Book of Common Prayer serves for Anglicans: uniting the high church and low in a formal or symbolic way rather than a doctrinally substantive one.

High church conservatives across the Atlantic, however, would be quick to observe that a constitution that fails to provide for continuity of culture may not succeed in perpetuating a form of government, either. To Coleridge, a national church, as a guardian of the national heritage and character, was as integral a part of the constitution as the state itself. Upon it depended "the morality which the State requires in its citizens for its own wellbeing and ideal immortality." This sounds very much like the "constitutional morality" that the American political theorist Willmoore Kendall argued was necessary for the operation of the Constitution—an ethical base to teach Americans how to select virtuous representatives, who in turn would exercise restraint and prudent deliberation in the wielding of power.

American high culture flourished in the 19th century in the absence of any substitute for the national church that Coleridge and Arnold desired, with New England in particular supplying a literature that aspired to be both world-class and quintessentially American. Yet New England's regional culture could not stand in for the constitutional ethos that Coleridge believed was necessary. Perhaps this lack of a national "constitutional" culture is one reason that Americans in the 20th century, waylaid by World War and Depression, drifted from their constitutional course.

The prime task of American conservatism should have been to correct that drift. In the 19th century there had been few self-conscious conservatives, but nomocratic traditions of politics remained strong, even after the disruption of the Civil War. America had discovered a back door to constitutional morality—not through a national church and culture but by way of another high church principle: federalism. The Anglican Communion itself is a federated body, while the Catholic Church has long endorsed the idea of subsidiarity—that needs should be met at the most local level possible, preferably through the institutions of civil society. Federalism was the matrix in which the impressive regional cultures of 19th-century America arose, and it accounts in large part for the survival of the constitutional ethic.

Once federalism had come under assault by successive waves of reformists and progressives, and as Leviathan extended its reach deeper into civil society, an energetic high church conservatism was needed to revitalize the constitutional order. But only the first intimations of such a thing arose in the 1950s, in the work of writers such as Peter Viereck, Russell Kirk, and Robert Nisbet. More than compensating for their salutary influence, however, was the advent of a militant Cold War conservatism. Although the intelligentsia of the Cold War Right was Catholic to a disproportionate degree—think of *National Review,* led not only by Catholic William F. Buckley Jr., but with senior editors Willmoore Kendall, L. Brent Bozell Jr., Frank Meyer, and James Burnham all crossing the Tiber sooner or later—it was also disproportionately populated by ex-radicals and ex-Communists. They retained the marks of their former faith even as they embraced a new one with zeal. The result was not low church conservatism but an ultramontane anti-Communist Right.

A high church Right might have taken its place after the fall of the Soviet Union. But before the end of the Cold War, conservatism in America experienced a Protestant Reformation, as the populist New Right of the 1970s opened the way for an evangelical influx into the Republican Party. For all the righteous energy the Moral Majority, Christian Coalition, and other

Religious Right groups brought to conservatism, they lacked the high church concern for prudence and order. They were teleocratically driven at a time when America needed nomocratic conservatism.

Today, the American Right is divided between low church and "no church" tendencies. On one side are tea-party activists who believe that a renewed commitment to core conservative issues—God, guns, gays, and now taxes—will return the Right to power. On the other side are *soi-disant* "reform conservatives" who are not conservatives at all but social liberals (in the case of David Frum) or social democrats (in the case of the tokens on the editorial page of the *New York Times*). These "no church conservatives" are analogous to the liturgical traditionalists within the Anglican communion who nonetheless want to revise—or really reject—the moral content of traditional theology.

High church conservatism remains to be rediscovered. It will not offer the Right an easy road to power, but then that is not what it is meant to do. More important than reclaiming Congress or the White House, or even "winning" on specific issues, is the task of restoring the constitution—not only the written Constitution but also the cultural framework that must undergird it. Without an institutional, national clerisy, high church conservatives are in the awkward position of having to anoint themselves for the task. But after 30 years of low church conservatism, some alternative must be found.

Fascism

Fascism is an example of a regressive ideology. A regressive ideology idolizes the past and seeks to recapture former values in a society. It appeals to myth and history and what many feel was a better time. Italy and Germany developed fascist ideologies that became dominant after World War I. In Italy, it was a harkening back to the glories of ancient Rome and the desire for empire. Many Italians felt they had been cheated at the Versailles Peace Conference after World War I. They felt Italy had been promised territorial gains that were not delivered. In German fascism, race was more prominent. Many people harkened back to what was viewed as a more stable time. After World War I, Germany lost territory, its colonies, its military was restricted, and it had to pay reparations and admit war guilt. For many Germans, the postwar experience was very chaotic and made worse by the Great Depression.

Qualities of Fascism

Militant Nationalism and the Glorification of the State
The passionate attachment to the nation-state features subordination of the self to the larger community.

Appeal to Myth
This is the glorification of the past and a harkening back to the heroes and myths of the culture. In Italy, the emphasis was on the glorification of ancient Rome. In Germany, the emphasis was on the purity of blood and the myths of German civilization as found in the music of Richard Wagner.

Militarization
The military is an important tool of foreign policy. There is a glorification of war, and the militarization of society. Examples of this include the indoctrination of young children into military-type organizations. In Nazi Germany, the Nazi Party dominated all organizations, with an emphasis on uniforms and military-type organization.

Racism

Part of fascist ideology is favoring some groups over others and justifying discrimination and genocide as well as military conquests. In Italian fascism, Mussolini used racism to justify building an empire in Africa. In Germany, Hitler used racism to justify his conquests in Eastern Europe and the Soviet Union to depopulate the territory and prepare it for German colonization.

Glorification of the Leader

In fascism, there is the central position and glorification of the leader. The leader is supported without question. In Nazi Germany, the military took an oath of loyalty personally to Hitler. This made it very difficult for some of them to go against Hitler, even when they knew World War II was lost.

Imperialism

The conquest of territory to expropriate resources and to have room for colonization was paramount in both Italian and German fascism. Nonfascist governments have practiced **imperialism** as well.

CHAPTER 3

Nationalism and the Development of Modern States

KEY TERMS

Nation

Unitary System

Federalism

Nationalism

Welfare State

Statism

Aristocracy

Divine Theory

Patriotism

Oligarchy

Democracy

State

Confederacy

Laissez-Faire

Monarchy

Natural Theory

Force Theory

Tyranny

Divine Right of Kings Theory

Social Contract Theory

DISCUSSION QUESTIONS

1. Define nationalism and discuss whether it has been a positive or negative force overall.

2. Identify the term "failed state" and discuss its implications. Discuss one or two examples.

3. Address the political and social implications of the divine right of kings theory. Compare and contrast with social contract theory.

4. Discuss the differences between federalism, confederacy, and unitary systems of government.

5. Define and discuss the characteristics of states.

INTRODUCTION: NATION VERSUS A STATE?

What Is a State?
A **state** is defined by four characteristics.

- Permanent population
- Defined territory
- Government with the ability to enforce laws
- Ability to have relations with other states

A state is a political unit with the symbols of government, such as a flag, national anthem, and representation at the United Nations and other international organizations.

What Is a Nation?

A **nation** is a group of people linked by abstract concepts. Nations are united by a common history, language, culture, or religion. Typically, a nation strives to be independent, and in many cases, a nation has a state that it can call its own.

However, in some cases, a society has a strong sense of national identity, but for whatever reason, it does not have a political state. Often, this is because the society's national aspirations conflict with other established states.

An example of this are the Kurds. They are a distinct nationality, and if Kurdistan were independent, it would encompass substantial parts of Turkey, Iraq, and Iran, along with smaller portions of Syria and Armenia.

Likewise, there are established states that have a weak sense of nationalism. An example of this is Afghanistan.

People in Afghanistan are more focused on their respective regions and local areas. Historically, they have viewed the central government with mistrust, as it has done little to help them, only making demands on the people.

WHAT IS NATIONALISM?

Nationalism is the passionate attachment to a nation-state. It has its origins in modern times with the American and French Revolutions. People ban together to fight a common foe. In the French Revolution, people thought of themselves as citizens of the state as opposed to subjects of a king. In the immediate aftermath of the revolution, royal titles were eliminated, and people addressed each other by the term "citizen." Napoleon inadvertently encouraged nationalism through his conquests. Even though he promised reforms many of the peoples of Europe that he conquered saw their country occupied by foreigners and their resources exploited.

Is Nationalism a Positive or a Negative Force?

There are positive examples of nationalism. People feel a sense of loyalty to each other and will support each other in the event of a natural disaster, for instance.

Nationalism can be a negative force as it emboldens people to be militantly nationalistic, which can lead to greater conflict. Nationalism has contributed to modern wars that are long-lasting and brutal.

A failed state is a state that has collapsed. There is no functioning government. Often, the state fragments into several components. An example of this was the former Yugoslavia. After Marshal Tito died and the Communist Party fell apart, Yugoslavia broke up into several states. This led to a period of sustained conflict and, ultimately, NATO intervention.

STATES AND STATEHOOD
K. F. Holsti

Source: *Taming the Sovereigns: Institutional Change in International Politics* (Cambridge University Press, Cambridge, 2004), pp. 28–72.

Holsti identifies the sovereign state as the foundational actor of international relations. Having outlined its essential features, he traces how the practices, ideas, and norms that help to define the state have evolved from the seventeenth century through to the present day. Although now the prevailing form of political authority, Holsti accepts that not all states are successful. But he challenges the widely accepted view that states are becoming obsolete and argues instead that states are becoming more complex.

Societies and smaller groups throughout history have formed organizations that provide and sustain them with security, access to resources, social rules, and means of continuity. Frequently they also devised, embodied, or sought more ephemeral objectives or qualities such as identity, glory, renown, and reputation. The institutional forms they have taken have varied greatly. Even terms we commonly use to designate polities—tribes, clans, empires, principalities, city-states, protectorates, sultanates, or duchies—would not begin to cover the actual diversity of political forms. [...]

Our concern, however, is with states, the only contemporary political organizations that enjoy a unique legal status—sovereignty—and that, unlike other types of polities, have created and modified enduring public international institutions. They are thereby the foundational actors of international relations. Other types of polities may ultimately become states but until they have transformed themselves into public bodies—moral agents representing some sort of community—they do not have the legal standing of states. [...]

Polities that had many but not all the features of states include the Han Empire, the Greek city-states, the Roman state, the Aztec and Inca empires, the Byzantine Empire, and the Italian city-states. We would not include in this list thousands of polities that once may have been politically and militarily formidable but otherwise lacked most of the critical attributes of statehood. The Visigoths, Lombards, Franks, Vandals, and Huns, for example, are better known for their depredations than for political continuity and the creation of international institutions. Others such as the Cimbri, Knights Templars, Samnites, Taurisci, Tigurini, Carbo, or Frisians, have disappeared into the mists of history. They lacked the essential qualities of statehood that provide polities with both legitimacy and longevity. What are these? A non-inclusive list would contain at least the following: (1) fixed position in space (territoriality); (2) the politics of a public realm (differentiation between private and public realms); (3) institutionalized political organizations (continuity independent from specific leaders or other individuals); (4) and a multiplicity of governmental tasks and activities (multifunctionalism), based on (5) legitimizing authority structures. [...]

The Late Seventeenth-Century Westphalian State

At the beginning of the fifteenth century, Europe remained dotted with hundreds of different polities, overlapping jurisdictions, a low degree of differentiation between private and public realms, and divided loyalties. No prince could predictably prevail over his feudal barons, independent towns, or even church authorities. To muster military strength he had to rely on purchasing armies or making alliances with subordinates who had their own—though seasonal—military capacities. By 1700, in contrast, most princes could effectively suppress most challenges to their authority, although the costs of doing so were often ruinous. [...]

Practices: The Great Power Grab

The struggle to establish central authority—to bring to life the various assertions of internal sovereignty—could not be conducted unilaterally by the royal figures. They faced resistance and opposition from a variety of sources, including towns and cities, the landed aristocracy, the church, and the peasantry. In order to prevail they had to make alliances, concede charters and grants of autonomy, buy off the aristocracy, purchase loyalty through the sale of offices, put down rebellions and resistance with force, and, as in the case of Peter's Russia, physically annihilate the opposition. Power and authority during the medieval era had resided in many centers, including the church, local assemblies and councils, and in the various landed estates, towns, duchies, and principalities. In the construction of the Absolutist State, those claiming sovereignty had to curtail the ancient rights and privileges of these bodies. [...]

The issue of taxation was thus critical. Until the fifteenth century, approximately, princes could pay for most of the very limited functions of government from income deriving from their own estates. By the seventeenth century, the costs of administration and war had grown dramatically and no royal household had the means to sustain them.

The strategies for obtaining the necessary funds and support varied. In France, Richelieu ordered the destruction of all town fortifications, thus rendering them defenseless against royal troops. Louis XIV initiated the "court" at Versailles, an institution widely copied in other centralizing monarchies. [...]

By the end of the seventeenth century the centralizing authorities prevailed throughout much of Europe. The polity increasingly had those characteristics we listed as essential for statehood. It was fixed in space and time; the idea of patrimony—the state as a private realm—was in decline everywhere but in France and Spain; governance was becoming increasingly institutionalized as a vehicle distinct from the dynast or dynasty; and the state was well along the way to becoming multifunctional. [...]

No account of the growing multifunctionality of the state would be complete without mention of two intertwined "services" that became fully concentrated under central authority. Taxation and the military, each of which fed upon the other in a closed symbiotic relationship, were perhaps the most important characteristics of the seventeenth-century state. [...]

Most experts now agree that the geopolitical competition and war were the main motors driving the development of bureaucracy and public finance in the seventeenth-century state. Braun notes that almost every major taxation change in Europe during this epoch was occasioned by the preparation and commissioning of wars.[1] There were four main sources of revenues for these expanding requirements: (1) the personal possessions of the crown, (2) sale of offices, (3) public taxation, and (4) income from colonies. The first was inadequate in relation to the vastly increasing expenditures required to create and sustain permanent bureaucracies and armies. The second, perfected in France and Spain, generated only about 15 percent of the state's needs. The third was the predominant source, but it was never adequate to meet growing needs. Colonies were available only for some countries (particularly Spain). To meet the shortfalls, crowns often mortgaged their kingdoms to private financiers. Most seventeenth-century states were thus fundamentally weak: they had to extort, tax, and borrow to pay for their growing armies and bureaucracies, all with the result that loyalty (except among those with sinecures), legitimacy, and credit-ratings were compromised. They thus had to have myths, ideas, and ideologies to prop up their legitimacy.

Ideas

The extension of state activities in the seventeenth century was accompanied by a number of ideas that explained and justified them. We cannot say that ideas caused the practices or vice versa. Both were closely intertwined. In some cases ideas seemed to precede practices; in others, the reverse was the case. We have to see both ideas and practices as reinforcing each other.

The most important ideas associated with the seventeenth-century state reflected declining patrimonialism. Already in the fifteenth-century Italian city-states the concept of *raison d'état*—the differentiation between the private interests of the ruler and the welfare of the state—developed. Although Machiavelli's great *problematique* in *The Prince* was how leaders can retain power, the text is filled with references to the notion of public responsibility. In seventeenth-century thinking, the prince was not free to do as he pleased. He was constrained by law, by God's intentions, and by the welfare of the body politic. All his or her actions had to be undertaken within the context of an obligation to the state.

To legitimize the great power grabs and taxation for supporting armies and bureaucracies, the monarchs required ideological justifications. Theories of the divine origins of royal rule provided the main ideas. Robert Filmer (1588–1653) developed the most exhaustive treatment of the issue, although his ideas were mainly expansions of notions appearing already in the sixteenth century. […]

But it may be a paradox that while publicists and ideologues of the royal houses were busy developing theories of absolutism against the claims of local authorities and bodies, another theory of rights was also becoming established. This was the right to private property, another revolutionary concept and one that placed serious constraints on the royal prerogative to tax. It also distinguished the European form of absolutism from its parallels in the Ottoman Empire, Shogun Japan, or Imperial China. The age of absolutist public authority in Europe was, as Perry Anderson suggests, also the age in which 'absolute' private property was progressively consolidated. To the extent that this was the case, absolute rule was inherently limited.[2]

In addition to the basis of their rule, European dynasts also needed ideas to justify and explain the significant increases in seventeenth-century state extraction. The Cameralists and Mercantilists provided them. Reason of state—the long-term welfare of the community—requires public finances and economic leadership. Only the state can provide it, and thus it must become the main productive force. Everything within an organic society requires its own proportionate place in a complex economic and social structure. […]

We see here a notion of a contract: the government can extract, but it can do so only to redistribute what it takes in terms of government functions to provide security from external threats and to protect the life and property of royal subjects. This is a distinctly public view of finances and implies constraints on frivolous spending. The state is an agent of redistribution, not an agent for the personal gain of the monarch. So, despite terms such as absolutism and the venal practices of the Spanish and French kings of the period, the political vocabulary and discourses of the seventeenth century abound with notions of constraint, obligations, and responsibilities. The distinction between the public and dynastic interests in government was becoming more common, although in France it did not become firmly established until the 1789 revolution. […]

But perhaps the most influential ideas surrounding statehood in the early modern period derived from the logic and political demands of the Reformation. The Lutheran claims against the Roman church constituted a major assault on the bases of Catholic influence (and even authority) throughout Europe. The idea that the princes should have the authority to determine the religion of their subjects (the Peace of Augsburg, 1555), and thus that religion is essentially a *local* affair, undermined the medieval cosmology of a united and organic Christian community. And in order to make claims to freedom of religious choice stick, the Lutheran and Calvinist rulers in the Holy Roman Empire and elsewhere had to mobilize all resources available to turn themselves into powerful states. […]

Norms

The main moral and legal canon surrounding the seventeenth-century state was sovereignty, or supreme rule within the realm. It was at once an aspiration, a fragile fact, and a norm in the sense that it provided a standard against which royal behavior and status could be measured and judged. Europe's rulers had been making assertions of sovereignty for several centuries, often without much effect either internally or externally. By the seventeenth century, however, sets of ideas had defined in considerable detail that which was sought, for example, by fourteenth-century kings in their long efforts to free themselves from the competition and control of the church. Henry VIII's final takeover of the church and its properties, his establishment of the Church of England, and the extension of his authority over numerous ecclesiastical matters was a major watershed, one that others sought to emulate later. By the sixteenth century, writers and publicists had begun to enunciate what was appearing in practice: the increased concentration of power and authority around the royal figure. Jean Bodin (1530–96) was among the first to offer a conceptual solution to the wars, revolutions, and general chaos of the times: a clear-cut statement that order must rely upon some continuous and legitimate authority that transcends a particular ruler. Sovereignty, he suggested in his *Six Books on the Commonwealth* (1576), is an "absolute and perpetual power vested in the commonwealth" but exercised by one center, whether a monarch, an assembly, or an aristocracy. Sovereignty does not lie with an individual or group, but is an attribute of the commonwealth. Bodin rejected medieval notions of shared sovereignty—as between landed estates, town assemblies, and territorial princes—and insisted it is indivisible. The essential idea is that there can be no competing authority (as distinct from power) either within or exterior to the realm. The facts may differ, but sovereignty is the norm. Anything that deviates from the norm is thus a violation, an injustice, a wrong, or an error that must be remedied. Sovereignty is not a status or condition that fluctuates (a variable) with the rising and falling fortunes of individual leaders. It is an attribute of a continuous and distinct political community inhabiting a defined realm. It cannot wax and wane, be shared, or diluted. States may be big or small, weak or strong, peaceful or chaotic, but so long as there is exclusive legal authority—the *right* to make and apply laws for the community—there is sovereignty. By the end of the seventeenth century, town assemblies might draft or alter local laws but such initiatives required implicit or explicit royal consent. And, finally, only sovereigns could send diplomatic delegations abroad, establish embassies, and make treaties with other sovereigns.

The Peace of Westphalia

Ideas, practices, and norms of stateness and sovereignty were intermingled in the two treaties negotiated at Osnabrück and Münster that comprised the 1648 Peace of Westphalia. The lengthy document includes a long list of territorial revisions, exchanges of towns, castles, and fortifications, compensation for some of the noble victims of war, a nascent scheme for conflict resolution, the elevation of France and Sweden as guarantors of the treaty, and many other matters. It does not, however, mention the word sovereignty. Yet the 1648 settlement was a watershed because it engraved in Europe's first great multilateral treaty the essential ideas of sovereignty. [...]

The late seventeenth-century state in many parts of Europe now contained most of the ingredients of our definition of a state: territoriality, at least the beginning of a distinction between private and public realms (the distinction between dynastic and state interests), the institutionalization of political bodies guaranteeing continuity through time, multifunctional tasks, and legitimate authority. It lacked, nevertheless, a sound basis in a sense of community or loyalty. Individuals may or may not have felt loyalty to the royal figure—most were probably indifferent—but there was little sense of a national community. Hobbes' "commonweal" was made up of atomistic individuals, not of a society as we understand the term today. Indeed, most political thought of the era was highly individualistic, whether discussing political and property rights, or the duties of obedience to the absolute ruler. The nation part of the state, the idea of group solidarity and identity, did not appear widely until the nineteenth century.

Nation and State in Nineteenth-Century Europe: Growing Complexity

The English and French revolutions of 1688 and 1789 largely destroyed the normative bases of royal rule and substituted for them the novel idea that authority derives ultimately from the people. The ideas of popular sovereignty and rule by consent were truly revolutionary and helped pave the way for the concept of citizenship (resurrected by the French from Roman usage) which in turn was linked to the rights of individuals.

The concept of the citizen, while still individualistic, nevertheless suggests a larger body, a community of citizens. At the time of the French Revolution, those who had been royal subjects automatically became French citizens. Theorists and politicians of the age now portrayed France as a community of citizens transcending the diversity of languages, dialects, religions, and races that existed within the traditional boundaries of the French kingdom.

This community was not, however, a spontaneous emanation from revolutionary citizens. Throughout Europe, the state itself took the lead in creating a sense of national community. It did this through its control of education, through the promotion and/or suppression of local languages and dialects, and through military conscription. It also employed the traditional means of military displays and pomp to inculcate feelings of loyalty. The development of a sense of nationhood took many different forms and occurred in different places at different times. […]

Among the other innovations of the nineteenth century, we can add the following:

- a single currency and fiscal system
- a national language(s) that superseded or supplemented local languages
- national armies based on conscription from among the entire male population
- national police organizations to enforce a disarmed public and to engage in various forms of social surveillance and coercion against criminal (and sometimes political) activity
- the greatly expanded social and commercial services provided by the state, to include education and some elementary welfare services, all of which in the seventeenth century had been provided through private means such as extended families and the church
- state leadership in organizing, funding, and regulating industrialization
- the direct involvement of citizens in local, regional, and national governance through legislative and other types of deliberative bodies.

Two other characteristics of the nineteenth-century state were particularly important. Governance became increasingly based on legal means and deliberative processes, and less on royal whims, prejudices, and status considerations that were so prominent in seventeenth-and eighteenth-century rule. […]

The second extraordinary characteristic of the late nineteenth-century state was its militarization. Between 1880 and 1914 most European states built massive military machines costing an ever-increasing proportion of national wealth. Finer cites a few figures that are symbolic of the trend. British military expenditures in the last decade of the nineteenth century amounted to about £36 million.[3] In the next decade they increased to £876 million, that is, more than a twenty-fold expansion within less than twenty years. […]

The Contemporary State

The critical importance of states as the main agents of international relations and the essential format for protecting, promoting, and sustaining the national community is revealed in part by their numbers. In the medieval era, there were about five hundred polities with some state-like characteristics. Through the processes of aggregation, integration, marriages, and conquests these units eventually emerged as twenty-one states, principalities, and independent cities in Europe in 1875. […]

In the twentieth century there were three major explosions of state-making: the first in 1919, the second in the three decades after World War II, and the third in the early 1990s. In all cases, war was the main engine of historical change. In 1918–19 a number of constituent nationalities within the great empires of central Europe and the Balkans revolted and achieved independence. The new states ran from Finland in the north to Yugoslavia in the south. Now Europe suddenly had eight more states, actually nine since Norway had peacefully seceded from Sweden in 1905. The second great wave of state-making followed World War II. It started in 1947 with India's independence and was essentially completed by 1975 with the withdrawal of Portugal from Angola and Mozambique. Fifty-one governments signed the Charter of the United Nations in 1945. By 1970 the organization had 150 members. During this same period Cyprus, Malta, East Germany, Greenland, and Iceland joined the roster of European states, which, however, had lost Estonia, Latvia, and Lithuania through Soviet conquests in 1940.

After the end of the Cold War, a raft of new states appeared, including thirteen former republics of the Soviet Union. They achieved independence primarily through peaceful means. Yugoslavia, however, broke up into its constituent republics through violence and massive orgies of killing and ethnic cleansing. If we include Russia, Ukraine, Belarus, and the rest of the former Soviet republics, today Europe is composed of fifty-one countries compared with twenty-one in 1875. Worldwide, candidates for future statehood include Montenegro, Palestine, the Faroe Islands, Turkish Cyprus, and Somaliland. Any number of armed secessionist movements in what used to be known as the Third World could push the number higher. United Nations membership will probably reach 200 within the next decade. [...]

The Practices of Contemporary Statehood

Among the many new and growing functions of the state, moral and ethical leadership, regulation, and instruction are significant. In the European context at the time of the early Westphalian state, religious institutions sustained these tasks. Today, in states where religious and government institutions are separate, they share these functions, but with one big difference: religious institutions do not have enforcement capacity. Most contemporary states set limits, regulate, or otherwise define policies relating to population growth and sexual relations, and to the sale and/or possession of alcohol, tobacco, and drugs. They propagate norms relating to behaviors of citizenship, and define a host of regulations governing other private activities. In states where religious and state institutions are not separated (e.g., Iran) the state may establish regulations that guide the full range of public and private behavior, from codes of dress, through appropriate relationships between the sexes, to what individuals may read or watch on television. As the name implies, in states with totalitarian regimes (e.g., North Korea) there is no realm of "private" behavior; the state regulates every facet of individuals' lives, including what, where, and how much they eat! The state is much more than an administrative or justice-providing institution. It has become the great moral teacher and regulator.

The multifunctional tasks of governments have to be paid for. State practices in the twentieth century included massive intervention in the market economy and dramatic growth of taxation. The standardized universal income tax is an invention of the twentieth century—imposed in most countries as a temporary measure to finance participation in World War I—and has grown to extract prodigious proportions of personal wealth. In a typical OECD country today, government receipts, mostly through taxes, constitute more than 40 percent of the Gross Domestic Product (GDP). [...]

Ideas

The ways we look at the world, perceive events, and conduct our daily activities—our mental frames of reference—are highly conditioned by statehood and our ideas about states. So are our identities. Nationality and occupation are among the main forms of identity today as anyone learns quickly when traveling abroad. They were not several centuries ago, when religion and family lineage were of greater importance. Our statistics, our political systems, and our plethora of political symbols all derive from "stateness." Most people are roughly familiar with the geography and history of their own country The further one moves away however, the more public knowledge dissipates. Even among political elites, knowledge of other countries and cultures is often rudimentary, highly stereotyped, and often just plain wrong. Large numbers of people throughout the world maintain suspicious attitudes toward anything that is "foreign." [...]

Norms

The predominant norm of statehood today is self-rule. We no longer tolerate one "people" ruling over others, even if it is not in a colonial-type relationship. In the seventeenth and eighteenth centuries there was nothing peculiar about a German from Hanover becoming the king of England, or a Swedish king exercising sovereignty over Lübeck, a German city, or of the Spanish king as sovereign over Naples. This was normal practice. In contrast, the norms of statehood in the Versailles Treaty and the League of Nations Covenant sustain a view of the state as a contiguous entity based on distinct peoples who have self-rule, that is, government by "one's own". Under contemporary international law, a polity that does not have self-rule cannot become a state. It is some sort of dependency, and thus does not have a crucial element of statehood. [...]

The norms of self-determination and self-rule have helped to create more than 140 new states since 1945, and to de-legitimize all forms of imperial or suzerain-type relationships. The self-ruling state is now universally recognized and assumed to be the "natural" form of political organization. But in some cases the realities of statehood are not consistent with the norms. Some states have collapsed, others, like some of their seventeenth-century predecessors, cannot establish effective authority over their territories, and still others remain states primarily by virtue of outside support. While the state is the predominant form of legitimate authority over distinct societies, it is by no means universally successful.

The Problem of Weak States

[...] Unlike their European predecessors, however, most post-1945 states began with democratic constitutions, and with an international set of norms that promoted and sustained self-determination, self-government, and independence. Many of these paraphernalia of popular sovereignty were "delivered" as part of the de-colonization process. But the problem was that many of the colonies-turned-states were in fact fictions. They had the appurtenances of states—flags, armies, capital cities, legislatures, and ambassadors—but they did not have the other requisites of statehood, such as a clear distinction between public and private realms, government institutionalization, and effective multifunctionality Most had only weak civil societies. Many were polities, but not functioning states as we have defined them. Few populations had deeply ingrained senses of national identity; most, in fact, remained primordial, fixed around clans, tribes, religious groups, or limited geographic regions. The fiat of the "national" government often extended no further than the suburbs of the capital city, beyond which local leaders, based on a variety of claims to legitimacy, ruled. The modern symbol of sovereignty, a monopoly over the legitimate use of force, plus the effective disarmament of society, existed more in rhetoric than in fact.

These and other characteristics of some new states constitute a syndrome that Barry Buzan has called the *weak state* and Robert Jackson has termed *quasi-states*.[4] The terms may differ, but the phenomena to which they direct attention are similar. Weak states have all the attributes of sovereignty for external purposes—they are full members of the international community and have exactly the same legal standing as the oldest or most powerful states in the system—but they severely lack the internal attributes of sovereignty. [...]

Weak and failed (or collapsed) states became the object of considerable attention during the 1990s. With the end of the Cold War, analysts began to acknowledge that rebellions, civil wars, and massacres taking place in the Third World and elsewhere were not just the manifestations of great power competition or ideological incompatibilities. Suddenly, observers discovered the phenomenon of "ethnic wars," overlooking the fact that wars within states having nothing to do with Cold War competition had been part of the Third World landscape for many years. Civil wars and wars of secession in Burma, Sudan, Eritrea, Nigeria, and elsewhere long preceded the collapse of the Berlin Wall.

Some states have moved from original weakness to collapse. They are the ultimate failures of contemporary statehood. In 1991, Somalia became the symbol of the *collapsed state,* ostensibly a new phenomenon in international politics. Lebanon in 1976, Angola and Mozambique (perhaps more aborted than collapsed states because they began to fall apart immediately upon independence) and Chad between 1980 and 1982 all had the symptoms of the state moving toward collapse. [...]

On the other hand, many originally weak states have avoided or overcome the syndrome and today function much as their European forebears. Singapore, Malaysia, Mauritius, Tanzania, Barbados, and Trinidad are prominent examples. But a fair number of former colonies cannot yet sustain the qualities of statehood outlined earlier, including effective control over a defined territory, a clear distinction between public and private realms, political institutionalization, and effective multifunctionality

One final characteristic of weak states needs emphasis because it is largely an artifact of the twentieth century and finds no predecessors in the state-building enterprise in Europe during the early modern period. Unlike Hobbes' Leviathan, which had the main purpose of maintaining order and providing security for members of the commonwealth, many weak states have been a major threat to their populations. The state, instead of being a vessel of security and national community, has become a menace to parts of its population. Since World War II, more people have been killed by the agents of their own state than by foreign invaders. Where the state is captured by one individual or a political clique that has no foundation in popular legitimacy, opposition to arbitrary rule is often met by widespread oppression and killing. The citizens of Kampuchea, Equatorial Guinea, China, or Uganda in the 1970s, of South Africa at the height of apartheid in the 1980s, or of Rwanda in 1994 and Sudan today faced murderous regimes that in some cases have counted their victims in the hundreds of thousands, and even in millions. Such are the sources of secessionism. The seventeenth century did not have precedents for the many politicides of the past one hundred years.

The State and Change: The Case for Transformation

[…] The literature on this question is notable more for its volume and scope of assertions than for systematic empirical inquiry. Much is claimed, but not much has been verified according to the methodological canons of the social sciences. Yet, the case has become so prominent that it has almost become conventional wisdom. The state is in the process of transformation toward weakness. If present trends continue, the transformation will be toward obsolescence.

Transformationalists approach the problem from two perspectives. The first suggests that the authority of the state is "leaking," "moving up," or "evaporating" toward forces, agents, and entities beyond it, including international organizations, transnational associations, the global market, or the global civil society. The second suggests that *individuals within* states are increasingly questioning the authority of the state, withholding loyalty to it, and developing new loyalties toward more accommodating or psychologically satisfying identity groups such as ethnic associations, churches, and regional groupings. […]

The late Susan Strange, a noted international political economist, presents an exemplary and robust case for the first type of state transformation in her study *The Retreat of the State*.[5] Her main thesis is that state power and authority are "leaking" to globalized markets and their main agents, transnational corporations (TNCs), to international criminals, and to international organizations. […]

Strange examines recent trends in the three sectors to support this basic position. There are numerous interesting and compelling illustrations as, for example, the multi-billion-dollar international drug trade that not only escapes government efforts to curtail it, but actually involves collusion because governments have been unwilling to regulate the banks through which the profits of the trade are "laundered." […]

In addition to the cases Strange discusses, we might add the role of the World Bank (IBRD) and International Monetary Fund (IMF), both international organizations that help sustain the globalizing world economy. A weak developing country seeking outside support has little choice but to accept the "conditionality" attached to loans. […] Can we then speak of states as critical agents in the international political realm when the real locus of authority and power today resides outside the country? Overall, in Strange's estimation, the authority of the state is "retreating," a trend that in the long run portends obsolescence.

James Rosenau has made one of the most interesting arguments regarding the erosion of state authority through shifting loyalties and the appearance of various particularisms—the second approach to state obsolescence or regression.[6] He emphasizes phenomena such as declining loyalties to the state as seen, for example, in resistance to conscription, in tax cheating and evasion, migration, and declining voter participation. Increasingly people judge states not on the basis of presumed authority, but by performance. When states fail to perform according to expectations, people resist, withdraw, or shift their loyalties in other ways. The explanation lies in the increased analytical skills of people gained through universal education, increased literacy, and the availability of new information technologies. If many people no longer submit automatically to state authority, then either loyalty will be directed elsewhere to polities that can effectively challenge the state, or in the extreme, the state may become obsolete or in some other way become transformed. The trend is already well on the way, for authority is escaping both to the outside and within the state. [...]

Critique of the State Transformation/Obsolescence Argument

The arguments for transformation and/or obsolescence are partly persuasive, even if based on highly selected indicators and cases. Five major theoretical difficulties come to mind, however: (1) confusion of influence and power with authority; (2) conceptions of power based on zero-sum assumptions; (3) lack of benchmarks; (4) confusion of the legitimacy of the state with the performance of governments; and (5) setting the bar of state authority too high. There are also a number of empirical difficulties. [...]

To claim that TNCs, financial markets, drug cartels, and international organizations all have power in international political relationships and over states is undeniable. But that is not the same as having authority over states and it does not mean that state authority is retreating. It may mean, however, that states are increasingly constrained in their freedom to make policy choices. States may be losing autonomy (although this is also arguable), but this is not the same as losing authority.

A second problem is that Strange assumes a zero-sum quality to power and influence. If TNCs have political influence today, she implies, it must mean that someone has lost it, and that someone is the state. In her view, it does not seem conceivable that both states and transnational actors and agents of various kinds may be increasing their power simultaneously, or that states voluntarily and purposefully increase the stature and possible influence of transnational or international bodies so as to promote their own purposes. [...]

Another problem with the state transformation or obsolescence argument is that it offers no benchmarks. What is the standard against which states

are supposedly "eroding?" [...] If we use 1960 as our standard, then in some states there has been some retrenchment of state activities. But in most states the figures indicate a *slowing down of the rate of growth of state functions but no decline.* Indeed, for most industrial countries, social security transfers as a percentage of GDP actually increased through the 1970s and 1980s. This hardly comprises evidence of the transformation or obsolescence of the state. [...]

Rosenau's suggestion that shifting loyalties within the state are evidence of its erosion requires similar interrogation. There is, first, confusion between loyalty to a state and support of a government. Increased political participation, a widespread sense of public confidence, and increasing intellectual skills that enable citizens to judge government performance and sometimes to oust them indicates little about loyalty to the state. In virtually every polity organized as a state, there are opponents of government. In parliamentary systems, they are organized as "the loyal opposition." Millions join political parties that seek to replace incumbents. This is normal. Only in cases of secession do we see the withdrawal of loyalty to the state. Here, separatists and secessionists deny legitimacy to the state and seek to create a state of their own. But this is the key point. They are not denying the legitimacy of statehood as such, but only of a particular state.

Does the illicit drug trade, estimated to involve purchases and profits close to one trillion dollars annually and directly costing taxpayers hundreds of million dollars to control (not very successfully), indicate the loss of state authority? [...] Only if we assume that states have been, are, and should be omnipotent—a standard against which we can measure—could we successfully argue that the inability to control the trade in *stupefiants* represents a retreat of the state.[7] If the state did for smoking or alcohol what it has done for *stupefiants,* we would have exactly the same problem but on a more massive scale. That a state cannot effectively enforce such bans hardly warrants the conclusion that it is declining, disappearing, or transforming. *The argument sets the bar of state capacity far too high.* The failure to control effectively all trafficking in drugs may be more indicative of impossible goals than of a "retreat" of state authority.

The Case for Complexity

The types of changes we have seen in the contemporary state have been primarily related to the extension and proliferation of government activities, that is, to growing complexity rather than to transformation. The odds are pretty good that states as we know them will be around for a lot longer than most TNCs, transnational criminal groups, and even international organizations. The state remains the primary agent of international relationships and is the only one that has the quality and status of sovereignty. It is primarily states that create and sustain international institutions such as diplomacy, trade, international law, and the like. It is primarily states, through their practices and the ideas, beliefs, and norms that underlie them, that sustain and change those institutions. Other types of entities (e.g., banks) may create private international institutions of various kinds, but they seek to regulate only a single domain. In many cases, these sets of regulations do not *replace* the activities of states, but supplement them, or are entirely new. Collapsed or failed states show us what life would be like without states. In the absence of other more attractive alternatives, none of which seems to be on the horizon, we remain the inhabitants of an international society of states. […]

Notes

1. R. Braun, "Taxation, Sociopolitical Structure, and State-Building: Great Britain and Brandenburg-Prussia" in C. Tilly (ed.), *The Formation of National States in Western Europe* (Princeton University Press, Princeton, 1975), p. 311.
2. P. Anderson, *Lineages of the Absolute State* (Verso, London, 1979), p. 429.
3. S. Finer, "State- and Nation-Building in Europe: The Role of the Military" in C. Tilly (ed.), *The Formation of National States in Western Europe* (Princeton University Press, Princeton, 1975), p. 162.
4. B. Buzan, *People, States and Fear: The National Security Problem in International Relations,* 2nd edition (Harvester-Wheatsheaf, London, 1991) and R. Jackson, *Quasi States: Sovereignty, International Relations and the Third World* (Cambridge University Press, Cambridge, 1990).
5. S. Strange, *The Retreat of the State: The Diffusion of Power in the World Economy* (Cambridge University Press, Cambridge, 1996).
6. J. Rosenau, *Turbulence in World Politics: A Theory of Change and Continuity* (Princeton University Press, Princeton, 1990).
7. I prefer the French term for mind-altering drugs because it more clearly indicates the consequences of their use and does not confuse them with legitimate medicines.

TYPES OF POLITICAL SYSTEMS AS ARTICULATED BY ARISTOTLE

- Monarchy: **Monarchy** is the hereditary rule of one family. Traditionally, monarchs were heads of state and heads of government. Historically, people believed that the kings were God's representatives, and there were no limits on their powers. This was known as divine right of kings theory. Today, with a few exceptions, monarchs have very limited power, and their rule is more symbolic.
- Aristocracy: **Aristocracy** is rule by the upper class. It takes its name from the Greek philosopher Aristotle. Aristotle viewed the upper class as suitable to rule because they had the wisdom and experience. Their duty is to look at the best interests of society.
- Polity: Polity is a constitutional democracy in which citizens have a voice in selecting leaders and framing the laws, but constitutional procedures protect individual rights.
- Tyranny: **Tyranny** is the arbitrary rule of one person who rules for his or her own interests.
- Oligarchy: **Oligarchy** is the rule of a small group of people who only look after their own interests.
- Democracy: **Democracy** means rule by the people. Aristotle was against this as he associated it with the rule of the "mob." Leaders would appeal to what is popular even if it is not in the best long-term interests of the society.

THE ORGANIZATION OF NATIONAL, REGIONAL, AND LOCAL GOVERNMENT

Unitary System
Unitary system is a type of government in which all power comes from the center. National government is supreme, and regional and local governments follow the directives of the national government. The former Soviet Union and India are examples of this type of government structure.

Federalism
Federalism is a form of government in which power is divided between the national and regional and local governments. While the national government is supreme, regional and state governments have some power and responsibility. The United States and Canada are examples of this type of system.

Confederacy
Confederacy is characterized by a weak national government. Most power is invested with regional and local governments. National government only performs very specific functions. A contemporary example would be Switzerland. From 1776 to 1789, the United States was governed by the Articles of Confederation. Some of the weaknesses of the national government were a lack of power to tax, develop infrastructure, and print and coin money. These were some of the factors that gave rise to demands for a stronger national government, which led to the adoption of the U.S. Constitution.

GOVERNMENT AND THE ECONOMIC SYSTEM

Laissez-Faire Capitalism
Laissez-faire is the idea that the marketplace should govern economic interactions. Governments should have a limited role in the economy. It comes from Adam Smith, the noted economists who wrote *On the Wealth of Nations* in 1776. He advocated that the economy works best when the free market is allowed to set the terms of trade and costs.

Welfare State
The **welfare state** is an idea that developed in the early nineteenth century that states it is a government's responsibility to ensure a certain standard of living for everyone. This makes a stronger government necessary to enforce regulations and provide an economic and social safety net.

Statism
Statism is a concept of government in which the state directs the economy in ways to enhance the power of the state. These include policies promoting trade and key strategic industries. While this type of government is most associated with fascist states, all governments do this in some form or another. An example of this in the United States is when a local government offers a company land or tax incentives to relocate to its city in the hopes of bringing in jobs, increasing the tax base, and gaining prestige.

Socialism

Socialism is a system that practices partial or full state ownership of businesses and extensive welfare benefits. Socialist states can vary. Some states like the old Soviet Union practiced strict socialism in which the government owned everything. Other states, such as many of the social democracies of Europe, had some state ownership, or joint ownership with the private sector, of some state industries but private ownership was present throughout the economy.

THEORIES OF THE ORIGINS OF THE STATE

The Natural Theory

The **natural theory** is drawn from Aristotle. People need to seek perfection and can only do that within a community. The state is greater than any single person.

Force Theory

Force theory is a glorification of the state, which is especially prominent in fascist thought. The state is created by conquest. Another aspect of the theory argues that the state was created by nationalism.

Georg Hegel's and Friedrich Nietzsche's views formed the basis of statism. They argued that the state is the most powerful form of human organization.

Divine Theory

Divine theory explains that God created the state. Therefore, religious authority was supreme over civil authority. This led to clashes between the church and some monarchs during the late Middle Ages and early modern periods.

Divine Right of Kings

The **divine right of kings** approach supported absolute monarchs. It was believed that the king was God's representative on Earth and had divine grace. It was very prominent in Europe from roughly the fifteenth to the nineteenth century. In Russia, it lasted until the twentieth century.

Most monarchs today in the West are ceremonial rulers. Monarchs in the Middle East still wield a great deal of political authority (Jordan, Kuwait, Saudi Arabia, Oman, United Arab Emirates, Qatar, Morocco).

Social Contract Theory

Social Contract Theory is often cited as the basis for modern government. This is an agreement between the ruler and ruled based on the concept of popular sovereignty. The people will support the government if the government itself agrees to abide by certain rules. So, for example, the social contract in the philosophy of John Locke is that people owe the government allegiance as long as the government protects the natural rights of the people. Therefore, the government must protect the life, liberty, and property of the citizens and cannot arbitrarily take these away.

Nationalism

Nationalism is the identification by people with a nation-state, which has been developing since the late middle ages. In the modern period, it became very significant as a result of the French Revolution, which was spread by Napoleon and became a global phenomenon. The attempt by Napoleon to conquer Europe helped to spawn other nationalisms in opposition.

Patriotism

Patriotism is an act or gesture of loyalty or commitment to the nation-state. An example of patriotism is saluting a national flag or honoring a country's national anthem. It is also feeling committed to a country and having a desire to protect it. Extreme forms of patriotism, however, can lead to chauvinism in which a person supports his or her country at all costs, even if this is detrimental to other countries.

■ CHAPTER 4

What Is Democracy?

KEY TERMS

Democracy

Glorious Revolution

Republican Democracy

Referendum

Capitalism

Social Contract Theory

Adam Smith

Laissez-Faire

Contemporary Liberalism

James Madison

Classical Conservatism

Separation of Powers

Federalism

Bills of Attainer

Bill of Rights

Social Democracy

Initiative

Natural Rights

Popular Sovereignty

Liberal/Constitutional Democracy

Mercantilism

Social Darwinism

Montesquieu

Jeremy Bentham

Edmund Burke

Thomas Jefferson

Checks and Balances

Writ of Habeas Corpus

Ex Post Facto Law

DISCUSSION QUESTIONS

1. Address the significance of social contract theory and relate it to John Locke's concept of natural rights.

2. Define and discuss the terms "separation of powers" and "checks and balances."

3. Discuss the differences between mercantilism and laissez-faire capitalism.

4. Discuss the differences and values between liberal and social democracy.

5. Address the values and assumptions of classical conservatism.

DEMOCRACY: COMES FROM THE GREEK

demos: the populace
Kratia: rule
Rule by the people

- Aristotle associated **democracy** with mob rule. It can turn into mob rule if the will and rights of the minority are not taken into account.
- Athens: Democracy rule of government. All free males served in the Athenian assembly on a rotation basis. Direct democracy is a system of government in which decisions are made by the people directly.
- Aspects of direct democracy include initiatives and referendums.

Initiative
Initiative is the process by which citizens can get public questions on an election ballot. Laws vary from state to state on how this can be done. In some states, it is comparatively easy and needs relatively few signatures. In other states, it is very difficult. California has a great many initiatives and propositions on the ballot.

Referendum
Referendum is the process by which political leaders put a question to the voters on a ballot. Some state constitutions require voter approval to issue bonds over a certain amount of money.

TYPES OF DEMOCRACY

Liberal/Constitutional Democracy
Liberal/constitutional democracy is the type of democracy in which individuals possess the freedom to achieve their personal happiness. The emphasis of society is on the concept of individual rights and a limited form of government.

- Abstract notations of equality and freedom rather than equality itself
- Equality of rights as opposed to actual equality
- Weaker central authority. National government shares power with regional and local governments
- Government more regulator and police power, as opposed to a provider

Social Democracy
In **social democracy**, the emphasis is on equality in practice, as well as abstract rights. Government is seen as a provider in establishing a strong public sector to limit inequalities in wealth.

Republican Democracy
Republican democracy is formed through elected representatives. It serves to diffuse passions and emphasizes mediation between various interests. It helps to safeguard the minority, as policies are more carefully considered. An important emphasis on republican democracy is universal suffrage: all adults, with some exceptions, such as those convicted of crimes, have the opportunity to vote.

In the United States, the concept of suffrage has progressed over time. In the colonial period and the early nineteenth century, only adult, white, male property owners could vote. Eventually, it was extended to most white males with the gradual elimination of property requirements. The amendments after the Civil War legally gave African American males the right to vote. However, with the end of Reconstruction, many African American males were disenfranchised. It was only with the Civil Rights Act of 1964 and the Voting Rights Act of 1965 that African Americans systemically gained the right to vote. Women suffrage was achieved in 1920 with the Nineteenth Amendment. Tennessee was the state that enabled this amendment to be ratified. It was decided by one vote. A state legislator was persuaded by his mother to change his vote at the last minute.

LIBERALISM

Qualities/Supporters of Liberalism
- Those elements in society who were opposed to the landed nobility.
- Those who wanted to eliminate restrictions on the free pursuit of profits.
- Liberals wanted to extend the French Revolution and its reforms.
- Those who emphasized the individual as opposed to social class and the society at large.
- Those who emphasized individual rights and a limited government.
- Liberalism was opposed to classical conservatism.

These all appealed to the growing middle class of merchants and business people who were benefitting from the development of the industrial revolution beginning in the 18th century.

Factors that Shaped Liberalism
- **Glorious Revolution**
- John Locke's concept of **natural rights** which was the basis of his social contract theory
- Enlightenment and the thought of philosophers such as Montesquieu
- **Separation of powers**
- French and American Revolutions

DEVELOPMENT OF CAPITALISM: CHARACTERISTICS

- Private enterprise
- Free trade
- Markets dictate production, selling, price, etc.

CAPITALISM WAS IN DIRECT OPPOSITION TO MERCANTILISM

Mercantilism
Mercantilism is the belief that wealth equated to power in international affairs. The state used its economy and resources not to enhance individual prosperity as a whole but to increase the power of the state over its rivals. Imperialism/colonialism are derived from this view.

Factors of Mercantilism

- The government acted as a stimulus for investment: governments acted like giant consumers. Examples would include large-scale infrastructure projects, such as canals and roads, as well as purchasing equipment for expanding militaries.
- The introduction of new forms of investment to raise revenues.
- The development of overseas market outlets for exports while supplying labor and raw materials.
- Wealth is measured in gold and silver. The goal was to be self-sufficient.
- The state subsidized new industries and chartered companies for overseas trade. An example is the trading empire the Dutch built in Asia by chartering the Dutch East India Company in 1602. This led to the establishment of trading posts and a commercial empire that lasted until World War II. The growth of commercial enterprises led to a power transition in both Holland and England. Commercial classes gained in importance at the expense of the aristocracy.

Adam Smith: 1732–1790

Adam Smith is considered the father of modern **capitalism**. He argued against mercantilism, as it protected inefficient monopolies and stifled individual initiatives. He developed the idea of the **laissez-faire** economic system. In this system, the government gets out of the economy and allows the citizens a free hand to conduct their own economic affairs. He valued the development of competition. Those who could adapt were economically successful, and those who could not lost out.

ADAM SMITH REVEALS HIS (INVISIBLE) HAND
Mark Skousen

"Adam Smith had one overwhelmingly important triumph: he put into the *center* of economics the systematic analysis of the behavior of individuals pursuing their self-interest under conditions of competition."

—George Stigler (emphasis added)

Critics of laissez faire—from Cambridge economic historian Emma Rothschild to British Labor Party leader Gordon Brown—have recently attempted to wrestle Adam Smith out of the hands of the free-market camp and into the camp of the social democrats. According to Iain McLean, professor of politics at Oxford University, and Samuel Fleschaker, professor of philosophy at the University of Illinois at Chicago, the Scottish philosopher was a "radical egalitarian" who, while endorsing economic liberalism, had a lively appreciation of market failure and ultimately rejected "ruthless laissez-faire capitalism" in favor of "human equality" and "distributive justice."

These critics are quick to claim that Smith was no friend of rent-seeking landlords, monopolistic merchants, and conspiring businessmen, and that he advocated an active State authority in support of free education, large-scale public works, usury laws, progressive taxation, and even limits on free trade.

Mark Skousen (editor@markskousen.com) is the editor of Forecasts & Strategies, *author of* The Making of Modern Economics, *and the producer of Freedom Fest (www.freedomfest.com). He is a former president of FEE. This article first appeared at TheFreemanOnline.org.*

Mark Skousen, "Adam Smith Reveals His (Invisible) Hand," Freeman, vol. 61, no. 4, pp. 22–24. Copyright © Foundation for Economic Education (CC by 4.0) at https://fee.org/articles/adam-smith-reveals-his-invisible-hand/.

What about the metaphor of the "invisible hand," the famous Smithian idea that "by pursuing his own self-interest, [every individual] frequently promotes that of the society"? Free-market economists from Ludwig von Mises to Milton Friedman have regarded it as a powerful symbol of unfettered market forces, what Adam Smith called his "system of natural liberty." In rebuttal the new critics belittle Smith's metaphor as a "passing, satirical" reference and suggest that he favored more of a "helping hand." They emphasize that Smith used the phrase "invisible hand" only once in each of his two major works, *The Theory of Moral Sentiments* (1759) and *The Wealth of Nations* (1776). The references are so sparse that commentators seldom mentioned the expression by name in the nineteenth century. No notice was made of it during the celebrations of the centenary of *The Wealth of Nations* in 1876. Until well into the twentieth century, no subject index listed "invisible hand" as a separate entry. It was finally added to the index in 1937 by Max Lerner for the Modern Library edition. Clearly, it wasn't until the twentieth century that the invisible hand became a popular symbol of laissez faire.

Could the detractors be correct in their assessment of Adam Smith's sentiments? Is the metaphor central or marginal to his "system of natural liberty"?

Friedman refers to Adam Smith's symbol as a "key insight" into the cooperative, self-regulating "power of the market to produce our food, our clothing, our housing … without central direction." Economist George Stigler calls it the "crown jewel" of *The Wealth of Nations* and "the most important substantive proposition in all of economics."

On the other hand, economist Gavin Kennedy contended in earlier writings that the invisible hand is nothing more than an afterthought, a "casual metaphor" with limited value. Rothschild, the Harvard University economic historian, even goes so far as to declare, "What I will suggest is that Smith did not especially esteem the invisible hand. … It is un-Smithian and unimportant to his theory" and was nothing more than a "mildly ironic joke."

Who's right?

A fascinating discovery by Daniel Klein, professor of economics at George Mason University, may shed light on this debate. Based on a brief remark by Peter Minowitz, the Santa Clara University political philosopher, that the "invisible hand" phrase lies roughly in the middle of both of Smith's books, Klein made preliminary investigations. He next recruited Brandon Lucas, then a doctoral student

> Some economists have begun to refer to the "invisible hand" reference as, at best, a "mildly ironic joke."

PERHAPS IF HE UNDERSTOOD THE INVISIBLE HAND, WE COULD GET HIM TO LIFT HIS BIG FOOT.

BIG GOV'T

ECONOMY

TheFreemanOnline.org

at Mason, to investigate further. Klein and Lucas reported in *Economic Affairs* (March 2011) that they found considerable evidence that Smith "deliberately placed 'led by an invisible hand' at the centre of his tomes" and that the concept "holds special and positive significance in Smith's thought."

Klein and Lucas base their conjecture on two major points. First, the physical location of the metaphor: The single expression "led by an invisible hand" occurs almost dead center in the first and second editions of *The Wealth of Nations*. (It moves slightly away from the middle after an index and other material were added to later editions.)

Moreover, it appears again "well-nigh dead centre" in the final edition of *The Theory of Moral Sentiments*. Klein and Lucas admit that it was not in the middle of the first edition in 1759, speculating that "physical centrality was not initially a part of his intentions ... [but that] by 1776, Smith had become intent on centrality." Indeed, Smith moved the phrase "invisible hand" closer to the center of the book, first by appending an important essay on the origin of language and finally by making substantial revisions in the final edition.

Second, they note that as a historian and moral philosopher, Adam Smith commented frequently on the importance of middleness in architecture, literature, science, and philosophy. For example:

- Smith wrote sympathetically about the Aristotelian golden mean, the idea that virtue exists "between two opposite vices." For instance, between the two extremes of cowardice and recklessness lies the central virtue of courage.

- In his essays on astronomy and ancient physics, he was captivated by Newtonian central forces and periodical revolutions.

- Klein discovered that in his lectures on rhetoric, Smith admired the poetry of the Greek poet Thucydides, who "often expresses all that he labours

so much in a word or two, sometimes placed in the middle of the narration."

In sum, according to Klein and Lucas, the invisible hand represents the centrality of Smith's "system of natural liberty" and is appropriately found in the middle of his works. By this discovery, if true, one goes from one extreme to the other—from seeing the invisible hand as a marginal concept to accepting it as the touchstone of his philosophy.

Klein and Lucas's list of evidence is what a lawyer might call circumstantial, or "impressionistic," to use their own adjective. Taken as a whole, the documentation is either an ingenious breakthrough or a "remarkable coincidence," to quote Kennedy.

A few Smithian experts have warmed up to Klein and Lucas's claim. Kennedy, who previously considered the invisible hand a "casual" metaphor, now sees a "high probability" in their thesis of deliberate centrality. Others are more skeptical. "We have no direct evidence for the conjecture," states Craig Smith, an expert on Adam Smith at the University of St. Andrews. The idea that Smith deliberately hid his favorite symbol of his philosophy "strikes me ... as very un-Smithian," he states, and runs contrary to his policy of expressing thoughts in a "neat, plain and clever manner." Placing the shorthand phrase "invisible hand" in the middle of his works may not be plain, but is it not neat and clever?

We may never know the truth, since we have no record of Smith's confession on the matter. Fortunately, one does not need to depend on the physical centrality of the "invisible hand" to recognize the doctrinal centrality of his philosophy.

There are many passages from *The Wealth of Nations* and *The Theory of Moral Sentiments* that elucidate the "invisible hand" theme, the idea that individuals acting in their own self-interest unwittingly benefit the public weal, or that eliminating

> # There are many passages from Smith's works that elucidate the "invisible hand" image.

restrictions on individuals' behaviors "better[s] their own condition" and makes society better off. Smith repeatedly advocated removal of trade barriers, State-granted privileges, and employment regulations so that individuals could flourish.

In *The Theory of Moral Sentiments*, Smith writes:

> The man of system … seems to imagine that he can arrange the different members of a great society with as much ease as the hand arranges the different pieces upon a chess-board. He does not consider that the pieces upon the chess-board have no other principle of motion besides that which the hand impresses upon them; but that, in the great chess-board of human society, every single piece has a principle of motion of its own, altogether different from that which the legislature might chuse to impress upon it. If those two principles coincide and act in the same direction, the game of human society will go on easily and harmoniously, and is very likely to be happy and successful. If they are opposite or different, the game will go on miserably, and the society must be at all times in the highest degree of disorder.

Smith's argument is comparative. To quote Klein: "Hewing to the liberty principle generally *works out better* than not doing so—in *this* respect, [Kenneth] Arrow, Joseph Stiglitz, and Frank Hahn *do* disfigure Smith when they identify the invisible hand with some rarified perfection. We need not rehearse Smith on the ignorance, folly, and presumption of political power, on the corruption and pathology of political ecology. … Smith sees the liberty principle as a moral, cultural, and political *focal point*, a worthy and workable principle in the otherwise dreadful fog of interventionism."

To think that Adam Smith, the renowned absent-minded professor, hid a little "invisible" secret in his tomes is indeed the ultimate irony. As Klein concludes, "That the phrase appears close to *the center*, and *but once*, in *TMS* and in *WN* might be taken as evidence that Smith did intend for us to take up the phrase."

I find Professor Klein's story compelling and have enjoyed showing copies of Smith's works with a bookmark in the key pages to students, faculty, and interested friends.

DEVELOPMENT OF SOCIAL DARWINISM

According to **social Darwinism**, the rich have wealth because they deserved it. Wealth was a sign of the individual's worthiness. This tied in with scientific theories about why certain species in nature were able to adapt and survive while others were not.

DEVELOPMENT OF CONTEMPORARY LIBERALISM

With the development of modern society and a capitalist economic system, problems developed. The growth of urbanization led to social and economic problems, such as overcrowding, poor housing conditions, and spread of disease. This required more regulation and the development of government services to deal with these issues. Politically, this led to the tendency in liberalism to argue that the government needed more authority to deal with social and economic problems. One of the proponents of **contemporary liberalism** was **Jeremy Bentham**. Bentham pioneered reforms such as a secret ballot and the development of a civil service. He developed the concept of utilitarianism. He advocated that public policy should be evaluated by studying what is the greatest good for the greatest number.

JEREMY BENTHAM (1748–1832)
Diane Collinson and Kathryn Plant

Jeremy Bentham propounded a moral doctrine based on what has become generally known as the Principle of Utility. The doctrine derives from the phrase 'the greatest happiness of the greatest number', which Bentham found in a pamphlet written by Joseph Priestley, chemist and Presbyterian cleric, concerning whom he wrote: 'Priestley was the first (unless it was Beccaria) who taught my lips to pronounce this sacred truth … that the greatest happiness of the greatest number is the foundation of morals and legislation.'

Bentham devoted much of his life to the work of reforming jurisprudence and legislation in accordance with the principle of producing the greatest happiness for the greatest number. His best-known philosophical work is the *Introduction to the Principles of Morals and Legislation,* published in 1789. His written output was enormous, but much of it was produced by him in manuscript or draft form to be worked over and completed by others. This has meant that writers on Bentham have had difficulty in distinguishing the fully authentic matter from that which has undergone significant editorial change. Bentham worked closely with James Mill, father of John Stuart Mill, on political and social issues and exerted a powerful influence on John Stuart Mill's education and development. As a part of his utilitarian doctrine he propounded a 'felicific calculus' that was devised to calculate the quantity of happiness likely to result from actions.

Bentham was born in London and was educated at Westminster School and Queen's College, Oxford. In 1763, when he was 15, he entered Lincoln's Inn and was called to the Bar in 1768. Three years later he published anonymously his *Fragment on Government,* a critical examination of Blackstone's *Commentaries on the Laws of England.* He visited his brother in Russia from 1785 to 1788 and published the *Introduction to the Principles of Morals and Legislation* on his return, having spent long periods of time working on it in a remote part of Russia. Thereafter, the range of his interests and activities expanded rapidly. Revolutionary events in France absorbed much of his attention and he became involved in a great many social and political activities. He planned a model prison, known as the Panopticon, and worked for many years to gain its acceptance and realisation, but without success. Meanwhile his legal reputation was becoming established on the Continent through the work of a Frenchman, Dumont, who had compiled and edited many of his papers to produce the *Traités de législation civile et pénale.*

The friendship with the Mill family began in 1808 and thereafter the two households were regularly amalgamated for several months each year. During these later years Bentham was preparing an enormous work, his *Constitutional Code,* and writing many pamphlets advocating law reform and criticising bad legislation. He died on 6 June 1832. After his death his close friends and followers, a number of whom attended the ceremonial dissection of his body in Webb Street, formed themselves into a Benthamite party within the House of Commons. Edwin Chadwick, who was living in Bentham's house at the time of his death where the two, it is reported, were 'surrounded by 70,000 sheets of manuscript on the theory of law and all conceivably related subjects', dedicated himself to working across the whole gamut of Bentham's reforming ideas. Thus a host of friends and followers made this great and indefatigable innovator's work important, among them John Stuart Mill, who developed Bentham's rather crude exposition of utilitarianism into an influential and widely subscribed-to ethical doctrine.

On first acquaintance, it is perhaps surprising to find that the Principle of Utility is in fact to do with happiness, and with happiness regarded as the supreme moral value. Bentham had adopted the term 'utility' from Hume, but he eventually came to feel that it was unfortunately chosen and said, 'the word "utility" does not so clearly point to the ideas of *pleasure* and *pain* as the words *happiness* and *felicity* do'.[1] In the *Fragment on Government,* his first published work, he maintained that all actions tend to aim at producing happiness 'and this *tendency* in any act we style its *utility*'; but later, in the 1820s, he made it clear that he preferred the utilitarian principle to be called 'the Greatest Happiness Principle' and added footnotes to this effect in new editions of his earlier works. The two terms link together informatively once it is understood that Bentham's 'utility', or usefulness, is a usefulness for producing happiness.

The happiness principle became the foundation of all Bentham's work of legislative reform and the tool he used to criticise all social institutions and practices. For him, it was to be the shaping force for resolving large issues in society. Later, in the hands of John Stuart Mill, it was explored and developed as a principle of personal and individual morality.

The fullest account of Bentham's utilitarianism is in *An Introduction to the Principles of Morals and Legislation.* Central to his account is, first, a psychological theory asserting that human behaviour is governed by pain and pleasure, and that each person acts to secure his or her own good; second, a moral theory that asserts that happiness, or pleasure, is the supreme good for humanity, and that the greatest happiness of the greatest number is the end of right action. Since, according to Bentham, each person is psychologically disposed to seek his or her own happiness, but morality requires that one acts to bring about the greatest good for everyone, his task is to show how legislation can effect a coincidence of individual and societal interests. He has to present a system 'the object of which is to rear the fabric of felicity by the hands of reason and law'.[2] The legislator must therefore be able to gauge the relative values of pleasures and pains in order to impose sanctions in accordance with what Bentham calls the Duty-and-Interest-Juncture-Producing-Principle. Punishment, he maintains, is 'primarily mischievous'; it has utility only if it serves to minimise pain and increase pleasure. To calculate amounts of pain and pleasure, Bentham identifies seven properties that he believed were quantifiable: intensity, duration, certainty, propinquity, fecundity, purity and extent. He also distinguishes different kinds of pleasures and pains and points out that in estimating their quantities in particular cases it is necessary to take into account the fact that people vary enormously in their individual capacities and predilections. This is the basis of the 'felicific calculus', probably the most stringently criticised element of Bentham's utilitarianism. The doctrine was strongly disapproved of for other reasons as well, chief among them its uncompromising secularity. It made no appeal to religious authority or revelation in the formulation of its happiness principle, nor did it invoke religious motives for actions. Bentham believed that his principle accorded with reason and that moral mistakes arose simply from mistakes in calculation. Moreover, he held that from the legislative point of view 'quantity of pleasure being equal, push-pin is as good as poetry', a remark that engendered heated debate when John Stuart Mill produced his own version of utilitarianism and tried to transpose the doctrine from the public to the personal domain.[3]

Bentham was thoroughly detested by opponents such as Thomas Arnold, Carlyle and Macaulay. Yet the heart of his doctrine was the urgent desire to benefit all humankind; and his followers, the Benthamites, were upright and earnest men of the same persuasion. Bentham bequeathed his body for the purposes of dissection to the Webb Street School of Anatomy at a time when only the bodies of executed murderers were legally procurable for teaching purposes. The campaign for change succeeded soon after his death when the Anatomy Act made it legal for bodies to be given for dissection, thereby realising Bentham's hope that humanity 'may reap some small benefit by my disease'.

See also: **Hume, Mill.**

Notes

1. Bentham, *An Introduction to the Principles of Morals and Legislation,* Chapter 1, 1.
2. Ibid., Chapter 1.
3. See J. S. Mill's essay, 'Bentham', in *Dissertations and Discussions,* vol. I, and his *Utilitarianism,* Chapter 2. Both are in M. Warnock (ed.), *Utilitarianism* (Fontana, London, 1962).

Bentham's Major Writings

Fragment on Government (1776) Cambridge: Cambridge University Press, 1988.

Introduction to the Principles of Morals and Legislation (1789), ed. J. H. Burns and H. L. A. Hart, London: Methuen, 1982.

Traités de législation civile et pénale (1802).

The Book of Fallacies (1824), ed. H. A. Larrabee, Oxford: Oxford University Press, 1952.

Bentham's *The Book of Fallacies* is also in *Bentham's Political Thought,* ed. B. Parekh, New York: Barnes and Noble, 1973.

Bentham's writings are in *The Collected Works of Jeremy Bentham,* Oxford: Clarendon Press, 1983.

Further Reading

Dinwiddy, J., *Bentham,* Oxford: Past Masters Series, Oxford University Press, 1980.

Eisenach E.J., *Narrative Power and Liberal Truth: Hobbes, Locke, Bentham and Mill,* Lanham: Rowan and Littlefield, 2002.

Harrison, R., *Bentham,* London: Routledge, 1985.

Postema, G., (ed.) *Bentham: Moral, Legal and Political Philosopher,* Aldershot: Ashgate, 2002.

Waldron, J., (ed. and intro.) *'Nonsense on Stilts': Bentham, Burke and Marx on the Rights of Man,* London: Methuen, 1987.

A useful website for information on Bentham is University College, London's Bentham Project Home Page: http://www.ucl.ac.uk/Bentham-project/

CONSERVATISM

The idea was to maintain the status quo. Political change should only come gradually.

Edmund Burke (1729–1797)

Edmund Burke is considered the father of modern conservativism. He believed that a good government kept order. Burke believed in traditional institutions. Institutions represented an accumulation of wisdom over generations. Institutions had value. He believed in traditional institutions, such as the crown, church, and role of the aristocracy in society.

A Good Ruler Needs Three Qualifications

- Ability
- Property
- High birth (Burke believed that the upper class had the experience and education to make public policy)

His idea of representation was more of that of a trustee. Representatives needed to do what they thought was best in the long term for the good of the nation and not vote the way their constituents wanted them to vote solely.

James Madison (1751–1836)

James Madison is the "father" of the US Constitution. Madison believed in **popular sovereignty** but did not trust people to make the wisest decision for the long term. This is illustrated in the Constitution with the **checks and balances** that were put into place.

Concepts Behind the Constitution Separation of Powers

Each branch of the government has separate and distinct functions. Membership does not overlap. Government functions split into legislative, executive, and judicial functions.

Checks and Balances

Different branches of government interact with each other and need to cooperate to get things done. Each branch can also impede the others. It can best be described as separate institutions that share power. (Analysis of the noted political scientist Richard Neustadt.) An example of this in the United States is the president is commander in chief of the armed forces but Congress makes the rules for the military, has to approve their budget, and has the power to declare war.

Federalism

National government is supreme, but states have some rights where their laws do not conflict with national laws. In the United States, the national government is supreme but state and local governments are left with some powers and responsibilities. State boundaries are also guaranteed by the Constitution. States have to agree to relinquish territory, the national government cannot ultimately take territory from one state and either give it to other states or create a new state.

Natural Rights in the US Constitution

The powers of the government are limited by the following:

- **Writ of habeas corpus**: defendants must be informed of the charges against them by the state
- **Bills of attainer**: laws against specific individuals
- **Ex post facto law**: retroactively applying a new law and prosecuting individuals for doing it when it was legal
- **Bill of Rights**: limits government and establishes rights for citizens and states (This is collectively the first ten amendments of the US Constitution)

In the United States, each branch has checks over the others. French philosopher **Montesquieu** (*The Spirit of the Laws*) influenced this system. The process of restraining the government enhances liberty. A slow pace of action requires careful consideration. The purpose of this process was to make lawmaking difficult, to frustrate the majority, and to guarantee minority rights. The idea is that if it were too easy to make a law, it could lead to tyranny.

The president appoints members of the cabinet and appointments to the federal courts subject to Senate confirmation. Congress must approve all laws which are subject to presidential veto. Congress must appropriate funding for programs. The federal courts can strike down a portion of a law or presidential act as unconstitutional. Each branch has some control over the others. As the political scientist Richard Neustadt argues, it is really separate institutions that share power.

Thomas Jefferson (1743–1826)

Thomas Jefferson believed in the individual. He advocated a smaller government and emphasized state's rights. He was the writer of the Declaration of Independence, and he incorporated Locke's idea of natural rights into the document. He was the minister to France at the time of the Constitutional Convention, so he played no part in that. Ironically, as the third president of the United States, Jefferson expanded the powers of the federal government by sending the navy to the Mediterranean to fight the Barbary pirates and concluded the Louisiana Purchase.

CHAPTER 5

Anarchism

KEY TERMS

Haymarket Square Riot
Anarcho-Syndicalism
Mikhail Bakunin
Emma Goldman
Freedom Riders
Anarcho-Capitalism

Pacifism
William Godwin
Pierre Joseph Proudhon
Leo Tolstoy
Lumpenproletariat
Nihilist Movement

DISCUSSION QUESTIONS

1. Discuss the significance of the Haymarket Square Riot.

2. Define and discuss the significance of anarcho-syndicalism.

3. Address the beliefs and implications of the nihilist movement in Russia.

4. Discuss pacifism's influence on the tactics of the American civil rights movement.

INTRODUCTION

Anarchists argue that the focus of government should be that individuals are directly involved in governmental decision making. Anarchists believe that a large centralized state becomes oppressive either on purpose or as a result of not being in touch with the concerns of the people.

Most anarchists believe that some form of government is needed. Anarchists believe that human beings have outgrown government. They argue that government impedes individuals.

There is a misperception that anarchists advocate violence. In American history, anarchism was considered an alien ideology brought over by radical immigrants. While the United States needed immigrant labor to fuel the Industrial Revolution, there were concerns regarding the political and religious beliefs of the new immigrants. Events such as the Haymarket Square Riot, the assassination of President William McKinley, and the Sacco and Vanzetti case fueled these beliefs. Self-proclaimed anarchist Leon Czolgosz assassinated President McKinley in 1901. Sacco and Vanzetti were two Italian immigrants who were convicted of murder and executed in 1927. Doubt was cast after the executions as to whether they were guilty. There is a strong belief that their political views biased their case.

HAYMARKET SQUARE RIOT

The **Haymarket Square Riot** in early May 1886 confirmed for many the mistrust and violence of anarchism as a political ideology. This was a protest in Chicago for an eight-hour workday. A bomb was thrown, and several policemen were killed. Seven people were convicted. Several were executed, and one died in prison. The remaining three were exonerated and released from prison. The riot gained worldwide attention. The first of May is now an international holiday for labor in virtually every country, except the United States.

TYPES OF ANARCHISM

Pacifism
Pacifists do not believe in violence for any reason, even in self-defense. Many of the early anarchists were pacifists.

William Godwin (1756–1836)
Godwin believed that if people were left alone, they would develop a harmonious society. Godwin argued that modern society is exploitive. He not only criticized government but also, like many anarchists, was against social institutions as well, such as organized religion.

Anarcho-Syndicalism
This **anarcho-syndicalism** approach advocates that society should be restructured into voluntary associations of workers, which would take the place of government. These associations would negotiate with each other so that people would have the goods and services they needed.

The major initial advocate of this approach was **Pierre Joseph Proudhon**, 1809–1865. He believed that private property is theft. He advocated for workers to ignore the state, and, eventually, it would collapse.

Another prominent anarchist was the Russian writer **Leo Tolstoy**. He is best known for literary works such as *War and Peace*, which is set during Napoleon's invasion of Russia in 1812. He argued that Napoleon was defeated by the sacrifices of the Russian peasants and not the Russian state.

Tolstoy was a religious man; he wanted people to destroy the state without using violence. He also advocated the abandoning of the institutions that propped up the state, such as the Russian Orthodox Church.

Anarchism also had a violent strain. There were those anarchists who believed that the only way to destroy the state was with violence. This was especially true in Russia. Russia was an autocratic state where there were no legitimate outlets for free expression or opposition to government policy. Therefore, protests were often extreme and violent. A Russian anarchist who advocated violence was **Mikhail Bakunin** (1814–1876). He argued that a successful revolution comes from arming the underclasses, which he labeled the **lumpenproletariat**. He believed in absolute individual freedom. Bakunin influenced the **nihilist movement** in Russia from 1860 to 1880. The nihilists believed in nothing and advocated the destruction of the state through violence. The nihilists assassinated several high-ranking government officials, including Czar Alexander II. He was an enlightened despot who had great power but attempted to reform Russia. He granted freedom to the serfs and was attempting to open up the political system. He was about to sign a law allowing for parliamentary elections when he was assassinated.

ANARCHISM IN THE UNITED STATES: EMMA GOLDMAN, THE ASSASSINATION OF PRESIDENT MCKINLEY, AND SACCO & VANZETTI

A prominent American anarchist was **Emma Goldman** (1869–1940). Earlier in her life, she advocated violence. Later in her life, she questioned this. She advocated a network of communes based on mutual trust and consideration among individuals who remained free to think and act as they choose. She also questioned social institutions such as marriage. An American anarchist, Leon Colgosz, assassinated President McKinley in 1901 at the Pan-American Exposition in Buffalo, New York. The case of Nicola Sacco and Bartolomeo Vanzetti saw two Italian anarchists convicted of murder and armed robbery in 1920. This case was very controversial as many felt they were wrongfully convicted.

Largely as a result of the assassination of President McKinley and the Sacco and Vanzetti case, as well as the Haymarket Square riot, Anarchism was viewed as a foreign subversive ideology by most Americans.

EMMA GOLDMAN (1869–1940)
Peter Dreier

Emma Goldman did *not* say the famous line that is often attributed to her: "If I can't dance, I don't want to be in your revolution." But those words do express her sentiments. She was a serious radical, an anarchist, and she believed that she was fighting for people's right to enjoy themselves, free of unjust and inhumane restrictions.

"I want freedom, the right to self-expression, everybody's right to beautiful, radiant things," Goldman said. "Anarchism meant that to me, and I would live it in spite of the whole world—prisons, persecution, everything. Yes, even in spite of the condemnation of my own closest comrades I would live my beautiful ideal."

How did Goldman expect her ideal society to come about? Another quotation accurately summarizes her view: "If voting changed anything, they'd make it illegal." Goldman liked to party, but she did not believe in political parties or in achieving change through the slow, incremental process of elections, reforms, and policy debates. She did not have a blueprint or a roadmap to change the world, but she nevertheless encouraged Americans to join the revolutionary movement, not only to dance but to challenge arbitrary authority, even through violence if necessary.

Goldman was an eloquent and dazzling speaker and writer who advocated anarchism, free speech, women's suffrage, birth control, workers' rights, the eight-hour workday, and free universal education without regard to race, gender, or class. She preached a brand of uncompromising revolutionism and absolute personal freedom that won many converts but alienated many more radicals and reformers—and provoked the opposition of the political establishment, who frequently sought to silence, jail, or deport her.

Born in Lithuania to a family of Russian-Jewish shopkeepers, Goldman moved with her family in 1881 to St. Petersburg. There, she embraced Russia's revolutionary movement but lived in an atmosphere of fear, as the czar's secret police crushed any dissent. Her father put her to work in a corset factory and began pressuring her into an arranged marriage. She resisted, and in 1885 the sixteen-year-old Goldman set sail for America in the company of her older half sister, Helena. As they sailed into New York Harbor, Goldman rejoiced at "the free country, the asylum for the oppressed of all lands." "We, too," she thought, "would find a place in the generous heart of America."

Goldman ended up in Rochester, New York, where she worked in a clothing factory and had a brief, unhappy marriage to another worker. Conditions in America were better than they had been in Russia, but the pace of work was faster, the discipline was harsher, and the pay ($2.50 for a ten-and-a-half-hour day) made it nearly impossible to make ends meet.

Already a radical, Goldman was inspired by the events surrounding the Hay-market bombing in 1886. During a rally in Chicago's Haymarket Square protesting police brutality against workers striking for the eight-hour workday, someone threw a bomb and killed a police officer. Eight anarchists were tried and convicted of murder, triggering an international protest movement. Outraged by what she viewed as a travesty of justice, Goldman began to read everything she could about anarchism and soon embraced the cause.

She moved to New York City in 1889 and quickly became part of that city's bohemian and anarchist worlds. There she met her lifetime partner, Alexander Berkman, a fellow anarchist. In 1892 she was an accessory to Berkman's failed attempt to assassinate steel tycoon Henry Clay Frick in revenge for Frick's brutal treatment of workers during the Homestead Steel strike. Berkman spent fourteen years in prison for this crime, but Goldman escaped indictment because of insufficient evidence. She became a prominent public figure, promoting revolutionary anarchism in speeches, pamphlets, and books.

In 1893 she was arrested and tried again for urging a crowd of hungry unemployed workers in New York's Union Square to rely on street protest rather than voting to obtain relief. In court, Goldman based her defense on the right of free speech. She lost and spent ten months in jail on Blackwell's Island, where she apprenticed as a nurse to the inmates.

When President William McKinley was shot in 1901 by Leon Czolgosz, the police quickly sought to implicate Goldman, because Czolgosz had recently attended one of her lectures in Cleveland, Ohio. Goldman and other anarchists were arrested, but she was released, again for lack of evidence.

In 1903 Goldman helped found the Free Speech League in New York City in response to a new federal law that barred anarchists from entering the country. The group was one of several that laid the groundwork for what eventually, more than a decade later, became the American Civil Liberties Union.

Goldman claimed that she opposed violence in theory, but she often defended it in practice by blaming government and business leaders for instigating violence against dissidents. "As an anarchist, I am opposed to violence," Goldman said. "But if the people want to do away with assassins, they must do away with the conditions which produce murderers."

While working as a nurse and midwife among poor immigrant workers on the Lower East Side in the 1890s, Goldman became convinced that birth control was essential to women's sexual and economic freedom. She influenced the young **Margaret Sanger,** encouraging her campaign against the Comstock Law, which prohibited the distribution of birth control literature. Goldman was arrested at least twice for violating the anti–birth control law—and saw her arrests as yet more evidence that freedom of speech was linked to other causes.

Indeed, Goldman was frequently arrested and jailed while lecturing on such topics as birth control and opposition to the draft, and sometimes her talks were banned outright. Goldman edited an anarchist literary and political magazine, *Mother Earth*, from 1906 to 1917. Starting in 1917, Goldman spent two years in prison in Missouri for her opposition to the draft during World War I. She was often called "Red Emma."

In December 1919 the US government stripped Goldman of her citizenship and deported her, Berkman, and other radicals to Russia. Goldman and Berkman grew quickly disillusioned with the Russian Revolution, which they viewed as corrupt and authoritarian. After two years, they left Russia, moved to Europe, and determined to expose the persecution, terrorism, and harsh economic conditions they had witnessed. Goldman wrote a series of articles for the *New York World* that became part of her 1923 book *My Disillusionment in Russia*.

She and Berkman eventually settled in France, where she wrote her autobiography, *Living My Life* (1931). Except for a brief visit in 1934, she was denied entry into the United States for the rest of her life, but upon her death in May 1940 she was allowed burial in Chicago's Waldheim Cemetery, near the graves of the Haymarket martyrs.

ANARCHISM'S INFLUENCE TODAY

Anarchist thought is still influential today. **Pacifism** influenced the thought and practice of Mahatma Gandhi and the Indian independence movement. He, in turn, influenced the American civil rights movement and the teachings and actions of Dr. Martin Luther King Jr. Eventually, the tactics of nonviolence and civil disobedience won over many people, and laws and practices were reversed because of them.

The tactics of nonviolence during the American civil rights movement were symbolized by the **freedom riders**, groups of students who rode interstate buses throughout the South to bring to light the discrimination that African Americans endured in traveling and using public accommodations. They were frequently harassed and beaten.

In addition, other students participated in sit-ins to integrate department store lunch counters. They were frequently harassed and beaten and then arrested for inciting a riot. The publicity these events generated led to further actions and support for the civil rights cause.

A more recent interpretation of anarchism is looking at the state as holding people back through its priorities and redistributive policies. This has given rise to movements calling for the weakening of the centralized state and people advocating for the government to do less. In the United States, this has contributed to the movement toward downsizing government and fewer taxes and regulations.

Anarcho-capitalism is a concept popularized by Murray Rothbard and David Friedman. They claimed that the market can satisfy all human wants. It is a belief that the government can be abolished and replaced by unregulated market competition. The market can even regulate social interactions.

Anarchism has aspects in common with communism. They both support the belief that eventually the state should wither away and be replaced by more communal organizations. However, anarchism substantially disagrees with communism on some substantial points.

- Anarchism rejects the central notion of economics.
- Anarchism does not view only the industrial working class as revolutionary.
- They also disagree on political organization. Anarchism emphasizes mass participation.
- Anarchists also advocate that the state be abolished.

LIBERTARIANISM'S IRON CAGE: FROM AYN RAND TO RAND PAUL
Alan Wolfe

In the past decade, libertarianism in the United States has come in from the cold. Once a fringe political movement associated with cranks, conspiracy theorists, and a few economists, it is now an ascendant force within one of our two major political parties. The change can be measured in the difference between the trajectory of Ron Paul, the Texas congressman who ran for president once as a Libertarian and twice as a Republican, and that of his son Kentucky Sen. Rand Paul, a candidate for the 2016 Republican nomination. Despite having a devoted following, Paul *père* was never a real contender for the White House; he was always an outlier and long shot in the GOP field. Paul *fils*, by contrast, has been treated as a major player by the GOP establishment and the media alike. Meanwhile, causes long dear to libertarians have become nationally prominent, including same-sex marriage, the legalization of marijuana, and opposition to the government's surveillance programs—the last spurred by a self-described libertarian, Edward Snowden. In the United States today, libertarianism is hailed by many as the solution to an economy and society stuck in bureaucratic mud, and candidates of all stripes can be found flirting with libertarian themes.

The movement's growing momentum derives in part from the largesse of the billionaire brothers Charles and David Koch. The latter ran as the Libertarian Party's vice-presidential candidate in 1980, and the two brothers have continued to give generously to libertarian organizations like the Cato Institute, the D.C.-based think tank. The Kochs now spend even more money promoting Republican candidates who lean libertarian, and in the post–*Citizens United* era, this strategy has given them and their political philosophy enormous influence. But libertarianism has also been attracting converts from left of center, especially among younger voters who find its anti-political, live-and-let-live message a refreshing departure from the meddling of big-government liberalism and culture-war conservatism. Indeed, many advocates of libertarianism present their position as a pure form of liberalism, and describe themselves as "classical liberals," equally committed to economic and civil liberty, and equally opposed to state bureaucracy and the legal enforcement of moral codes.

Given such confusing alignments, it might be useful to sketch in some political terms and pedigrees. Is libertarianism in fact conservative, or liberal? In 1960, Friedrich von Hayek, the Austrian-born economist and political philosopher known for his unswerving advocacy of free markets, published an essay titled "Why I Am Not a Conservative." Though Hayek's work in economics has appealed enormously to the American right, his self-assessment was correct: the version of laissez-faire capitalism he promulgated allowed little room for tradition, religion, locality, or other core concepts embraced by conservative thinkers from Edmund Burke to Michael Oakeshott. This is not to say that Hayek's free-market fundamentalism is liberal, however. Where Adam Smith's free market would liberate individuals from the caprices of an inflexible mercantilism, Hayek's would chain individuals to a system of rules over which they have no control and which they cannot, by themselves, fully understand. As political philosophies, the liberal tradition to which Smith belongs, and the libertarian one, which includes Hayek, have little in common—and indeed are often mutually antagonistic.

Let me be clear that in criticizing libertarianism, I'm not dismissing its priorities wholesale. I am not condemning policies that break up monopolies in favor of a greater emphasis on choice, for instance; and while I have some misgivings about school vouchers, I also believe that inner-city parents should have the same flexibility of options enjoyed by wealthier, suburban parents. On another subject, there is nothing wrong with, and much right about, relying on private institutions such as churches to help those who cannot help themselves. A number

Alan Wolfe, "Libertarianism's Iron Cage from Ayn Rand to Rand Paul," Commonweal, vol. 142, no. 15, pp. 14–18. Copyright © 2015 by Commonweal Foundation. Reprinted with permission. Provided by ProQuest LLC. All rights reserved.

of libertarian intellectuals, including a number of gay thinkers, have enriched our understanding of the importance of personal liberty. And of course we should be open to a variety of ways of making government function better.

Libertarianism, however, is not just a set of policy prescriptions, but an ideology. It is, moreover, a *total* ideology, one that addresses every aspect of how people live. There is a libertarian way of riding a bicycle, of taking your medicine, finding a spouse, giving blood, and even calling a cab (can you say, "Uber?"). Where liberalism raises questions, libertarians seek answers, and always find the right ones. Their philosophy is an antidote to the doubt, inconsistency, and vagueness that has always been built into liberalism. Libertarians come in different forms, and can argue vehemently over concepts and applications. Yet there nonetheless does exist a general libertarian outlook on life—and it is very different from the liberal one.

Perhaps the best place to begin distinguishing these two outlooks is the same place that liberals and libertarians themselves invariably start—namely, with that mystery known as human nature. What is the relationship between fundamental human capacities and the challenges—and rewards—of freedom? "He who lets the world choose his plan of life for him," John Stuart Mill famously observed in *On Liberty*, "has no need of any other faculty than that of ape-like imitation." Published in 1859, ten years before Darwin's *The Origin of Species*, Mill's essay was inspired by the writings of Wilhelm von Humboldt, who had added a touch of German romanticism to English ideas about individualism. We live for more than simply being free, Humboldt reminded his readers. We live to improve, to make and then remake ourselves in a never-ending state of self-development. Apes do not.

Were Mill writing today, his points of comparison with human beings would likely come from technology rather than biology. Computers do many of the things we human beings do, after all, and often much better than we do. But even those impressed with computers' ability to play chess or translate a language are generally unwilling to predict the capacity of such machines to love, be influenced by conscience, or change their minds in response to the contexts surrounding them. How can a computer be "free"? Liberty is for people. Its exercise requires a being capable of knowing how to put that liberty to good use.

Computers "think" by following mathematical rules known as algorithms. So, in the libertarian view, do human beings. Indeed, the libertarian conception of human nature seems curiously, even paradoxically, machine-like. Seemingly free to make our own decisions, in the libertarian utopia we would in fact be little more than slaves of rules that conform our choices to the rigidities of marketplace rationality. We would not give special preference to our loved ones merely because we love them. We would honor and admire our country, but only insofar as it followed

Ron (Right) & Rand Paul

libertarian ideals; if it did not—if its citizens voted, say, for a system based on altruistic precepts—we would hate it and seek its destruction, as John Galt and his followers did in Ayn Rand's popular novel *Atlas Shrugged*. At a personal level, emotions such as envy, guilt, and sympathy would be forbidden us. Human nature, libertarians insist, is one thing and one thing only: the capacity to make choices based on the rational calculation of self-interest. Great creative capitalists, they believe, understand this; everyone else is suffering from collectivism's version of what Marxists used to call false consciousness.

Better than any other political philosophy, libertarianism embodies Max Weber's nightmare of an iron cage, the apotheosis and province of "specialists without spirit, sensualists without heart." But where Weber lamented the severe rationality that turns man into a "nullity," libertarians praise it. Any motive other than rationality is a lower one. We are born to think, and the best among us are those who think the hardest, no matter where their thoughts may lead. Consequences are irrelevant to the libertarian; one must never be distracted from the one true course.

If these ideas are familiar to Americans, it is mostly due to the ever-resurgent legacy of Rand (1905–1982), the Russian-born philosophical novelist, whose oeuvre established her as the quintessential libertarian and inspired a kind of pop philosophical cult. It is common among contemporary libertarians to deny Rand membership in the club, but that is mostly because her ideological stridency is so revealing of libertarianism's limits. Though Rand styled herself a heroic thinker about heroic thinkers, she did not in fact develop her ideas all by herself. As a young woman she met and befriended other libertarian thinkers, including Rose Wilder Lane (daughter of the author of *Little House on the Prairie*) and Isabel Paterson, a leading columnist for the *New York Herald Tribune*, who helped Rand's *The Fountainhead* become a bestseller. Rand eventually broke with Paterson, part of a lifelong habit of cultivating cult-like followers, only to renounce them once they showed themselves insufficiently devoted to her. Even Rand's most devoted follower (and eventual lover), Nathaniel Branden, would be forced out of the closed circle, as Rand indulged another of her Stalinesque purges.

It was ironic, to be sure, that this woman who fled the Soviet Union in its infancy, and excoriated its political oppression, would mimic in her own life the regime's worst features. Rand's habit of brutally excommunicating her followers was not merely a personal quirk, however, but rather a tactic inherent in libertarianism itself, a creed obsessed with ideological purity and given to ceaseless sectarian purges. As soon as the Koch brothers bought themselves influence in the Cato Institute, for instance, they immediately began to rid themselves of those big-tent libertarians, such as Cato's president Ed Crane, who wanted the organization to attract libertarians from the left as well as the right. Like Ayn Rand, the Koch brothers took a "my way or the highway" approach, surrounding themselves with those who were in complete agreement with them. And that agreement had to be *truly* complete. "Koch called out Milton Friedman and Alan Greenspan specifically as sellouts to the system, merely trying to make government work more efficiently when the true libertarian should be tearing it out at the root," Brian Doherty, a historian sympathetic to the movement, has written.

This sort of denunciation is endemic to the school Ayn Rand did so much to promote. Name a libertarian, no matter how extreme, and another will turn up who finds that person too wishy-washy. Murray Rothbard, one of those cast out of the Randian inner circle for nonconforming views, hated the sectarianism of those who worshiped on the altar of *The Fountainhead*, calling them "posturing, pretentious, humorless, robotic, nasty, simple-minded jackasses." But Rothbard himself had no patience for anyone he considered soft. "Milton Friedman is the Establishment Court's libertarian," he once opined, declaring it "high time to call … a statist a statist." Ayn Rand herself described Friedman and George Stigler, another Chicago economist, as "a pair of reds," and dismissed Hayek as "'real poison' who does more good to the Communist cause than to our own." In the world of libertarianism, everyone is a suspect until proven innocent.

Why this closed-minded and tightly guarded boundary maintenance in the libertarian movement? The key may lie in the term "libertarian organization," with its obvious contradictions. It is difficult to be a passionate advocate for freedom and also a member of a tightly knit group. Individualistic to the core, libertarians practice what Margaret Thatcher preached: there is no such thing as society. Yet while they despise the left, they often copy leftists in their behavior. Take, for example, Rothbard, an extreme-right libertarian who behaved in a sectarian manner characteristic of the extreme left. "Always conscious of movement strategy, he looked to ideological revolutionaries of the past, such as Lenin, for strategic insights into how to effect ideological change on a national level," Doherty writes. "One of Rothbard's pet Leninist tropes was the idea of the cadre—the dedicated inner circle of revolutionaries, 100 percent reliable in ideology and action, around which a movement could crystallize."

Rand, as we have seen, approached politics in much the same way. And, as one of her biographers points out, her fiction closely resembled Soviet realism. When John Galt and his friends leave society behind for their hiding place in the mountains, they are acting as any Leninist vanguard would. "In essence," concludes journalist Jonathan Chait, in one of the best analyses of Rand's ideas, "Rand advocated a reverse Marxism. In the Marxist analysis, workers produce all the value, and capitalists merely leech off their labor. Rand posited the opposite."

Libertarians like to see themselves, in the tradition of Montesquieu and Madison, as wary of power and ever eager to limit its reach. In reality, these are people who hate the state but love power; they typically seek to advance liberty by exercising a distinctly authoritarian personality and politics. Everything must be their way—or they will work to destroy it. Here, more than anywhere else, is where libertarianism and liberalism take different paths. As thinkers such as Cass Sunstein and Stephen Holmes have demonstrated, rights are indeed checks against the power of an arbitrary state. But in the absence of power to protect their rights, people have no such guarantees; they require the state, and its ability to further human development, in order to limit the State. No such paradoxes are available to the libertarian mind, which abhors the messy reality of modern liberal democracy. A is always A, Rand repeatedly proclaimed; A is never B.

Nowhere do libertarians express more passionate conviction than in their abhorrence of coercion. The great sin of government regulation, in their view, is not that it seeks to promote equality (misguidedly, they think), but that it involves coercion. Regulation, as the libertarian law professor Richard Epstein calls it, is a "taking," and therefore unconstitutional. Each individual is entitled to what he or she owns, and if that person does not give permission for the government to take it away, then any such action by government is coercive. (The paramount bête noire in the libertarian panoply of enemy principles is eminent domain. *Kelo v. The City of New London*, a 2005 Supreme Court ruling that allowed cities to acquire private property in order to promote economic development, is the movement's *Dred Scott* decision.) In reality, however, the true unrestrained power in the world of Ayn Rand is the power of acting only in one's own self-interest. The potential violence of the state pales beside the violence required to build Howard Roark's skyscrapers; indeed, it is only by seeking the state's power that individuals can find any protection against the rapaciousness to which they are subjected in the workplace. Laissez-faire capitalism is not a beneficial harmony of interests to which we will return if we can only get government out of our lives. Far from constituting a refuge from violence, laissez-faire is a regime imposed by force. Unlike the rest of us, the Koch brothers have sufficient funds to impose their vision of the good society on the rest of us. The Koch brothers do not hate the state; they crave its use.

And so while libertarianism may at first glance seem to have a fair amount in common with liberalism, in fact, a more revealing comparison from the history of political philosophy lies in the work of one of liberalism's greatest enemies—Carl Schmitt, the right-wing German political philosopher (and Nazi sympathizer) of the 1930s and '40s. Both worldviews divide the political world into two camps, friend and enemy. Both focus on times of emergency and crisis rather than on everyday life. No wonder that libertarians find in gun rights the ultimate vision of the good society: where the state is absent, vigilante violence will flourish. There are few pacifists among libertarian activists and thinkers; though the movement theoretically opposes force, it has no place in its ranks for those who reject war. At times a libertarian such as Rand Paul speaks in the language of isolationism; what he offers, however, are the sentiments not of a proponent of world peace, but of a loner hunkered down with his gun, waiting for catastrophe.

This dreary image reveals libertarianism's angst-laden vision of a society in perilous decline. It reminds us that libertarianism—like Puritan theology and unlike liberalism and progressivism—is declensionist, viewing our world as hopelessly tainted by sin, irretrievably distant from its Edenic origins. In libertarianism, the state is always growing, taxes are always rising, freedom is always disappearing, and the only hope lies in taking pride in being what libertarian social critic Albert Jay Nock called "a remnant." There is a reason all the good guys in *Atlas Shrugged* withdraw into their hiding place in the mountains. Libertarianism chooses exit over engagement. To work with a corrupt society is to be corrupted by it.

The overt preoccupation with decline leaves libertarianism politically vulnerable; citizens in a democracy want to hear a bit of good news every now and then. Although libertarianism is a more powerful political force in the United States than in Europe, its greatest thinkers were European by birth—Hayek, Mises, and Rand, but also Frederick Bastiat, Carl Menger, and Tibor Machan, among numerous others—and the Euro-pessimism that clings to it would seem foreign to the sunny American optimism that made Ronald Reagan so popular. It is surprising that Republicans today, especially those committed to libertarianism, view Reagan as a saint who did no wrong. Reagan's

> # There is a reason all the good guys in *Atlas Shrugged* withdraw into their hiding place in the mountains. Libertarianism chooses exit over engagement. To work with a corrupt society is to be corrupted by it.

actual record—he left the welfare state by and large in place while raising taxes—hardly reflects a libertarian credo; and his appeal to the better angels of our nature is just as alien. Both Ayn Rand and Ronald Reagan spent considerable years in Hollywood, and seemingly absorbed opposing aspects of its aesthetic: Reagan its sunny happy endings, Rand its ominous *noir*. The lesson that routinely eludes proponents of libertarianism—a lesson that American preachers, even those associated with evangelical churches, have learned—is that contemporary Americans generally resist making too many judgments of others, and *vehemently* resist others making judgments of them. By and large, uplift has replaced sin in American preaching.

And uplift is hardly the libertarian forte. Randians do not generally advocate violence in order to bring about the society they favor. But there is a violent side to libertarianism nonetheless, a ready hatred that many libertarians have difficulty keeping under wraps. Rose Wilder Lane once let it slip that she hated FDR so much that she hoped someone would kill him. And Ayn Rand's fiction is drenched in contempt for those peons who fail to appreciate the benefits they glean from the creative class. In one of the greatest lines ever to appear in a book review, the ex-Communist Whittaker Chambers penetrated Rand's utopianism to expose the rigid state power that lay behind it: "From almost any page of *Atlas Shrugged*," he wrote in the *National Review*, "a voice can be heard, from painful necessity, commanding, 'To the gas chambers—go.'" Men and women without a conscience, Chambers understood, are capable of doing anything.

Chambers comprehended both the rigidity of libertarian singlemindedness and the mercilessness it entailed. Such qualities, again, would seem to make the creed ill-suited to a diverse democracy. The political philosopher Isaiah Berlin grew up in much the same way—indeed, in some of the very same places—as Ayn Rand, but unlike her, he became a proponent of value pluralism. By all three criteria Berlin used to define pluralism, libertarianism fails, and does so via a threefold insistence: 1) that there is a true answer to all questions; 2) that such truths are discoverable through reason alone and will eventually be proven correct; and 3) that anything discovered as truthful cannot contradict anything else discovered as truthful. Take, for example, the Friedmanites who insisted that the free market would have worked in Chile if it had been given a real chance, or the current governor of Kansas, whose faith in supply-side economics cannot be shaken: no matter how contrary the evidence, libertarianism can never fail, but can only be failed. There is no trial-and-error method, because there is no error. Strikingly modern in many ways, libertarianism has nothing in common with the most modern of all methodologies, the scientific one.

Berlin's objection to this kind of intellectual monism paralleled his objection to totalitarianism. For him, the good society was not one that proclaimed itself the embodiment of everything virtuous. He was far too Kantian for that, habitually citing Kant's dictum that "out of the crooked timber of humanity, no straight thing was ever made." Rand, by contrast, viewed Kant as the most evil philosopher—her term—who ever lived. Beyond Rand's sometimes laughable efforts to appear Kant's equal in epistemology, it seems she was especially offended by the Kantian moral ideal of disinterest. In her view, the act of willing our actions to conform with a universal moral law marks the first step toward subjection.

Such dogged monism typifies a creed that goes out of its way to reduce the complexity of the world to one thing and one thing only—whether it be how we make decisions, what decisions we make, or what our decisions imply for others. The often-noted attraction of libertarianism to college students is, I believe, a reflection of this radically simplifying inclination. There is something deeply satisfying to young minds in the Faustian idea that all of reality can be unlocked with one simple key. Only when they grow out of that fantasy, and begin to understand just how complex the world actually is, do some adherents of libertarianism begin to realize the limits of what was once so appealing.

Finally, one must note libertarianism's abiding relationship to atheism. Ayn Rand hated God like she hated Kant, and for much the same reason. Not all libertarians necessarily follow suit; there is, for example, a certain kind of libertarianism that appeals to Baptists, who throughout their history often rejected the authority of the state. Among the many recipients of the Koch brothers' bounty, meanwhile, are the Acton Institute, an organization devoted to reconciling laissez-faire capitalism with Catholic orthodoxy, as well as those Catholic universities willing to establish special programs of study consistent with the Koch ideological agenda. Although the Kochs themselves are prochoice and pro–gay marriage, they have sought to make common cause with Catholic social conservatives willing to promote their creed of deregulation and privatization.

Still, Christian libertarianism is not a term one commonly hears—not least of all because the libertarian lineage traces to a form of Social Darwinism, embodied in writers such as Herbert Spencer and William Graham Sumner, that was aggressively atheistic in its very inception. Christian liberals, on the other hand, are plentiful, and have long been so. Indeed, it is because the social Darwinists so strongly endorsed the theory of evolution that religious believers of the time insisted on a Christian ideal of charity as an alternative: Walter Rauschenbusch, founder of the Social Gospel, and Leo XIII, who issued *Rerum novarum* with its justification of labor unions, filled the gap that social Darwinism left open. Some celebrated liberals, such as Mill, wrote rarely about God. Others, such as Thomas Hill Green and R. H. Tawney, did so frequently; even John Rawls grew up in a religious home and considered theology as a career. Liberals, in short, can opt to choose God. Libertarians either cannot—or must twist themselves in knots in order to do so. The church, to most libertarians, is just another state. If modern society witnesses a war between science and God, libertarians stand in opposition to both.

All of this helps explain the gyrations of those who insist on being both libertarian-minded and Christian. Take, for instance, Representative Paul Ryan of Wisconsin, a Catholic and fiscal conservative—and chair of the House Budget Committee—who is routinely touted as the brain behind Republican fiscal policy. In a speech in 2005, when very few people were watching (save one who managed to get it on tape), Ryan allowed that "the reason I got involved in public service by and large, if I had to credit one thinker, one person, it would be Ayn Rand." After gaining the Republican vice-presidential nomination, Ryan, of course, changed his tune: now Ayn Rand was only one of the thinkers who influenced him—in general rather than in the specifics, and in any case not really all that much. But cynics think the true Ryan is the one who takes *Atlas Shrugged* as his Bible, and I agree. Behind all the charts and tables, a Paul Ryan budget is a blueprint for social meanness, and those who delve deeply into it cannot be faulted for concluding that Ryan is a Randian through and through. Like those who came before him—and in my view, fortunately—Ryan is too much the social Darwinist to be a significant Catholic force in American life.

Has libertarianism had its day? As a political force, perhaps not. Democracy, after all, requires an opposition party; and as an ideology for those out of power, libertarianism, with its relentlessly oppositional appeal, makes for a near-perfect fit. Yet democracy also requires ideals to live by, and that, I think, is where the severity of libertarianism's limitations becomes clear. Of course it may turn out that Americans dismayed by political cynicism and discord increasingly opt for a dysfunctional political system, preferring that nothing get done by government—in many ways, the actual libertarian program. But if we do ever long once again for leadership, and in that longing regain and express at least a modicum of trust in governance, then whoever ends up governing us well will need something more than a political philosophy based in pitilessness, rigidity, and a desiccated view of human nature.

CHAPTER 6

Socialism

KEY TERMS

Claude Henri de Saint-Simon

Robert Owen

Theory of Self-Alienation

Humanitarian/Utopian Socialism

Surplus Value

Lenin

Stalin

Politburo

Great Leap Forward

Cultural Revolution

Xi Jinping

Charles Fourier

Karl Marx

Labor Theory of Value

Scientific/Orthodox Socialism

Russian Revolution

New Economic Plan

Nomenklatura System

Mao Tse tung

Mass Line

Tiananmen Square

DISCUSSION QUESTIONS

1. What are Karl Marx's five stages of human development?

2. What is the difference between Humanitarian/Utopian Socialism and Scientific/Orthodox Socialism?

3. What are some criticisms of Marx's idea of Communism?

4. What contributions did Lenin make to Marxist thought?

5. What are Mao's four principles of Communism?

6. What was the significance of the Cultural Revolution in China?

EARLY SOCIALISTS AND TYPES OF SOCIALISM

Noel Babeuf (1760–1797)

Babeuf felt that the French Revolution would fall through on its stated goals. Babeuf advocated social justice for the common people. He was executed in 1797. After his execution, socialism split into two wings.

Humanitarian/Utopian Socialism

Humanitarian/Utopian Socialism is the belief that people should be treated fairly, and workers should benefit materially from their labor. The Utopians are often criticized by orthodox socialists for facilitating capitalism by treating workers better and not working toward the ultimate goal of replacing capitalism through revolution.

Labor Theory of Value

The **labor theory of value** states that only workers create wealth; therefore, society should adjust its social, economic, and political systems to prevent the unequal distribution of wealth.

Claude Henri Saint-Simon (1760–1825)

Saint-Simon is considered the "father of French socialism." He was a critic of capitalism because he viewed competition as wasteful and leading to poverty. Saint-Simon supported universal education and wanted to eliminate property inheritance.

Robert Owen (1771–1858)

Owen was opposed to charity; however, he realized that capitalism had excesses. He stated that exploiting workers was unprofitable, and everyone benefits with an improved work environment. Among his reforms are the following:

- Raised wages
- Encouraged unions
- Created a company store
- Provided education

Owen was more of a liberal capitalist than a socialist. His initial attempt at a model community succeeded. Subsequent attempts did not fare as well.

Charles Fourier (1772–1837)

Fourier was a critic of capitalism but also a vocal opponent of traditional institutions, such as religion, marriage, and the family. His vision for society was that it should be broken up into thousands of self-sustaining communities. They would associate with each other in a confederation, each preserving its independence. His thought influenced other socialists. He helped influence the founding of several communes.

Scientific/Orthodox Socialism

Marxism

Karl Marx (1818–1883) was a nineteenth-century German social thinker. He studied history from a materialistic point of view.

Marxism: Primary component of the life of society is labor. He argued that the ownership of means of production gives rise to the creation of social classes.

Capitalism Has Two Major Social Classes

- Bourgeoisie
- Proletariat

The course of human history can be explained in terms of class relationships. According to Marx, there are five stages of human history:

1. Communal societies
2. Slave
3. Feudal
4. Capitalist
5. Communist

Karl Marx believed that capitalism resulted in the masses becoming alienated from society (**theory of self-alienation**). He argued that due to the nature of capitalism and industrial work people do not derive any satisfaction from their work and living conditions. Another component of this alienation was his idea of **surplus value**. Marx believed that workers create value above the original labor cost of the products they manufacture. He argued that workers are responsible for creating wealth while factory owners and managers claim most of the profits.

Marx argued that the root of capitalism's destruction is competition. Because of competition, more and more people are driven into the proletariat, and capital becomes concentrated in fewer and fewer hands.

THE CRITICISM OF MARX'S IDEAS

- Capital-intensive industrialization: Industrialization evolved to be more focused on capital and technology rather than relying only on labor.
- Ownership diverse: The proliferation of the ownership of stocks and profit sharing led to a larger percentage of the population owning shares.
- Historically inaccurate: Historical process steady stream of events, complex process. Critics argue that history is more than just economics and who owns the means of production.

VLADIMIR LENIN (1870–1924)

Lenin believed in firm leadership, as workers were not ready for radical revolution. He pioneered the concept of the vanguard party: a small core group needs to lead the workers rather than a mass-based party.

Lenin developed the idea of imperialism in Marxism. He argued that the development of imperialism, with countries seizing territories to gain resources, captive markets, and strategic advantages, led the capitalist states to buy off their own working classes. This forestalled the working-class revolution that Marx thought would happen. Lenin argued that Marx died before the full implementation of modern imperialism and, therefore, did not foresee it. Lenin believed that rivalries between the imperial powers would eventually lead to conflict. The resulting deprivations would lead to revolution.

This is what happened in Russia. Initially, World War I was very popular. Men enlisted in the army willingly and went off to war with the blessings of the church and the tsar. However, Russia was not prepared for war. It was still a semi-feudal agrarian society. Its advantage was in the amount of manpower it could put into the field. However, it lacked industry and infrastructure. As a result, the Russian army quickly ran out of basic equipment a few months into the war. Russia suffered a great deal of losses during the war.

Tsar Nicholas II took personal command of the armies at the front and left domestic politics to his advisers. Food shortages and other deprivations increased. The government in St. Petersburg was seemingly incapable of dealing with the situation. In addition, there was a great deal of corruption. The upper classes continued to live as they did prior to the war, despite the suffering of the general population.

The Social Democrats removed the tsar from office in February 1917. He and his family were put under house arrest. Alexander Kerensky led the Social Democrats. Kerensky advocated a continuation of the war. He was under a great deal of pressure from the Entente powers to continue the war. They desperately wanted to keep Russia in the war to tie down massive amounts of German troops and equipment on the Eastern Front. Their biggest fear was that if Russia quit the war, it would release an overwhelming force of German soldiers for duty in the west, which could overwhelm the Entente forces.

The Bolsheviks continued to agitate against the Social Democrats. They argued that they were not true revolutionaries. Lenin had been living in exile. He was assisted by the German government, which facilitated his return to Russia. Lenin continued to agitate against the government. Things continued to get worse. These factors made the **Russian revolution** possible.

THE BOLSHEVIKS WERE ABLE TO TAKE POWER IN OCTOBER 1917 WITH LITTLE OPPOSITION

- Peasants were hostile toward existing social and political conditions
- Most of the population was alienated
- The military and police were disintegrated

The Bolsheviks gained support through the slogan "Peace, Land, and Bread." They agreed to end the war with Germany, which was eventually negotiated in 1918 with the Treaty of Brest-Litovsk. While the treaty gave sizable territorial gains to Germany at Russia's expense, it was nullified once Germany lost the war.

However, the conflict did not end in Russia. The Bolsheviks controlled the major cities, but their control over the rest of the country was weak. A number of groups rose to challenge the Bolsheviks (Reds). These groups were collectively called the Whites (white is the color of counterrevolution in Europe). The Whites were a collection of groups that ranged from Social Democrats to monarchists. Initially, they controlled much of the country, and it looked as if they would overrun the Reds. Lenin tasked Leon Trotsky, who had negotiated the Treaty of Brest-Litovsk, to build the Red Army. He installed discipline and proper training. He also incorporated former imperial officers into the Red Army. Their training, discipline, and tactical knowledge eventually allowed the army to develop. The Whites were weakened by infighting and the inability to maintain popular support. The Bolsheviks were able to defeat the last of the White groups in 1921.

Lenin found that governing a country was more difficult than developing political theory. Toward the end of his life, he contemplated initiating economic reforms that would involve economic privatization of some aspects of the economy. He called this the **New Economic Plan**. However, he could not fully implement them. He was the victim of an assassination attempt, which wounded him. He subsequently suffered several strokes, which further debilitated him. Lenin died in 1924.

Leadership of the Bolsheviks would eventually pass to Joseph Stalin. **Stalin** had made a name for himself in the Bolshevik party by being in charge of the nationalities question. During the years before the revolution, Stalin helped raise money for the party by planning bank robberies.

Lenin did not trust Stalin and tried to warn others in the leadership to be wary of him. Stalin was shrewd in developing alliances with other leaders. He was able to gain control of the **Politburo**, the highest policy making body of the Communist party, by playing the other members against each other until he emerged with total power.

His goal for the Soviet Union was to build socialism in one country. By the time he came to power, he wanted to industrialize rapidly. His emphasis was on heavy industry and transportation. Stalin used the funds generated from agriculture to finance this development. One of his policies was forced collectivization of agriculture. This was the taking of land from the peasants and the development of state-run collective farms. This would make it easier for the government to keep control of agriculture while taking the resources derived from agriculture and plowing them into industry. This had ramifications, especially in Ukraine. Many peasants resented the confiscation of their land and farm animals. They slaughtered their animals rather than turn them over to the state. This and the confiscation of grain led to a forced famine in the region.

Despite his harsh policies and the deaths of millions, Stalin was able to make the Soviet Union into a global industrial power. Although World War II saw the Soviet Union suffer huge loses, 20 million dead and much of the western part of the country devastated and under occupation for several years, it emerged as a major global power. By the end of World War II, Stalin's Soviet Union occupied eastern and much of central Europe.

The Yalta Conference in February 1945 assured the Soviet Union of the occupation of part of Germany and a prominent place in the United Nations. The wartime cooperation with the United States began to break down because of mutual suspicion. Stalin was also very paranoid. He initiated several rounds of purges in the 1930s, which strengthened his political position but weakened the Soviet Union. His purge of the army contributed to Soviet defeats during the initial stages of the Nazi invasion in 1941.

The end of World War II saw a Cold War in the international system between the United States and the Soviet Union. Each power tried to gain economic, military, and political advantage over the other.

The Soviet Union sought to match the United States in nuclear weapons and was successful in testing a weapon in 1949. The two countries fought wars through proxies until the collapse of the Soviet Union in 1991.

Joseph Stalin died in 1953 and was succeeded by Nikita Khrushchev. He initiated a period of de-Stalinization, which discredited Stalin's policies, and the Soviet government began to admit the crimes of Stalin and opened up the prison camp system.

Khrushchev was removed as general secretary of the Communist Party in 1964, as many of his policies failed. Leonid Brezhnev succeeded him. Under Brezhnev, the party apparatus, the **nomen-klatura system** where party leaders formed alliances and were dependent on those above them, became entrenched. The command economy saw production quotas and economic centralization. This led to economic stagnation and a failure of innovation. By the 1980s, it was apparent that the Soviet Union needed to reform. After Brezhnev died, there was a succession of leaders whose formative years were during World War II—leaders until Mikhail Gorbachev.

Gorbachev was a much younger man than his predecessors. He was not as shaped by the Stalin era and World War II as his predecessors. He advocated two basic policies: glasnost and perestroika. Glasnost meant openness and perestroika meant restructuring. What he wanted to do was advocate a discussion of economic change that would allow new ideas to be put into place to change the Soviet economic system to make it more competitive globally.

However, once the easing of restrictions was accomplished, people began to discuss other issues besides the economy. In different parts of the Soviet Union, people began to agitate for independence. This was especially true in the Baltic Republics of Lithuania, Latvia, and Estonia. These areas gained their independence after World War I and were reoccupied by the Soviet Union in 1940 as part of the Nazi-Soviet pact of 1939. In this agreement, Germany and the Soviet Union agreed to divide Eastern Europe into spheres of influence. They were the wealthiest areas of the Soviet Union, and many people wanted independence. In addition, people began to challenge the supremacy of the Communist Party. The result was the collapse of the Soviet Union in 1991 and its replacement by 16 separate republics. The most significant of which was Russia.

For a period of time, Russia withdrew as a superpower, and economic conditions worsened. Russia remained a country dominated by a strong national government. It eventually reemerged as a state with a strong economy and military under Vladimir Putin.

MAO TSE TUNG REINTERPRETS MARXISM

China in modern times was weak and divided. It was at the mercy of imperial powers. Much of the eastern coastal part of China had been occupied by one or another power. The Chinese had attempted to throw off these foreigners without success.

The imperial system in China was overthrown in 1911. China for a time was in a state of civil war with warlords dominating different parts of the country. A nationalist movement emerged under Dr. Sun Yat-sen, which attempted to strengthen the national government. After his death, the leadership of the nationalist movement passed to General Chang Kai-Shek. While consolidating the country and eliminating the power of the warlords, he grew increasingly more authoritarian.

The communist movement arose in opposition to the nationalists. They would eventually be successful in taking control of the country in 1949.

Chinese Communist Ideology: Three Elements
1. Influence of the Chinese Revolution
2. The ideas of Marx and Lenin
3. The thoughts of Mao

Mao was born in 1893 to a peasant family in central China. At the end of World War I, he moved to Beijing to attend university and joined a Marxist study group.

The Communist Party of China was very obedient to the Comintern (Communist International through which Stalin sought to control other communist movements.). In 1927, Mao reported to the party the necessity of forming alliances with peasants and abandoning the urban strategy that the Soviets were pushing.

In 1931, the Communists decided to adopt Mao's strategy and rejected the Soviet model of building the movement in urban areas to the neglect of the countryside.

Mao's Military Strategy for Victory
- Creation of a strong and mobile peasant-based Red Army for a protracted struggle
- Selection of a strategic terrain
- Establishment of a self-sufficient economic base

In 1935, Mao became the elected leader of the Chinese Communist Party. There was a series of truces with the nationalist government in an effort to deal with the Japanese invasion during World War II. Mao was able to use this time to build up his forces and prestige. After the war, the civil war commenced with the Communists emerging victorious in 1949.

Mao's Four Principles of Communism

Populism
Populism meant giving the peasants a leading role in the revolution. This was a break from Orthodox Marxism and the Soviet model, which favored emphasizing the industrial working classes. Mao, however, believed in the value of peasants and sought to win them over to the Communist cause. This served as a model for other Asian Communist movements, such as Ho Chi Minh's in Vietnam.

Permanent Revolution
The permanent revolution was a belief in violence to further the development of socialism. The idea of constant revolution would keep the population motivated.

Mass Line
Mao rejected the idea of elitism. He felt that peasants could be mobilized around socialism through education and inclusiveness. The concept of the **mass line** featured the following:

- Party cadres list the scattered views of the masses
- Study and put into systemic form
- Higher authorities evaluate and return ideas to the masses

Guerrilla Warfare
An unconventional strategy, guerrilla warfare featured small-unit attacks to tie down opponents and force them to expend resources to defend the territory. Mao was initially successful against the Japanese and the nationalists by not challenging them directly. He chose the terrain to fight on that favored his forces. He fought isolated units in hit-and-run attacks until they had built up their forces. This also served as a model, especially, for the Viet Minh in Vietnam.

The Great Leap Forward
This was an attempt to mobilize the people behind industrialization by creating small-scale industry throughout the country. This largely failed because China was still a largely agrarian, peasant society. Most people did not have industrial skills.

Cultural Revolution
The **Cultural Revolution** was an attempt to purify Chinese Communism by eliminating links with the past that were viewed as decadent and corrupt. Unfortunately, many ancient Chinese statues and works of art were destroyed during this period. The Red Guards were composed of young Communist radicals who were tasked with carrying this out. They sought to eliminate any shred of the old order and capitalist influence. This included turning on many Communist leaders. Radical leaders loyal to Mao supported them, and they were fueled by access to confidential information about the Communist leaders. In response to the excesses, the military assumed more control through the supervision of local government and party institutions.

CHINA POST-MAO: A QUICK SUMMARY

In 1976, Mao died, and the radicals were purged. This began an evolution of more pragmatic leadership.

This leadership would become more economically pragmatic, adopting market-oriented reforms. At the same time, the Communist Party retained its grip on society politically and socially. Diplomatic relations were established with the United States.

In 1986, China initiated new policies that welcomed foreign investment and the beginnings of a private-sector market economy.

In 1989, students protested in **Tiananmen Square** in Beijing. These protests were eventually crushed by the government. The Communist Party took steps to ensure its political control while increasing market reforms. Essentially, the message to the people was that they could engage in economic activity, partner with foreign companies, and make money as long as the political supremacy of the Communist Party was not questioned. In 2011, China became the world's second-largest economy, overtaking Japan. The Chinese economy has slowed in recent years. The year 2015 marked its lowest economic growth level in 20 years.

Xi Jinping became party chief in 2012 and assumed the presidency in 2013. In 2018, the National Party Congress of the Communist Party removed the two-term limit on the presidency. The assumption is that Xi Jinping will continue as president of the People's Republic of China for the foreseeable future. In recent years, China has asserted itself regionally by building up its military and asserting territorial claims to several island chains in the Pacific. Beijing is also using its control of reefs to build artificial islands to use as naval and air bases.

THE COMMUNIST MANIFESTO
Karl Marx

Bourgeois and Proletarians

The history of all hitherto existing society is the history of class struggles. Freeman and slave, patrician and plebeian, lord and serf, guild-master and journeyman, in a word, oppressor and oppressed, stood in constant opposition to one another, carried on an uninterrupted, now hidden, now open fight, a fight that each time ended, either in a revolutionary re-constitution of society at large, or in the common ruin of the contending classes.

In the earlier epochs of history, we find almost everywhere a complicated arrangement of society into various orders, a manifold gradation of social rank. In ancient Rome we have patricians, knights, plebeians, slaves; in the Middle Ages, feudal lords, vassals, guild-masters, journeymen, apprentices, serfs; in almost all of these classes, again, subordinate gradations.

The modern bourgeois society that has sprouted from the ruins of feudal society has not done away with clash antagonisms. It has but established new classes, new conditions of oppression, new forms of struggle in place of the old ones.

Our epoch, the epoch of the bourgeoisie, possesses, however, this distinctive feature: it has simplified the clash antagonisms: Society as a whole is more and more splitting up into two great hostile camps, into two great classes directly facing each other: Bourgeoisie and Proletariat.

Karl Marx, "Bourgeois and Proletarians: Part One of the Manifesto of the Communist Party," The Communist Manifesto: Bourgeois and Proletarians, pp. 1–10, 1969.

From the serfs of the Middle Ages sprang the chartered burghers of the earliest towns. From these burgesses the first elements of the bourgeoisie were developed.

The discovery of America, the rounding of the Cape, opened up fresh ground for the rising bourgeoisie. The East-Indian and Chinese markets, the colonisation of America, trade with the colonies, the increase in the means of exchange and in commodities generally, gave to commerce, to navigation, to industry, an impulse never before known, and thereby, to the revolutionary element in the tottering feudal society, a rapid development.

The feudal system of industry, under which industrial production was monopolised by closed guilds, now no longer sufficed for the growing wants of the new markets. The manufacturing system took its place. The guild-masters were pushed on one side by the manufacturing middle class; division of labour between the different corporate guilds vanished in the face of division of labour in each single workshop.

Meantime the markets kept ever growing, the demand ever rising. Even manufacture no longer sufficed. Thereupon, steam and machinery revolutionised industrial production. The place of manufacture was taken by the giant, Modern Industry, the place of the industrial middle class, by industrial millionaires, the leaders of whole industrial armies, the modern bourgeois.

Modern industry has established the world-market, for which the discovery of America paved the way. This market has given an immense development to commerce, to navigation, to communication by land. This development has, in its turn, reacted on the extension of industry; and in proportion as industry, commerce, navigation, railways extended, in the same proportion the bourgeoisie developed, increased its capital, and pushed into the background every class handed down from the Middle Ages.

We see, therefore, how the modern bourgeoisie is itself the product of a long course of development, of a series of revolutions in the modes of production and of exchange.

Each step in the development of the bourgeoisie was accompanied by a corresponding political advance of that class. An oppressed class under the sway of the feudal nobility, an armed and self-governing association in the mediaeval commune; here independent urban republic (as in Italy and Germany), there taxable "third estate" of the monarchy (as in France), afterwards, in the period of manufacture proper, serving either the semi-feudal or the absolute monarchy as a counterpoise against the nobility, and, in fact, corner-stone of the great monarchies in general, the bourgeoisie has at last, since the establishment of Modern Industry and of the world-market, conquered for itself, in the modern representative State, exclusive political sway. The executive of the modern State is but a committee for managing the common affairs of the whole bourgeoisie.

The bourgeoisie, historically, has played a most revolutionary part.

The bourgeoisie, wherever it has got the upper hand, has put an end to all feudal, patriarchal, idyllic relations. It has pitilessly torn asunder the motley feudal ties that bound man to his "natural superiors," and has left remaining no other nexus between man and man than naked self-interest, than callous "cash payment." It has drowned the most heavenly ecstasies of religious fervour, of chivalrous enthusiasm, of philistine sentimentalism, in the icy water of egotistical calculation. It has resolved personal worth into exchange value, and in place of the numberless indefeasible chartered freedoms, has set up that single, unconscionable freedom—Free Trade. In one word, for exploitation, veiled by religious and political illusions, it has substituted naked, shameless, direct, brutal exploitation.

The bourgeoisie has stripped of its halo every occupation hitherto honoured and looked up to with reverent awe. It has converted the physician, the lawyer, the priest, the poet, the man of science, into its paid wage-labourers.

The bourgeoisie has torn away from the family its sentimental veil, and has reduced the family relation to a mere money relation.

The bourgeoisie has disclosed how it came to pass that the brutal display of vigour in the Middle Ages, which Reactionists so much admire, found its fitting complement in the most slothful indolence. It has been the first to show what man's activity can bring about. It has accomplished wonders far surpassing Egyptian pyramids, Roman aqueducts, and

Gothic cathedrals; it has conducted expeditions that put in the shade all former Exoduses of nations and crusades.

The bourgeoisie cannot exist without constantly revolutionising the instruments of production, and thereby the relations of production, and with them the whole relations of society. Conservation of the old modes of production in unaltered form, was, on the contrary, the first condition of existence for all earlier industrial classes. Constant revolutionising of production, uninterrupted disturbance of all social conditions, everlasting uncertainty and agitation distinguish the bourgeois epoch from all earlier ones. All fixed, fast-frozen relations, with their train of ancient and venerable prejudices and opinions, are swept away, all new-formed ones become antiquated before they can ossify. All that is solid melts into air, all that is holy is profaned, and man is at last compelled to face with sober senses, his real conditions of life, and his relations with his kind.

The need of a constantly expanding market for its products chases the bourgeoisie over the whole surface of the globe. It must nestle everywhere, settle everywhere, establish connexions everywhere.

The bourgeoisie has through its exploitation of the world-market given a cosmopolitan character to production and consumption in every country. To the great chagrin of Reactionists, it has drawn from under the feet of industry the national ground on which it stood. All old-established national industries have been destroyed or are daily being destroyed. They are dislodged by new industries, whose introduction becomes a life and death question for all civilised nations, by industries that no longer work up indigenous raw material, but raw material drawn from the remotest zones; industries whose products are consumed, not only at home, but in every quarter of the globe. In place of the old wants, satisfied by the productions of the country, we find new wants, requiring for their satisfaction the products of distant lands and climes. In place of the old local and national seclusion and self-sufficiency, we have intercourse in every direction, universal interdependence of nations. And as in material, so also in intellectual production. The intellectual creations of individual nations become common property. National one-sidedness

and narrow-mindedness become more and more impossible, and from the numerous national and local literatures, there arises a world literature.

The bourgeoisie, by the rapid improvement of all instruments of production, by the immensely facilitated means of communication, draws all, even the most barbarian, nations into civilisation. The cheap prices of its commodities are the heavy artillery with which it batters down all Chinese walls, with which it forces the barbarians' intensely obstinate hatred of foreigners to capitulate. It compels all nations, on pain of extinction, to adopt the bourgeois mode of production; it compels them to introduce what it calls civilisation into their midst, *i.e.,* to become bourgeois themselves. In one word, it creates a world after its own image.

The bourgeoisie has subjected the country to the rule of the towns. It has created enormous cities, has greatly increased the urban population as compared with the rural, and has thus rescued a considerable part of the population from the idiocy of rural life, just as it has made the country dependent on the towns, so it has made barbarian and semi-barbarian countries dependent on the civilised ones, nations and peasants on nations of bourgeois, the East on the West.

The bourgeoisie keeps more and more doing away with the scattered state of the population, of the means of production, and of property. It has agglomerated population, centralised means of production, and has concentrated property in a few hands. The necessary consequence of this was political centralisation. Independent, or but loosely connected provinces, with separate interests, laws, governments and systems of taxation, became lumped together into one nation, with one government, one code of laws, one national class-interest, one frontier and one customs-tariff. The bourgeoisie, during its rule of scarce one hundred years, has created more massive and more colossal productive forces than have all preceding generations together. Subjection of Nature's forces to man, machinery, application of chemistry to industry and agriculture, steam-navigation, railways, electric telegraphs, clearing of whole continents for cultivation, canalisation of rivers, whole populations conjured out of the ground—what earlier century had even a presentiment that such productive forces slumbered in the lap of social labour?

We see then: the means of production and of exchange, on whose foundation the bourgeoisie built itself up, were generated in feudal society. At a certain stage in the development of these means of production and of exchange, the conditions under which feudal society produced and exchanged, the feudal organisation of agriculture and manufacturing industry, in one word, the feudal relations of property became no longer compatible with the already developed productive forces; they became so many fetters. They had to be burst asunder; they were burst asunder.

Into their place stepped free competition, accompanied by a social and political constitution adapted to it, and by the economical and political sway of the bourgeois class.

A similar movement is going on before our own eyes. Modern bourgeois society with its relations of production, of exchange and of property, a society that has conjured up such gigantic means of production and of exchange, is like the sorcerer, who is no longer able to control the powers of the nether world whom he has called up by his spells. For many a decade past the history of industry and commerce is but the history of the revolt of modern productive forces against modern conditions of production, against the property relations that are the conditions for the existence of the bourgeoisie and of its rule. It is enough to mention the commercial crises that by their periodical return put on its trial, each time more threateningly, the existence of the entire bourgeois society. In these crises a great part not only of the existing products, but also of the previously created productive forces, are periodically destroyed. In these crises there breaks out an epidemic that, in all earlier epochs, would have seemed an absurdity—the epidemic of over-production. Society suddenly finds itself put back into a state of momentary barbarism; it appears as if a famine, a universal war of devastation had cut off the supply of every means of subsistence; industry and commerce seem to be destroyed; and why? Because there is too much civilisation, too much means of subsistence, too much industry, too much commerce. The productive forces at the disposal of society no longer tend to further the development of the conditions of bourgeois property; on the contrary, they have become too powerful for these conditions, by which they are fettered, and so soon as they overcome these fetters, they bring disorder into the whole of bourgeois society, endanger the existence of bourgeois property. The conditions of bourgeois society are too narrow to comprise the wealth created by them. And how does the bourgeoisie get over these crises? On the one hand by enforced destruction of a mass of productive forces; on the other, by the conquest of new markets, and by the more thorough exploitation of the old ones. That is to say, by paving the way for more extensive and more destructive crises, and by diminishing the means whereby crises are prevented.

The weapons with which the bourgeoisie felled feudalism to the ground are now turned against the bourgeoisie itself.

But not only has the bourgeoisie forged the weapons that bring death to itself; it has also called into existence the men who are to wield these weapons—the modern working class—the proletarians.

In proportion as the bourgeoisie, *i.e.,* capital, is developed, in the same proportion is the proletariat, the modern working class, developed—a class of labourers, who live only so long as they find work, and who find work only so long as their labour increases capital. These labourers, who must sell themselves piece-meal, are a commodity, like every other article of commerce, and are consequently exposed to all the vicissitudes of competition, to all the fluctuations of the market.

Owing to the extensive use of machinery and to division of labour, the work of the proletarians has lost all individual character, and consequently, all charm for the workman. He becomes an appendage of the machine, and it is only the most simple, most monotonous, and most easily acquired knack, that is required of him. Hence, the cost of production of a workman is restricted, almost entirely, to the means of subsistence that he requires for his maintenance, and for the propagation of his race. But the price of a commodity, and therefore also of labour, is equal to its cost of production. In proportion, therefore, as the repulsiveness of the work increases, the wage decreases. Nay more, in proportion as the use of machinery and division of labour increases, in the same proportion the burden of toil also increases, whether by prolongation of the working hours, by increase of the work exacted in a given time or by increased speed of the machinery, etc.

Modern industry has converted the little workshop of the patriarchal master into the great factory of the industrial capitalist. Masses of labourers, crowded into the factory, are organised like soldiers. As privates of the industrial army they are placed under the command of a perfect hierarchy of officers and sergeants. Not only are they slaves of the bourgeois class, and of the bourgeois State; they are daily and hourly enslaved by the machine, by the over-looker, and, above all, by the individual bourgeois manufacturer himself. The more openly this despotism proclaims gain to be its end and aim, the more petty, the more hateful and the more embittering it is.

The less the skill and exertion of strength implied in manual labour, in other words, the more modern industry becomes developed, the more is the labour of men superseded by that of women. Differences of age and sex have no longer any distinctive social validity for the working class. All are instruments of labour, more or less expensive to use, according to their age and sex.

No sooner is the exploitation of the labourer by the manufacturer, so far, at an end, that he receives his wages in cash, than he is set upon by the other portions of the bourgeoisie, the landlord, the shopkeeper, the pawnbroker, etc.

The lower strata of the middle class—the small tradespeople, shopkeepers, and retired tradesmen generally, the handicraftsmen and peasants—all these sink gradually into the proletariat, partly because their diminutive capital does not suffice for the scale on which Modern Industry is carried on, and is swamped in the competition with the large capitalists, partly because their specialised skill is rendered worthless by new methods of production. Thus the proletariat is recruited from all classes of the population.

The proletariat goes through various stages of development. With its birth begins its struggle with the bourgeoisie. At first the contest is carried on by individual labourers, then by the workpeople of a factory, then by the operatives of one trade, in one locality, against the individual bourgeois who directly exploits them. They direct their attacks not against the bourgeois conditions of production, but against the instruments of production themselves; they destroy imported wares that compete with their labour, they smash to pieces machinery, they set factories ablaze, they seek to restore by force the vanished status of the workman of the Middle Ages.

At this stage the labourers still form an incoherent mass scattered over the whole country, and broken up by their mutual competition. If anywhere they unite to form more compact bodies, this is not yet the consequence of their own active union, but of the union of the bourgeoisie, which class, in order to attain its own political ends, is compelled to set the whole proletariat in motion, and is moreover yet, for a time, able to do so. At this stage, therefore, the proletarians do not fight their enemies, but the enemies of their enemies, the remnants of absolute monarchy, the landowners, the non-industrial bourgeois, the petty bourgeoisie. Thus the whole historical movement is concentrated in the hands of the bourgeoisie; every victory so obtained is a victory for the bourgeoisie.

But with the development of industry the proletariat not only increases in number; it becomes concentrated in greater masses, its strength grows, and it feels that strength more. The various interests and conditions of life within the ranks of the proletariat are more and more equalised, in proportion as machinery obliterates all distinctions of labour, and nearly everywhere reduces wages to the same low level. The growing competition among the bourgeois, and the resulting commercial crises, make the wages of the workers ever more fluctuating. The unceasing improvement of machinery, ever more rapidly developing, makes their livelihood more and more precarious; the collisions between individual workmen and individual bourgeois take more and more the character of collisions between two classes. Thereupon the workers begin to form combinations (Trades Unions) against the bourgeois; they club together in order to keep up the rate of wages; they found permanent associations in order to make provision beforehand for these occasional revolts. Here and there the contest breaks out into riots.

Now and then the workers are victorious, but only for a time. The real fruit of their battles lies, not in the immediate result, but in the ever-expanding union of the workers. This union is helped on by the improved means of communication that are created by modern industry and that place the workers of different localities in contact with one another. It was just this contact that was needed to centralise the numerous local struggles, all of the same character, into one national struggle between classes. But every class struggle is a political struggle. And that union, to attain which the burghers of the Middle Ages, with their miserable highways, required centuries, the modern proletarians, thanks to railways, achieve in a few years.

This organisation of the proletarians into a class, and consequently into a political party, is continually being upset again by the competition between the workers themselves. But it ever rises up again, stronger, firmer, mightier. It compels legislative recognition of particular interests of the workers, by taking advantage of the divisions among the bourgeoisie itself. Thus the ten-hours' bill in England was carried.

Altogether collisions between the classes of the old society further, in many ways, the course of development of the proletariat. The bourgeoisie finds itself involved in a constant battle. At first with the aristocracy; later on, with those portions of the bourgeoisie itself, whose interests have become antagonistic to the progress of industry; at all times, with the bourgeoisie of foreign countries. In all these battles it sees itself compelled to appeal to the proletariat, to ask for its help, and thus, to drag it into the political arena. The bourgeoisie itself, therefore, supplies the proletariat with its own elements of political and general education, in other words, it furnishes the proletariat with weapons for fighting the bourgeoisie.

Further, as we have already seen, entire sections of the ruling classes are, by the advance of industry, precipitated into the proletariat, or are at least threatened in their conditions of existence. These also supply the proletariat with fresh elements of enlightenment and progress.

Finally, in times when the class struggle nears the decisive hour, the process of dissolution going on within the ruling class, in fact within the whole range of society, assumes such a violent, glaring character, that a small section of the ruling class cuts itself adrift, and joins the revolutionary class, the class that holds the future in its hands. Just as, therefore, at an earlier period, a section of the nobility went over to the bourgeoisie, so now a portion of the bourgeoisie goes over to the proletariat, and in particular, a portion of the bourgeois ideologists, who have raised themselves to the level of comprehending theoretically the historical movement as a whole.

Of all the classes that stand face to face with the bourgeoisie today, the proletariat alone is a really revolutionary class. The other classes decay and finally disappear in the face of Modern Industry; the proletariat is its special and essential product.

The lower middle class, the small manufacturer, the shopkeeper, the artisan, the peasant, all these fight against the bourgeoisie, to save from extinction their existence as fractions of the middle class. They are therefore not revolutionary, but conservative. Nay more, they are reactionary, for they try to roll back the wheel of history. If by chance they are revolutionary, they are so only in view of their impending transfer into the proletariat, they thus defend not their present, but their future interests, they desert their own standpoint to place themselves at that of the proletariat.

The "dangerous class," the social scum, that passively rotting mass thrown off by the lowest layers of old society, may, here and there, be swept into the movement by a proletarian revolution; its conditions of life, however, prepare it far more for the part of a bribed tool of reactionary intrigue.

In the conditions of the proletariat, those of old society at large are already virtually swamped. The proletarian is without property; his relation to his wife and children has no longer anything in common with the bourgeois family-relations; modern industrial labour, modern subjection to capital, the same in England as in France, in America as in Germany, has stripped him of every trace of national character. Law, morality, religion, are to him so many bourgeois prejudices, behind which lurk in ambush just as many bourgeois interests.

All the preceding classes that got the upper hand, sought to fortify their already acquired status by subjecting society at large to their conditions of appropriation. The proletarians cannot become masters of the productive forces of society, except by abolishing their own previous mode of appropriation, and thereby also every other previous mode of appropriation. They have nothing of their own to secure and to fortify; their mission is to destroy all previous securities for, and insurances of, individual property.

All previous historical movements were movements of minorities, or in the interests of minorities. The proletarian movement is the self-conscious, independent movement of the immense majority, in the interests of the immense majority. The proletariat, the lowest stratum of our present society, cannot stir, cannot raise itself up, without the whole superincumbent strata of official society being sprung into the air.

Though not in substance, yet in form, the struggle of the proletariat with the bourgeoisie is at first a national struggle. The proletariat of each country must, of course, first of all settle matters with its own bourgeoisie.

In depicting the most general phases of the development of the proletariat, we traced the more or less veiled civil war, raging within existing society, up to the point where that war breaks out into open revolution, and where the violent overthrow of the bourgeoisie lays the foundation for the sway of the proletariat.

Hitherto, every form of society has been based, as we have already seen, on the antagonism of oppressing and oppressed classes. But in order to oppress a class, certain conditions must be assured to it under which it can, at least, continue its slavish existence. The serf, in the period of serfdom, raised himself to membership in the commune, just as the petty bourgeois, under the yoke of feudal absolutism, managed to develop into a bourgeois. The modern labourer, on the contrary, instead of rising with the progress of industry, sinks deeper and deeper below the conditions of existence of his own class. He becomes a pauper, and pauperism develops more rapidly than population and wealth. And here it becomes evident, that the bourgeoisie is unfit any longer to be the ruling class in society, and to impose its conditions of existence upon society as an over-riding law. It is unfit to rule because it is incompetent to assure an existence to its slave within his slavery, because it cannot help letting him sink into such a state, that it has to feed him, instead of being fed by him. Society can no longer live under this bourgeoisie, in other words, its existence is no longer compatible with society.

The essential condition for the existence, and for the sway of the bourgeois class, is the formation and augmentation of capital; the condition for capital is wage-labour. Wage-labour rests exclusively on competition between the labourers. The advance of industry, whose involuntary promoter is the bourgeoisie, replaces the isolation of the labourers, due to competition, by their revolutionary combination, due to association. The development of Modern Industry, therefore, cuts from under its feet the very foundation on which the bourgeoisie produces and appropriates products. What the bourgeoisie, therefore, produces, above all, is its own grave-diggers. Its fall and the victory of the proletariat are equally inevitable.

Discussion Questions

1. What is the critical difference between "bourgeoisie" and "proletarians"?

2. What factors increased the political power of the bourgeoisie?

3. Explain the revolutionary effect of the rise of the bourgeoisie on the nation-state.

4. Explain this statement: "The bourgeoisie itself … furnishes the proletariat with weapons for fighting the bourgeoisie."

5. To what extent does Marx's analysis reflect today's world? What's the same, and what's different?

CHAPTER 7

Fascism

KEY TERMS

Mussolini

Hitler

Treaty of Versailles

Richard Wagner

Elitism

Corporate State

Militarism

Lebensraum

Georges Sorel

Weimar Republic

Irrationalism

Friedrich Nietzsche

Totalitarianism

Imperialism

Social Darwinism

DISCUSSION QUESTIONS

1. Identify the factors that led to the rise of fascism during the interwar period.

2. Define and discuss the qualities of fascism.

3. Discuss the impact that the Treaty of Versailles had on the rise of fascism in Europe.

4. Discuss whether the Nazi seizure of power was inevitable in Germany.

5. Address the significance of the Spanish Civil War on the development of fascism.

FASCISM

Fascism derives from the term fasces. This means a bundle of rods carried before consuls in Ancient Rome to signify their authority.

Mussolini

Benito **Mussolini** was a socialist who was influenced by the thoughts of Georges Sorel. He believed that great historical events were set in motion by a small group of people. Mussolini was a schoolteacher and then became a journalist. He was initially against Italy's entry into World War I but later advocated for the war. After the war, Mussolini played on the frustrations of the people and advocated for policies of imperialism. He formed his Blackshirt militia as a part of his party to promote violence. In 1922, he called for a march on Rome, which led him to be named prime minister by the king.

Germany and Hitler

The **Treaty of Versailles** was a harsh peace for Germany. Among the terms were the following:

- Limited the size of the German military
- Banned the development of an air force
- Took away Germany's colonies
- Required the payment of war reparations
- Demanded admission of war guilt

The successor government after World War I was the **Weimar Republic**. It was controlled by Social Democrats. It had weak legitimacy, as it was forced to conclude the armistice, which ended World War I, as well as the Treaty of Versailles.

Treaty of Versailles

Adolph **Hitler** was born in Austria. He settled in Germany and received permission to enter the German army during World War I. Hitler was wounded several times. He spent the last few months of the war in the rear area recovering from wounds he received in a gas attack. After the war, Hitler worked for the military in Bavaria and was assigned the task of investigating political groups. One of these groups was a small political party called the German Workers Party. Hitler was attracted to the party and quickly became one of its leaders. It was renamed the National Socialist German Workers Party. He was involved in planning the Beer Hall Putsch in 1923 in which the group tried to take over the Bavarian state government. The revolt was put down. At the trial of the putsch leaders, Hitler emerged as the leader of the movement. He spent a short time in prison and after his release became involved in politics. Hitler and the Nazis appealed to the disaffected in society and blamed Germany's defeat and the subsequent social and economic dislocation on Communists. He and the party were also very anti-Semitic. He scapegoated Germany's Jewish population for all its problems. Like Mussolini, Hitler established a group of enforcers to secure party rallies and break up opponents' meetings. These were the Storm Troopers, also known as the Brownshirts.

The Nazi Party was not doing well in elections until the depression. They were able to play on people's frustrations and increased their numbers in Parliament in the 1932 election from 7 to 230. With the Social Democrats being unable to deal with the economy and political instability in the country, Hitler was appointed chancellor (prime minister) of a conservative government where the Nazis were a minority.

Hitler and the Nazis used the governmental apparatus to consolidate control and increase their position. Hitler assumed total power in 1934. He purged the Nazi Party, as well as gained the loyalty of the military and big industrialists. Everyone thought that he would be controllable, but he asserted his independence.

REASONS WHY FASCISM GAINED SUPPORT

- Democratic governments representing a coalition of interests or parties often appeared weak and unstable when confronted by economic or political crises. The attraction of strong leadership became compelling.

- European society had been disrupted by the experience of industrialization, which had, in particular, threatened a lower middle class composed of shopkeepers, small businessmen, farmers and craftsmen who were squeezed between the growing might of big business on one hand and the rising power of organized labor on the other. Fascists got most of their support from the lower middle class.
- The post-World War I period was deeply affected by the Russian Revolution and a fear among propertied classes that social revolution was about to spread throughout Europe. Fascist groups drew political and economic support from business interests.
- The world economic crisis of the 1930s provided the final blow to already fragile democracies.
- World War I had failed to resolve international conflicts and rivalries, leaving a bitter inheritance of frustrated nationalism and the desire for revenge. Nationalist tensions were strongest in those have-not nations, which had either, like Germany, been defeated in war or, such as Italy and Japan, were deeply disappointed by the terms of the post-World War I peace settlement.

QUALITIES OF FASCISM

Irrationalism

Irrationalism is an appeal to myth and emotion. The idea is to mobilize the masses around symbols and themes they can relate to. Nazis used the work of **Richard Wagner** (music and operas), which glorified the German nation and appealed to irrational ideals. Johann Fichte (1762–1814) argued for the German states to form a single state well before it actually happened. Heinrich von Treitschke (1834–1896) claimed Germans were a superior race. **Friedrich Nietzsche** (1844–1890) discussed a race of supermen who would one day rule the world. Nietzsche argued that pain was good, as it toughened people up. He also argued that people should not show compassion for others.

Struggle

Social Darwinism is related to fascism. It is the belief that some individuals and nations were destined to rule. Struggle is the natural and inevitable condition of both social and international life. Life is an unending struggle, and states are naturally expansionist.

Hitler advocated **lebensraum**—living space. Germans were in competition with other nationalities for land and felt because they were the superior race that gave them legitimacy.

Leadership and Elitism

Both Hitler and Mussolini advocated that people were not equal. People varied in terms of intelligence, strength, and talent, as well as physical features. Some were more prized than others. Fascism advocates a highly stratified society. The masses are shown a certain degree of contempt. At the end of the war, Hitler blamed the people for losing the war and ordered that infrastructure in the country be destroyed regardless of the consequences to the civilian population. (Most of these orders were not carried out.)

Racism

Racism varies with different fascist movements. However, it was a central theme with the Nazis. There is a long history of ethnocentrism in Europe. This served as justification for wars, such as the crusades and the slave trade.

Totalitarianism

Totalitarianism is a political system in which the government controls every aspect of life in a society. All institutions are subject to state control. Mussolini coined the term, although Italian fascism, for the most part, was less totalitarian than in Germany. Mussolini had to contend with the power of the Catholic Church centered in the Vatican. In Italy, the king was the head of state, not Mussolini.

Corporate State

Fascism bases some of its economic doctrine on syndicalism, advocated by Pierre Joseph Proudhon and **Georges Sorel**. This was especially true in Mussolini's Italy. It was the belief that people should channel their political ideas through giant trade unions. Mussolini advocated that the government should run the syndicates.

Imperialism

Fascism views society in terms of human conflict. **Imperialism** is one nation dominating others. Imperialism can take many forms: political, economic, social, and cultural. Ideas of racism justified imperialism. The strong should dominate the weak. Looking at the German occupation of Europe, in particular Eastern Europe, imperialism was used to justify harsh occupation policies, as well as the Holocaust.

Militarism

Militarism is the idea of war for its own sake. Keeping society militarized maintains a certain level of control by the state. This was symbolized by a proliferation of uniforms for government employees, as well as demonstrations of military equipment. Many societal organizations took on a paramilitary tone. This was especially true of organizations for young people. Fascists looked upon war as a positive thing, as a way for the strong to exercise control over the weak.

POPULISM IS NOT FASCISM

But It Could be a Harbinger

Sheri Berman

As right-wing movements have mounted increasingly strong challenges to political establishments across Europe and North America, many commentators have drawn parallels to the rise of fascism during the 1920s and 1930s. Last year, a French court ruled that opponents of Marine Le Pen, the leader of France's National Front, had the right to call her a "fascist"—a right they have frequently exercised. This May, after Norbert Hofer, the leader of Austria's Freedom Party, nearly won that country's presidential election, *The Guardian* asked, "How can so many Austrians flirt with this barely disguised fascism?" And in an article that same month about the rise of Donald Trump, the Republican U.S. presidential candidate, the conservative columnist Robert Kagan warned, "This is how fascism comes to America." "Fascist" has served as a generic term of political abuse for many decades, but for the first time in ages, mainstream observers are using it seriously to describe major politicians and parties.

Sheri Berman, "Populism Is Not Fascism: But It Could Be a Harbinger," Foreign Affairs, vol. 95, no. 6, pp. 39–44. Copyright © 2016 by Council on Foreign Relations, Inc. Reprinted with permission.

Fascism is associated most closely with Europe between the world wars, when movements bearing this name took power in Italy and Germany and wreaked havoc in many other European countries.

Although fascists differed from country to country, they shared a virulent opposition to democracy and liberalism, as well as a deep suspicion of capitalism. They also believed that the nation—often defined in religious or racial terms—represented the most important source of identity for all true citizens. And so they promised a revolution that would replace liberal democracy with a new type of political order devoted to nurturing a unified and purified nation under the guidance of a powerful leader.

Although today's right-wing populists share some similarities with the interwar fascists, the differences are more significant. And more important, what today's comparisons often fail to explain is how noxious politicians and parties grow into the type of revolutionary movements capable of fundamentally threatening democracy, as interwar fascism did. In order to understand this process, it is not nearly enough to examine the programs and appeal of right-wing extremist parties, the personalities of their politicians, or the inclinations of their supporters. Instead, one must carefully consider the broader political context. What turned fascists from marginal extremists into rulers of much of Europe was the failure of democratic elites and institutions to deal with the crises facing their societies during the interwar years. Despite real problems, the West today is confronting nowhere near the same type of breakdown it did in the 1930s. So calling Le Pen, Trump, and other right-wing populists "fascists" obscures more than it clarifies.

The Birth of Fascism

Like many of today's right-wing movements, fascism originated during a period of intense globalization. In the late nineteenth and early twentieth centuries, capitalism dramatically reshaped Western societies, destroying traditional communities, professions, and cultural norms. This was also a time of immense immigration. Peasants from rural areas, which had been decimated by new agricultural technologies and the inflow of cheap agricultural products, flocked to cities, and the citizens of poorer countries flocked to richer ones in search of better lives.

Then, as now, these changes frightened and angered many people, creating fertile ground for new politicians who claimed to have the answers. Prominent among these politicians were right-wing nationalists, who vowed to protect citizens from the pernicious influence of foreigners and markets. Fascist movements arose in almost all Western countries, from Argentina to Austria and from France to Finland. Fascists became disruptive forces in some countries and influenced policymaking in others, but they did not fundamentally challenge existing political orders before 1914. Their policies and appeal alone, in other words, did not make them truly dangerous or revolutionary. It would take World War I to do that.

That conflict killed, maimed, and traumatized millions of Europeans, and it physically and economically devastated much of the continent. "The lamps are going out all over Europe; we shall not see them lit again in our lifetime," British Foreign Secretary Edward Grey remarked at the beginning of the war. And indeed, by the time the war was over, an entire way of life had vanished.

The year 1918 brought an end to the war, but not to the suffering. Europe's continental empires—Austro-Hungarian, German, Ottoman, and Russian—collapsed during or after the conflict, creating a variety of new states that lacked any experience with democracy and featured mixed populations that had little interest in living together. Meanwhile, in many of Europe's older states, such as Germany and Spain, old regimes also collapsed, making way for democratic transitions. But like the new states, most of these countries also lacked experience with popular rule—and thus the habits, norms, and institutions necessary for making it work.

To make matters worse, the end of the war, rather than ushering in a period of peace and reconstruction, brought with it an unending stream of social and economic problems. New democracies struggled to reintegrate millions of soldiers back into society and reconstruct economies that had been distorted and disrupted by the fighting. Austria and Germany had to respond to the humiliation of a lost war and a

Ain't nothing like the real thing: Mussolini and Hitler in Munich, 1940

punitive peace, and both were hit with hyperinflation. Across the continent, lawlessness and violence quickly became endemic as democratic governments lost control of the streets and parts of their territories. Italy suffered through almost two years of factory occupations, peasant land seizures, and armed conflicts between left- and right-wing militias. In Germany, the Weimar Republic faced violent left- and right-wing uprisings, forcing the government to send in troops to recapture cities and regions.

Despite these and other problems, fascists at first remained marginal forces. In Italy, they received almost no votes in the country's first postwar election. And in Germany, Hitler's 1923 Beer Hall Putsch flopped, ending with him and many of his coconspirators in jail.

But as time passed, problems persisted. European economies had trouble getting back on their feet, and street brawls, assassinations, and other forms of social disorder continued to plague many European countries. By the late 1920s, in short, many Europeans' faith in democracy had been badly shaken.

Democracies in Crisis

Then came the Great Depression. What proved so catastrophic about that event was not the economic suffering it caused—although that was bad enough—but the failure of democratic institutions to respond to it. To understand the difference, compare the fates of Germany and the United States. These two countries were hit the hardest by the Depression, experiencing the highest levels of unemployment, rates of business collapse, and drops in production. But in Germany, the Weimar Republic then fell to the Nazi onslaught, whereas in the United States, democracy survived—despite the appearance of some pseudo-fascist leaders such as the Louisiana politician Huey Long and the radio preacher Father Charles Coughlin. Why the different outcomes?

The answer lies in the two governments' divergent responses to the economic crisis. German leaders did little to ease their society's suffering; in fact, they pursued policies of austerity, which exacerbated the economic downturn in general and the horrifically high rates of unemployment in particular. Strikingly, even the main opposition party, the Social Democrats, sat meekly by, offering little in the way of an attractive alternative program. In the United States, meanwhile, democratic institutions and norms were longer lived and therefore more robust. But also critical to staving off fascism was President Franklin Roosevelt's insistence that the government could and would help its citizens, by laying the foundations of the modern welfare state.

Unfortunately for Europe, too many governments there proved unable or unwilling to respond as actively, and most mainstream political parties offered little in the way of viable alternative plans. By the early 1930s, liberal parties had been discredited across much of the continent; their faith in markets, unwillingness to respond forcefully to capitalism's downsides, and hostility to nationalism struck voters as completely out of synch with interwar realities. With the exception of Scandinavia's, meanwhile, most socialist parties were also flummoxed, telling citizens that their lives would improve only once capitalism had fully collapsed—and that they could do little to help them in the interim. (Socialists were also indifferent or hostile to concerns about national identity and the evisceration of traditional norms—another politically unwise stance during a period of immense social upheaval.) Communists did at least put forth a compelling alternative to the status quo, but their appeal was limited by an almost exclusive focus on the working class and their hostility to nationalism.

And so in all too many European countries, it was the fascists who were able to take advantage of the declining faith in democracy that accompanied the Depression. Fascists offered both a strong critique of the reigning order and a powerful alternative to it. They criticized democracy as inefficient, unresponsive, and weak and promised to replace it altogether.

The new system would use the state to protect citizens from capitalism's most destructive effects by creating jobs, expanding the welfare state (for "true" citizens only, of course), eliminating supposedly exploitative capitalists (often Jews), and funneling resources instead to businesses that were deemed to serve the national interest. Fascists promised to end the divisions and conflicts that had weakened their nations—often, of course, by ridding them of those viewed as not truly part of them. And they pledged to restore a sense of pride and purpose to societies that had for too long felt battered by forces outside their control. These positions enabled fascism in Germany, Italy, and elsewhere to attract an extremely diverse constituency that cut across classes. Although fascist parties received disproportionately high support from men, the lower-middle class, and former soldiers, they enjoyed a broader base of support than any other type of party in interwar Europe.

Despite all these advantages, the fascists still lacked the strength to take power on their own; they also needed the connivance of traditional conservatives. These conservatives—who sought to preserve the power of the traditional elite and destroy that of the people—lacked mass constituencies of their own and believed they could use the fascists' popularity to achieve their long-term goals. So they worked behind the scenes to maneuver Mussolini and Hitler into office, believing that they could later manipulate or get rid of these men. Little did they know that the fascists were playing the same game. Soon after being appointed chancellor, in 1933, Hitler did away with his erstwhile conservative allies, whom he correctly viewed as a hindrance to his long-planned revolutionary project. Mussolini, who had been appointed prime minister in 1922, took a little longer to completely secure his position—but he, too, eventually pushed aside (or simply killed) many of the traditional conservatives who had helped make him Il Duce in the first place.

Lessons for Today

So what does all of this say about Le Pen, Trump, and today's other right-wing extremists? They certainly share some similarities with the interwar fascists. Like their predecessors, today's right-wing extremists denounce incumbent democratic leaders as inefficient, unresponsive, and weak. They promise to nurture their nation, protect it from its enemies, and restore a sense of purpose to people who feel battered by forces outside their control. And they pledge to stand up for "the people," who are often defined in religious or racial terms.

But if the similarities are striking, the differences are even more so. Most obvious, today's extremists claim they want not to bury democracy but to improve it. They critique the functioning of contemporary democracy but offer no alternative to it, just vague promises to make government stronger, more efficient, and more responsive.

Current right-wing extremists are thus better characterized as populist rather than fascist, since they claim to speak for everyday men and women against corrupt, debased, and out-of-touch elites and institutions. In other words, they are certainly antiliberal, but they are not antidemocratic. This distinction is not trivial. If today's populists come to power—even the right-wing nationalists among them—the continued existence of democracy will permit their societies to opt for a do-over by later voting them out. Indeed, this may be democracy's greatest strength: it allows countries to recover from their mistakes.

But the more important difference between today's right-wing extremists and yesterday's fascists is the larger context. As great as contemporary problems are, and as angry as many citizens may be, the West is simply not facing anything approaching the upheaval of the interwar period. "The mere existence of privations is not enough to cause an insurrection; if it were, the masses would be always in revolt," Leon Trotsky once wrote, and the same logic applies to the appearance of fascism. In the United States and western Europe, at least, democracy and democratic norms have deep roots, and contemporary governments have proved nowhere near as inept as their predecessors in the 1920s and 1930s. Moreover, democratic procedures and institutions, welfare states, political parties, and robust civil societies continue to provide citizens with myriad ways of voicing their concerns, influencing political outcomes, and getting their needs met.

For these reasons, the right-wing extremists in the United States and western Europe today have much more limited options and opportunities than their interwar counterparts did. (On the other hand, in eastern and southern Europe, where democratic norms and institutions are younger and weaker, movements have emerged that resemble traditional fascism much more closely, including Golden Dawn in Greece and Jobbik in Hungary.) As the scholar Theda Skocpol has stressed, revolutionary movements don't create crises; they exploit them. In other words, true revolutionary threats to democracy emerge when democracies themselves create crises ready to be exploited by failing to deal with the challenges they face.

Things can change, of course, and the lack of true fascist movements in the United States and western Europe today is no excuse for complacency. But what the interwar period illustrates is that the West should worry more about the problems afflicting democracy than about right-wing populists themselves. The best way to ensure that the Le Pens and Trumps of the world go down in history as also-rans rather than as real threats is to make democratic institutions, parties, and politicians more responsive to the needs of all citizens. In the United States, for example, rising inequality, stagnating wages, deteriorating communities, congressional gridlock, and the flow of big money to campaigns have played a bigger role in fueling support for Trump than his purported charisma or the supposed authoritarian leanings of his supporters. Tackling those problems would no doubt help prevent the rise of the next Trump.

History also shows that conservatives should be particularly wary of embracing right-wing populists. Mainstream Republicans who make bogus claims about voter fraud, rigged elections, and the questionable patriotism and nationality of President Barack Obama in order to appeal to the extremist fringes are playing an extremely dangerous game, since such rhetoric fans citizens' fear and distrust of their politicians and institutions, thus undermining their faith in democracy itself. And just like their interwar counterparts, these conservatives are also likely enhancing the appeal of politicians who have little loyalty to the conservatives' own policies, constituencies, or institutions.

Right-wing populism—indeed, populism of any kind—is a symptom of democracy in trouble; fascism and other revolutionary movements are the consequence of democracy in crisis. But if governments do not do more to address the many social and economic problems the United States and Europe currently face, if mainstream politicians and parties don't do a better job reaching out to all citizens, and if conservatives continue to fan fear and turn a blind eye to extremism, then the West could quickly find itself moving from the former to the latter.

CHAPTER 8

Legislative Branch of Government

KEY TERMS

James Madison
Prime Minister
Enumerated Powers
Magna Carta
Habeas Corpus Act
Bundestag
Common Law
Liberal Democratic Party

Implied Powers
Progressive Era
Standing Committees
Conference Committees
House of Commons
French Fifth Republic
Glorious Revolution

DISCUSSION QUESTIONS

1. To what extent do you think congressional term limits will aid in representation and lawmaking?

2. Discuss how the committee system in the US Congress contributes to decentralization?

3. Discuss the differences between a parliamentary system and the America congressional system. Discuss the impact on representation and lawmaking.

SIGNIFICANCE OF LEGISLATURES

Legislatures connect people with their respective governments. Legislatures represent citizens of a given area. They are assigned the function politically of crafting laws. Legislatures are at every level of government: county, state/region, and national. Legislatures often serve as a contact point between people and the government.

Countries have different legislative structures. Some legislatures are bicameral, two houses, while others have a single house. In the United States, there is a history of bicameralism. The Connecticut Compromise established two houses of the US Congress. The House of Representatives is based on population. By law, the number of representatives is fixed at 435 members divided by the 50 states. In the Senate, each state, regardless of its population, has two senators. At the state level, 49 out of the 50 states, Nebraska is the exception, also has a bicameral state legislature. At the local level in cities and counties, there are legislatures that can vary in size.

CONGRESS: HISTORY

Originally, the House of Representatives was designed as a more democratic institution, with members elected for short terms and traditionally had rapid turnover. Up until the twentieth century, most politicians used Congress as a stepping stone to state/local offices. The House was designed by **James Madison** to be more responsive to public opinion, as members would be popularly elected.

The Senate was viewed as the more aristocratic body, as state legislators appointed it for members. It was felt that senators would be less responsive to public opinion and take the long-term view on public policy. Senators would be aided in this by a longer term (six years), as well as not having to face election. (This was changed with the ratification of the Seventeenth Amendment on April 8, 1913. This was a significant reform of the **Progressive Era**.)

The members of the House of Representatives are more specialists, as there are 435 representatives. This allows them to focus on specific committees in detail. Also, they represent, by and large, smaller geographical and more homogeneous districts. This allows them to build up a great deal of influence and win reelection year after year. Typically, there is not a great deal of turnover, as most districts are heavily either Democrats or Republicans. The one hundred senators are spread much thinner regarding their committee responsibilities. Also, greater constituent responsibilities mean senators have to represent a whole state with many different populations. Senators also have to campaign statewide. Senators are more high profile, which means they tend to attract better-funded, stronger challengers, even within their own parties. Their elections also get more media attention, both within an individual state and nationally.

POWERS OF CONGRESS

Enumerated Powers
- Right to impose taxes and import tariffs
- Borrow money
- Regulate interstate commerce and international trade
- Establish procedures for naturalizing citizens
- Make laws regulating bankruptcies
- Coin money
- Establish standards of weights and measures
- Punish counterfeiters
- Establish post offices
- Regulate copyrights and patents
- Establish a federal court system
- Punish piracy
- Declare war
- Raise and regulate an army and a navy
- Regulate the state militias (National Guard)
- Suppress insurrections and repel invasions
- Govern the District of Columbia

Implied Powers

Article I Section 8 of the Constitution states, "To make all laws which shall be necessary and proper for carrying into Execution the foregoing Powers and all other Powers vested by this Constitution in the Government of the United States, or in any Department or Officer thereof." This is referred to as the necessary and proper clause or the elastic clause of the Constitution because it has historically been interpreted very broadly.

FUNCTIONS OF CONGRESS

- Lawmaking: Before a bill becomes a law the same version must pass both houses of Congress and then not be vetoed by the President. If it is vetoed a 2/3 vote by both houses is necessary to override the veto.
- Service to constituents: Members of congress meet with constituents about issues and provide assistance to their constituents in dealing with the bureaucracy such as assisting them with social security or veterans benefits.
- Representation: Members of the House and Senate are expected to represent the interests of their districts/states. In that regard they do town halls and do meetings with their constituencies. They are also expected to advocate for the dominant interests in their districts/states.
- Oversight: Members of Congress sit on committees. One of the functions of the committees is to oversee components of the bureaucracy. An example are the House and Senate Armed Services Committee overseeing the Department of Defense.
- Public education: Through town hall meetings, newsletters, and other forms of communication members of Congress educate the public on political issues. It should be noted that in communication with constituents politicians put their political spin on the information they share.
- Conflict resolution: Often members of Congress have to mediate disputes between different interest groups and with each other in an effort to build coalitions.

ASPECTS OF CONSIDERATION IN THE VOTING BEHAVIOR OF CONGRESS

Members of Congress must weigh a number of considerations in determining how to vote. First is the view in their respective districts/states. This is often the most important criteria guiding a member's decision making. Another consideration is the wishes and goals of party leaders. Members' positions in the respective houses of Congress, how much influence they have, or whether they chair committees is dependent on whether their party is in the majority. They have an incentive to be loyal to their respective party leaders. Another consideration, in particular for members of the president's party, is the power and status of the president. If the president is popular in their respective districts/states, then the president can exert a certain degree of pressure for them to vote the way the president wants. However, if the president's popularity is weak, then the president's fellow party members in Congress may be more likely to defect. Finally, another determinant of congressional voting behavior is a member's own policy agenda. People initially get involved in politics because they are passionate about a particular issue, and this motivates them to run for office.

HOW CONGRESS IS ORGANIZED: THE IMPORTANCE OF THE COMMITTEE SYSTEM

Types of Committees

- **Standing committees**: Supervise specific policy areas and are permanent from Congress to Congress. These committees supervise policy areas, such as agriculture, commerce, defense, and foreign affairs. Most of the work of Congress is done in committee. Bills are marked up and changed. Committees are further divided up into subcommittees. Members of Congress generally serve on several committees, and if their party is in the majority, they will at a minimum chair at least one subcommittee.

Other committees in Congress include joint committees, composed of members of both houses, which are concerned with oversight. These are temporary committees.

- Special ad hoc committees deal with specific major pieces of legislation.
- **Conference committees** consist of members of both houses of Congress who are brought together to work out a compromise of different versions of legislation that have passed both houses of Congress. Only a single version of a bill can be presented to the president.

PARLIAMENTARY SYSTEMS

Characteristics

One of the characteristics of a parliamentary system is a fusion of executive and legislative power (the prime minister is first among equals). In addition, the parties are centralized, controlled from the center, and illustrate strong party discipline. Strong party discipline is defined as representatives being required to vote as their leadership instructs them. Parliamentary systems often have some form of proportional representation in which voters cast votes for a party and seats are awarded to parties based on their percentage of the total vote. As a result, there are usually several parties that win seats in a parliament. Frequently, no one party controls a majority, so two or more parties enter into a coalition to form a parliamentary majority. Coalition governments are common in Germany, Israel, and Italy, for example. Many parliamentary systems have a weak chief executive. For example, in Germany, Israel, and Italy, the presidents are selected by their parliaments, and they have ceremonial political roles. Other parliamentary systems in the West are monarchies and have only ceremonial roles. An example of this is the United Kingdom.

The United Kingdom

In the United Kingdom, Queen Elizabeth II (1926–) became the reigning monarch in 1952.

There has been a growth in the power of Parliament historically at the expense of the monarchy as a result of events and customs in English history.

Common Law

Common law was developed in the Middle Ages and is law based on judicial precedent. As a result, it changes slowly and serves as a check on the state/king, as the leader cannot simply change laws at a whim.

Magna Carta, 1215

The **Magna Carta** began the idea of developing due process. The king was forced to agree that before he punished a nobleman for a crime, other nobles had to sit as a jury, and the crown had to present the evidence against the accused. Essentially, this meant that noblemen were entitled to a jury of their peers. (A noble title in Great Britain is known as a peerage.)

Habeas Corpus Act, 1679

Habeas Corpus was an act of Parliament that mandated that the government inform defendants of the charges against them. This is essential for defendants to do some form of defense.

Glorious Revolution, 1688

The **Glorious Revolution** overthrew James II. James II was a Catholic and very autocratic. It was called the Glorious Revolution because James II had very few supporters in England. However, because of his Catholicism, he was able to raise an army in Ireland, and there were several bloody battles between his forces and the army of William of Orange.

English Bill of Rights, 1689

The English Bill of Rights was passed by Parliament in the immediate aftermath of the Glorious Revolution. It essentially helped establish the power of the **House of Commons**, which continued to increase over time.

The Prime Minister of the United Kingdom

The **prime minister** is first among equals in the cabinet. The cabinet is made up of the senior members of the ruling party. The prime minister holds his/her position by virtue of the person's role as the leader of the majority party. If the person loses the party leadership position, then he/she is no longer prime minister. The majority party elects a new leader who becomes prime minister. Most recently, David Cameron resigned because of his losing a vote on the United Kingdom staying in the European Union. The Conservative Party elected Theresa May as their leader. Because they were the majority party in the House of Commons, she became prime minister.

The French Fifth Republic

The **French Fifth Republic** was created in 1958 during the crisis in Algeria. The idea was to create a strong executive branch to counterbalance what had frequently been a divided Parliament. The French political system is a dual executive: the prime minister is the head of government and the president is the head of state but is elected independently from Parliament. The president can appoint and dismiss the prime minister, dissolve Parliament, call new elections, declare a state of emergency, issue decrees that have the force of law, and preside over cabinet meetings. The president is also the chief diplomat of the country.

Germany

In Germany, at the top of the political system is the chancellor/prime minister. The chancellor is the leader of the largest party in the Parliament. Parliament is divided into two houses. The most significant is the **Bundestag**, which is the lower house of Parliament. Half the members are elected directly, and the other half are elected by party lists using proportional representation. Parties that gain five percent of the vote on the party lists or win at least three constituencies are allocated seats in the chamber based on the total percentage of their vote. This has led to a robust party system in which a number of different parties representing various ideologies are able to win seats. Historically, the Christian Democrats, a moderate conservative party, and the Social Democrats, a left-leaning party, have been the top two parties. The Free Democrats, a classical liberal free-market-oriented party, has historically been the third party. More recently, the Greens, who emerged out of the peace movement of the 1970s, have become a significant party. The Greens are now called Alliance 90/Greens. Other political parties that have become significant in recent years are the Left, which is the successor to the East German Communist Party, and Alternative for Germany, which is a very far-right political party.

Japan

Modern Japan started with the Meiji Restoration in 1868. A new emperor introduced reforms that included economic and governmental modernization. This led to industrialization and the development of a modern governmental bureaucracy.

The US occupation authorities wrote the Japanese postwar constitution of 1947. The constitution renounced war. The emperor remained as a figurehead but political primacy resided with Parliament. Today, the Parliament is elected with a mixture of single-member districts and proportional representation.

From 1955 to 2009, Japan was dominated by the **Liberal Democratic Party** (LDP). Japan was essentially a dominant party system in which there were several parties, but one party tended to win overwhelmingly.

The LDP forged an alliance with government bureaucrats and interest groups, which included business and agricultural interests.

Japanese politics were characterized by patron-client relations. People were willing to put up with a certain degree of this when the economy was robust. When the Japanese economy faded in the 1990s, the fortunes of the LDP suffered.

INSTITUTIONS AND LEADERSHIP:
A COMPARISON OF PARLIAMENTARY AND PRESIDENTIAL SYSTEMS
Oliver H. Woshinksky

Americans are at a disadvantage in trying to understand democratic politics elsewhere, because their system differs from the others. Unlike Americans, most people in stable polyarchies live under **parliamentary government**. Knowing how their own system works, they can readily grasp the general nature of politics in similar countries.

Americans, however, are different. They live in what's variously referred to as a separation-of-powers, checks-and-balances, or (simply) **presidential system**. *No other stable, long-term polyarchy operates*

this way. Scholars have long debated why. Some believe that structural factors make parliamentarism more compatible with democracy than presidentialism.[1] Others see the correlation between polyarchy and parliamentarism as an historical accident. Parliamentary systems, they say, just happened to be introduced in cultures whose values were compatible with democracy.[2]

We cannot resolve that debate here. Since both systems exist in at least one strong polyarchy, it is clear that nothing inherent in either system makes it

Oliver H. Woshinksky, "Institutions and Leadership: A Comparison of Parliamentary and Presidential Systems," Explaining Politics, pp. 209–227, 356–357. Copyright © 2008 by Taylor & Francis Group. Reprinted with permission.

incompatible with democracy. We will now focus on differences in the two systems as they operate within stable polyarchies. What, if any, political effects do these different systems produce?

How do these Systems Differ?

The quickest way to illustrate the difference between **presidentialism** and parliamentarism is to ask this question. When will the next election for national leader occur in the USA? When will it occur in the UK, Italy, Norway, and Holland? In answering, you must be precise. Name the exact day on which each election will occur.

This is an easy question for Americans, but impossible for citizens in *any* parliamentary system. I can name the very day when Americans will vote for President in 2172. Assuming that there is still a USA and that the Constitution and the election laws have not changed, then that date will be Tuesday, November 3. In 2284 Americans will be voting on November 4, and in 2416 it'll be November 8.

How do I know this? Simple. The Constitution says that the President will be elected every 4 years (starting in 1788), and federal law says that the election for president will take place on the first Tuesday after the first Monday in November. Once you know those two facts, it is a simple matter of heading to a universal calendar and checking for that particular Tuesday in 2008, 2012, 2016, and so forth.

Ask the same question for any nation with a parliamentary system, and *it can't be answered*. The reason lies at the heart of the way this system works. Once we understand that system, we will see why election dates are rarely firm until a few months (or even a few weeks) before any election.

The Parliamentary System Explained

We will start with the strangest fact (for Americans). There is *no* election to fill the country's top post. National elections occur for the legislature only. That body then goes on to choose the national leader, always one of its own. In parliamentary systems, executives *must* be members of the legislature. In the USA

the president *cannot* hold a seat in either house of Congress. It is constitutionally forbidden.

Thus, executives in parliamentary systems are not independent of the legislature. They run for a legislative seat like all other candidates for parliament. To become the national leader (usually termed Prime Minister), you must be chosen to head your political party, and you must then run and win a parliamentary seat at election time. Once in parliament, you must get a majority of legislators to back you. This will occur automatically if your party has a majority of seats. You are its leader, after all, and you helped it gain that majority in the recent campaign. Even if your party fails to win a majority of seats, you can still become Prime Minister if you and your party form coalition alliances sufficient to produce a majority.

In any case, the road to executive leadership always runs through the legislature.

That difference between systems is just the beginning. Let's return to our original way of showing the central difference between parliamentarism and presidentialism. Remember that no one can pinpoint the date of the next election in a parliamentary system. True, elections must be held every 4 or 5 years, depending on the country (as we explain below).[3] Otherwise, there is no "term of office" for a Prime Minister, and there's great uncertainty about how long any leader will last.

You become Prime Minister because your party or the coalition you head represents a majority of legislators. You remain Prime Minister as long as you can keep that majority support. Lose the majority, and you're out. At that point a new election could take place, whether it's 6 months or 5 years since the last one. In addition, Prime Ministers can call for new elections pretty much whenever they want. Because we can't know in advance when Prime Ministers will (a) lose their majority or (b) decide to call an election, we can never know exactly when the next election will be.

That's the short version of parliamentary politics. Now we will look at the operation in detail.

In most parliamentary systems, ultimate power rests in one institution: the popularly-elected house of the legislature.[4] There are no "checks and balances"—at least, not as Americans conceive them. In the USA, relatively equal independent political units are chosen in different ways, endowed with different legal and political powers, and given a variety of ways to check each other's actions. In most parliamentary systems, "the buck stops" in the more powerful house of the legislature. When a majority there decides on a policy, that policy *will* take effect.

This is a key point, and one quite unfamiliar to Americans. If the US House of Representatives passes a bill, the Senate can stop the bill dead in its tracks by refusing to vote for it. If both House and Senate pass a bill, the President can veto it (and vetoes are very hard to override). If House and Senate pass a bill, and the President signs it, the Supreme Court could declare it unconstitutional in a later court case. On it goes. Each of the four most powerful institutions of American politics must be in accord for a policy to go forward.

It is quite different in most parliamentary systems. Once a bill is passed in the most powerful body of the legislature, no other political entity can stop it. The second house, if there is one, is much weaker and can, at best, slow down ratification of the bill. The Prime Minister cannot veto the bill. Remember that Prime Ministers are members of the legislature and have just one vote like all other members. And in most parliamentary systems, courts cannot overturn laws passed by the legislature. Either by law or by convention (sometimes both), they just do not have that power, which Americans call **judicial review**.[5]

Only parliament itself can amend or abolish its original policy. That usually happens after the voters have spoken in a new election and chosen a different set of leaders. In any case, power in parliamentary systems is *concentrated*. It is tied to one key institution rather than dispersed among several, as Americans expect it to be.[6]

Elections in a parliamentary system center on the choice of members of the "popular" house of parliament (the one elected by the people). It is this house that chooses the Prime Minister. Its members are directly elected, something that is usually not true of the second and weaker house.[7] We concentrate here on operations in the dominant legislative body.

The name of this entity varies widely. It is the House of Commons in English-speaking countries (Britain, Canada, Australia, New Zealand, even India), the National Assembly in France and other French-speaking countries (including Canada's province of Québec), the Bundestag in Germany, the Folketing in Denmark, the Diet in Japan, and the Knesset in Israel. We will refer to this body from now on simply as "parliament."

All democratic parliaments share some key characteristics. First, members are chosen in a widely-publicized vote via free and fair elections. Second, the election struggle involves multi-party competition. More than one party (almost always several) strive to get candidates elected. Finally, once elected, members of parliament (specifically, members of the majority party or majority coalition) get to name the **Prime Minister**.[8]

Let's start with the day after an election, to illustrate just how parliament uses its power to name the country's top official. Parliament has been chosen and is now composed of members of various parties. There are two main possibilities, as described below.

Majority Government

In the first scenario, one party wins a majority of seats. That party on its own can now name the Prime Minister. This person will be no stranger to the nation. Each party's leader is well known long before the campaign, and voters know that a vote for party X is a vote for the leader of party X.

Party X's leader, now Prime Minister, goes on to name the entire Cabinet. Again, no surprises. Most cabinet members (known as **ministers**) are leading members of the majority party. They themselves have just been elected (or re-elected) to parliament after promoting the party's fortunes in the just-concluded campaign. The Prime Minister and the other ministers now govern the country in their executive capacity, but they all remain members of parliament. They attend its sessions, report to it on a regular basis, propose the major pieces of legislation that have any chance of passage, and are subject to lengthy and hostile interrogation about the course of their developing policy decisions. At the same time, each of these ministers runs a government department: defense, education, social services, and so on.

Here we see a major difference between parliamentarism and the presidential/checks-and-balances system. In the USA, it is unconstitutional to be a member of both the legislative and executive branches. A Senator who's appointed to the Cabinet must resign the Senate seat. A Secretary of Agriculture who runs for and wins a Senate seat must resign from the Cabinet. These two branches are truly separate from each other.

It is the opposite in a parliamentary system, where they are intertwined. The leaders of the executive branch (the prime minister and the cabinet) are *also* the leaders of the legislature. They do not stand apart from parliament, but are chosen by it, answerable to it, and deposable by it. They also remain members of it until the next election. If they are "deposed" by the legislature (that is, defeated in a vote and forced to resign—about which, more later), they do not go away, they simply change where they sit.

Coalition Government

In a second (and common) scenario after any parliamentary election, there may be *no* majority party. Several parties win seats, but none attain that crucial fifty-percent-plus-one threshold. At this point, a coalition of parties comprising a majority of legislators will form, and the leader of the largest of these parties is usually named Prime Minister.[9]

It is standard practice in parliamentary systems for the Prime Minister to name members of the cabinet. That is always a delicate operation, but is even more complex under coalition circumstances. First, each party's numerical strength must be considered. Party A provides, e.g., one-fifth of the coalition members, so it would expect a fifth of the cabinet seats.

Beyond numerical considerations is the fact that cabinet positions vary in power. The Defense Ministry is a plum. The Ministry for Sports is a consolation prize. Cabinet positions also vary in their significance to each party. The Green Party, for instance, would place great value on the Environment post, while the pro-business party would maneuver instead for a Finance or Commerce ministry.

The composition of each coalition will depend on party numbers in parliament, historical relations among the parties, and numerous other factors. The most stable coalition outcome is usually an alignment of two parties that are ideologically close. Typical of this situation was the alliance between two Left parties in Germany, the Social Democrats and the Greens, between 1998 and 2005. In the same vein, two Right parties in France, the Gaullists and the UDF,[10] have frequently found themselves in parliamentary coalitions. On the other hand, coalitions of three or more parties are often unstable, especially if they comprise parties of diverse tendencies.

The Life and Death of Governments in a Parliamentary System

Once named, whether representing a majority or a coalition, the Prime Minister and the Cabinet proceed to govern until they lose power. Note this phrase: "until they lose power." Unlike the USA, the phrase is not "until the next election" or "until the end of their term." In a parliamentary system, there *is* no term for the Prime Minister and his or her government. They can remain in power for years and years … or for just a few days. They remain in control of government until, to repeat, "they lose power." How does that happen? In just one way: when the Prime Minister loses control of their majority.

As long as Prime Ministers retain support from a majority of legislators, they can remain in office indefinitely.[11] But once a parliamentary majority loses confidence in the government and refuses to support it, the Prime Minister, with the entire Cabinet, must resign. Journalists usually refer to this development as "the fall of the government" after "losing parliament's confidence." When is a **no-confidence vote** likely to occur?

If a government was formed as a coalition of parties, its chances for long-term survival are slim. To govern, a coalition must retain all (or nearly all) of its members for votes on all major issues, but what are the chances that members of two or three parties (sometimes more) will all agree on all the major policy matters that governments must deal with?

It is hard enough to get all members of just one party to stick together!

So coalition governments are inherently shaky. They usually last less than 2 years. For a while, the parties may be able to cobble together compromise agreements on some key matters, and they may find ways to put off dealing with policies on which they could never see eye to eye. Eventually, however, some tough issue will arise which they cannot finesse and cannot resolve. The Prime Minister will have to propose a policy, and one of the coalition partners will be unable to support it. That party will pull out of the coalition and vote against the government, ensuring a parliamentary expression of no-confidence and forcing the government's downfall.[12]

A second and less common end to a government occurs when one party has *majority* status in parliament. Normally, the party will remain united and give the Prime Minister a string of victories until the next election. A particular Prime Minister may, however, prove so unpopular that the party decides to make a change. This is a delicate operation, usually achieved by forcing a Prime Ministerial resignation, followed by the immediate selection of a successor from the same party.

Britain in 1940 provides a clear example. The majority of Conservatives forced the resignation of their discredited leader, Prime Minister Neville Chamberlain, replacing him with another Conservative, Winston Churchill.[13] Conservatives followed this same pattern in 1990, replacing an unpopular Margaret Thatcher with another of their members, John Major. In the summer of 2007, the majority Labour Party replaced its long-serving Prime Minister, Tony Blair, with a top party official, Gordon Brown. None of these cases of national leadership change derived from a popular election.

The most common end to a parliamentary government comes after a national vote. In democracies, the parties that control government are bound to lose elections on a regular basis. Let's say that Party A holds 57 percent of the seats in parliament before a general election (and has thus served as governing party for several years). Its policies were not terribly popular, however, and after the next election it finds itself with just 41 percent of the seats. No

longer controlling a majority, the Prime Minister (and the entire Cabinet—that is, the government) must resign immediately. The new majority party (or coalition) takes over, forms a new government, and the game continues.

To summarize, *governments in parliamentary systems last as long as they retain the ongoing support of a majority of legislators, but must resign when they no longer have that support*. This lack of support most commonly reflects a government's unpopular policies. The government then falls after being punished by legislators through no-confidence motions (most likely to occur during periods of coalition government) or after being punished by voters at the polls.

When do Elections Occur in Parliamentary Systems?

We now arrive at a central question, and the one Americans find most curious about parliamentary systems. When do these elections, the primary event that can cause a change in government, take place?

As we already know, there is no set election date in parliamentary systems. Concerning these dates, there are two basic rules. First, Prime Ministers may call an election whenever they want. Second, there is a major exception to that rule; elections cannot be put off indefinitely. Parliaments everywhere are elected for a set number of years. The number varies, but is usually four or five.[14] In other words, Prime Ministers have wide leeway in determining the date of an election, but they cannot postpone it forever. In keeping with democratic principles, voters must be allowed to state, on a regular basis, how they feel about the job their rulers are doing.

Let's look more closely at this process. Say an election occurs in North Ruratania on March 7, 2028, and the parliamentary term under Ruratanian law is 5 years. Now let's consider the most likely outcomes of the election. First, a stable government majority exists. Either one party has gained a majority, or a stable coalition forms between two closely-allied parties. In this case, the Prime Minister can usually count on retaining that majority for the entire term of the legislature, and an election need not be called for several years.

Note, however, that the Prime Minister is unlikely to wait until the final days of the 5-year term before calling that election. She or he is more likely to call the election after 3.5–4.5 years in office. That's because prime ministers wish to call an election at the most advantageous time. They wish, naturally, to bolster their chances of being returned to office with a continuing majority. If they wait until the last minute, they will have lost all their options.

Like all good politicians, prime ministers know that the public is fickle. It may love you today, but despise you tomorrow. Everyone knows that "a week is a long time in politics." George W. Bush's popularity soared (2001) after his strong response to the 9/11 tragedy. Similarly, his poll numbers plummeted in the wake of Hurricane Katrina (2005) and the mishandling of that crisis. All politicians have ridden the popularity roller coaster, both up and down. Prime ministers know that waiting until the last minute is a gamble. Better call an election when you're high in the polls.

Under this reasoning, one might ask why Prime Ministers don't remain in power forever. Wouldn't savvy leaders call for a national vote every year or two, just as soon as pollsters assure them that they are bound to win?

To ask this question is to see the likely answer. Citizens don't particularly *enjoy* political campaigns and the folderol connected with an election. They would resent being called to the polls every year or two, especially for no reason. A popular Prime Minister with a solid majority has no plausible justification for calling an **early election**. Doing so might backfire, as opponents take advantage of the public's annoyance. ("He's called an unnecessary election to satisfy his excessive ambition," and so forth.)

Thus, calling an election "too soon" could prove unpopular and therefore dangerous. Remember that fickle public. But waiting "too long" could leave you with no options and might also be dangerous. What to do: find some middle course.

Around the 3-year mark of a 5-year term, government leaders start thinking seriously about the next election. If the signs are favorable, they might call an election at the 3.5-year point. More likely, they would wait until 4 years have passed. That's far enough from

the last election that voters won't be annoyed. (The government can claim a need to "renew our mandate," "let the people speak," and so forth.) It is also far enough from a term's end that leaders won't be boxed into a specific date by the force of circumstance.

Only when a government has been unpopular for a long period of time, will it wait until the last minute to call an election. If the governing party is likely to lose an election called after 3, 3.5 or even 4 years, it will continue to hold onto power to the bitter end, hoping for an eventual turn in public sentiment. John Major did this in Britain in the 1995–1997 period, hanging on to power as long as possible in unpopular circumstances. It did him no good. His party was trounced when he was finally forced by law to call the election.

Americans sometimes claim it's "unfair" that Prime Ministers can "call their own balls and strikes" by shopping around for the best election date. Oddly, this seeming advantage makes no difference at all in leadership longevity. If we compare the UK with the USA, for the 110-year period from 1896 to 2006, we find that 20 Britons and 19 Americans held their country's top post. These men spent an almost identical number of years of in office: an average of 5.5 (UK) and 5.8 (USA).

In other parliamentary systems, leaders with the supposed advantage of being able to name the date of the next election fare generally worse than in the UK, as Table 11.1 shows. During these same 110 years, New Zealand had 23 national leaders, Holland 26, and Denmark 31. The timeframe for other countries varies a good deal because of varying historical experiences, but it is clear that parliamentary leaders in polyarchies do not often have the longevity of American presidents in a fixed-term system. Only Canada, of the major parliamentary systems had fewer leaders than the USA during the 110-year period of time, and it had only three fewer, at 16. Germany has clearly been quite stable since the Second World War, but for decades before that it alternated between rigid authoritarianism and unstable democracy.

In any case, the evidence is clear. The ability to choose your election date *doesn't* necessarily produce longer stays in office than the fixed-term system.

TABLE 8.1 Time in Office of Executives in Polyarchal Systems: A Comparison of Selected Countries.*

Country	Period	Number of national political leaders (presidents/prime ministers)†	Average time in office (mean no. of years)
Germany	1949–2006	8	7.1
Canada	1896–2006	16	6.9
USA	1896–2006	19	5.8
UK	1896–2006	20	5.5
New Zealand	1896–2006	23	4.8
Norway (post-WWII)	1945–2006	13	4.7
Holland	1896–2006	26	4.2
Australia	1901–2006	25	4.2
Denmark	1896–2006	31	3.5
France (5th Republic)	1959–2006	17	2.8
Italy	1946–2006	24	2.5
Japan	1956–2006	20	2.5
Norway (pre-WWII)	1905–1940	15	2.3
France (3rd Republic)	1878–1938	44	1.4

* The timeframes were selected to reflect lengthy periods during which each country experienced polyarchal governance.

† This number includes "repeats." For example, Giulio Andreotti is counted just once, even though he held the premiership of Italy in three different time periods. If the number of different *governments* were counted instead of just individual leaders, then all countries except post-Second-World-War Germany would fall behind the USA, including Canada (22 governments, but only 16 leaders, since 1896).

Of the many possible reasons why leaders cannot "game the system" to get themselves re-elected, perhaps the most obvious is that day-to-day politics is complex and unpredictable. Reading the public's mind is still an art form, subject to much slippage. Many a Prime Minister has chuckled happily at having chosen an advantageous polling date, only to awake sorely disillusioned on the day after the election.

Perhaps the most dramatic example of an unexpected polling result occurred in July 1945. After leading his country to victory over Hitler, thereby (in his own mind) "saving the world," Winston Churchill called an election expecting to win handily. Instead, voters unceremoniously booted him from office in favor of the Labour Party and his uncharismatic rival, Clement Attlee. The reasons they did so are many, but two stand out. First, Churchill's Conservatives had been in power for over a decade, and people were ready for a change. Second, they

were especially eager for change after having suffered years of severe economic deprivation. True, one might "objectively" trace their troubles to wartime conditions that would have obtained no matter who was in power, but people living in "hard times" look for someone to blame, and there's no better scapegoat than a long-time governing party.

Parliaments with Unstable Coalitions

So far, we have been discussing parliaments with stable majorities (one party or a cohesive coalition). Let's now see how parliamentary politics work when an unstable coalition forms the government.

Quite frequently after an election, several parties with differing programs get together to form a majority-supported cabinet. Sometimes, it is just two parties, but they don't share many common aims. Reasons vary for the unlikely combinations that form a government. They range from agreement on at least one major issue of the day to friendships among the particular leaders, pure opportunism, or stark necessity (the country's in crisis and some government *has* to be formed).

Whatever the reason, governments formed in these conditions usually fail soon. Long before the official end of the parliamentary term—in a few months, 2 years at the most—prime ministers lose a vote of confidence. They then find themselves with two options. They could dissolve the legislature and call for new elections. Or they could forego elections and simply resign. That's the path most frequently taken. Someone else then puts together a majority coalition, a new government takes power, and the game continues.

There are several reasons why leaders of unstable, short-lived governments will not call elections. Remember, first, that voters do not like elections that follow too soon after the last one. They might well punish the Prime Minister and the party that's identified with the early-election decision.

In addition, *legislators* like elections even less than voters. Every election creates job insecurity. Everyone is vulnerable, no matter how safe a district appears to be, so every election produces anxiety and the possibility of a career-ending defeat for every politician. In any case, even if you're sure of winning your own seat, every election disrupts normal life. Instead of living nicely in the capital and debating grand policy matters, you must now enter the whirlwind of campaign activity. You have got to make pleading calls for money, give speeches, travel far and wide, knock on doors, and beg for support from all and sundry. It is a necessary part of political life, but few people want to do it every year or two.

So legislators will resent anyone calling an election that seems "unnecessary." The person who does so will not be popular with the political class. The Prime Minister who heads a fragile coalition in a fragmented government and calls for a new election after just 18 months will definitely be unpopular. Legislators will see this person not just as someone who put them to a lot of trouble and endangered their careers, but also as someone who acted quite foolishly.

After all, why would anyone call an election after losing the confidence of the legislature? The only purpose would be to *win* the election, to be returned by the people with a decisive victory. But what are the odds that *any* Prime Minister would win majority support in a fractionated political system with numerous parties? Very slim. Remember, for starters, that the Prime Minister's party never did have a majority. That's why it needed the help of other parties to form the government. After 18 months, it is not likely to be *more* popular than it was at the last election. Popular leaders do not lose votes of confidence. Beyond that, many voters will be unhappy with the Prime Minister just for calling that early election, if for no other reason.

So what could you, as a Prime Minister losing a vote of confidence, be thinking in calling an election? You are already unpopular (as illustrated in that no-confidence vote). Then you irritate the public further by calling a snap election just 18 months after the last one. Not a good strategy. The Prime Minister who does this could emerge from that election worse off than before.

There's more. Remember that we are in a multi-party system, so the Prime Minister's party probably won between 20 percent and 35 percent of the votes in the last election. In these already shaky circumstances (the government has fallen, its leader calls an early election), the odds are practically nil that the leader's party will be returned with a resounding show of public support. Much more likely is that this party will lose votes and find itself with a reduced number of seats. No matter what happens, the party won't have anything approaching a majority.

Knowing all this, most Prime Ministers will *not* call a new election. They are rational beings, after all. Following a no-confidence vote, they will ask themselves, "What is now best for me and my party?" They will realize that dissolving parliament won't help them and could insure their long-time absence from the seats of power. They won't win enough seats to form the next government, and the other legislators will be so mad at them for having called the election that they won't be invited to take part in the next coalition government. The discredited Prime Minister's own party will probably choose a new leader, and when that party eventually gets back into government, the disgraced former Prime Minister may well be overlooked when top cabinet posts are handed out.

No, the sensible thing to do, after losing a confidence vote in a multiparty system, is to resign and wait for a new government to form. It is possible that your party will be invited to participate in that government (this time as a junior partner, but at least you are still a key player). By taking the easy path (of resignation), you keep possibilities open for the future. You are, after all, still the leader of an important party. It is entirely possible that you'll be named to a top cabinet post in the next government (Minister of Foreign Affairs, say, or Defense). And if not now, then surely in a later government (and governments come and go, after all, in this unstable system).

Since most leaders think this way in fragmented parliaments, the "rules of the game" dictate the current government resigning and a new government forming, rather than the current government dissolving parliament and calling a new election. Eventually, an election *will* have to be called, but only after several governments have come and gone, and the date nears for the mandatory end of parliament's term. When 4 years have passed and the fifth government of that parliament loses a vote of confidence, then no one would be surprised to see that particular Prime Minister call for new elections. All will agree that there is no working majority to be found in this particular parliament, its term is almost up anyway, and it's about time for the people to be given another chance to express their wishes.

We now see why it is impossible to predict the precise date of an election in a parliamentary system. True, if an election occurs on April 17, 2026, we know that the next election must occur by April 17, 2031 (in a system with a 5-year term for parliament). But we also know it's unlikely that an election will take place on that *particular* date. Few Prime Ministers will wait until the last possible minute to place their fate in the voters' hands. Elections could occur in less than a year if the situation within parliament is particularly volatile. (Britain had *two* elections in 1974, one in February, one in October.) Elections might occur in a year and a half to two if an unexpected vote of no-confidence occurs (Canada held an election in June, 2004, and another in January, 2006).

What is most likely in a parliamentary system is that elections will occur after 70–85 percent of the term has been completed. It all depends on circumstance. The day after any election, we simply cannot know what circumstances of the next few years will be. Therefore, we can never know exactly when that next election will occur.

Effects of the Parliamentary System and Its Election Uncertainty

The seemingly arcane fact that the timing of elections in a parliamentary system is always unknown has an enormous impact on how politicians operate. We know that environment is a central variable for understanding behavior, and uncertainty about the time of the next election is a key element in the environment of any politician. American Senators (with a fixed term of 6 years) can act like "statesmen" for the first 2 or 3 years after their election. They can "take the long view," consider broad theoretical matters, and avoid automatic responses to constituent demands. Representatives, who run every 2 years, pay continuing attention to mundane constituent wants. (Many are called "errand-boys" for good reason.) We would expect politicians in parliamentary systems, people who might have to run for re-election *at any minute* (so to speak), to behave differently from those operating in a fixed-term system. Just how differently is worth exploring.

Among stable, long-term democracies, only the USA has a fixed-term system for all national officials. Presidents serve 4 years before having to face another election. House members serve 2 years, Senators six, and federal judges serve for life (specifically, "during good behavior"). Once in office practically nothing can force someone out until the next election—or until death, in the case of judges. (Yes, impeachments and ousters are technically possible, but almost never happen.)

The impact of these fixed terms is dramatic. They reinforce (even make possible) the desire of the writers of the Constitution for a separation-of-powers, checks-and-balances system. How? They keep the members of each center of power independent of each other. Think, after all: short of violence, what is the most important hold you can have over someone? It is the threat to dislodge them from their cherished job. High political office is valued, and those who can give it, or take it away, have great power.

In the USA, Presidents simply cannot give someone the job of senator, nor can they fire any senator. Supreme Court justices cannot make anyone a member of the House of Representatives. Senators cannot appoint presidents, and House members cannot name Supreme Court justices. It is true that the President *and* the Senate *combined* can put someone on the Court, but once there they cannot remove that person. (No justice has *ever* been forced from office.)

Of course, presidents and senators, representatives and justices, all have ways of influencing each other. They all have varied power resources to wield in the ongoing political struggle. But the fixed-term system shelters members of each unit from total control by members of another. It gives them all some leeway for independent action. In the end, it creates a system with multiple points of access to the powerful, while limiting the power of any one leader.

American politicians think like this about members of another branch: Since I did not get my job because of you (at least, not directly because of you), and since in any case you cannot fire me from my job, you cannot order me around. Yes, you have various resources and tactics you can bring to bear against me, including persuasion, but so do I against you, meaning you have to pay some attention to my interests, just as I do to yours. Neither you nor I are forced slavishly to follow each other's desires.

Relationships under these conditions center on bargaining and negotiation rather than on command and obedience. In the end, each political unit has power, and each can block the wishes of the other units. Sometimes Congress wants something that the President opposes. In that case, he can veto their legislation. Sometimes Congress and the President want something that the Supreme Court does not like, in which case the court can thwart both institutions by declaring a law unconstitutional. On it goes. No person or institution is "supreme" in the American system.

The lack of a single center of power in the USA is hard for non-Americans to absorb. In most countries (democracy or otherwise), there is one clear power point.

In parliamentary systems, it is the popularly-elected house of parliament. There's no "separation of powers." Indeed, the core principle is *concentration of power*. Power is centered on the legislative majority. Whoever controls that controls politics in that system.

Now let's return to our crucial point. None of the legislators in a parliamentary system have fixed terms, including the leaders they have chosen (prime minister and cabinet, usually referred to as "the government"). The political fortunes of legislators and executive officials are interdependent to a much greater degree than they are in the presidential, fixed-terms system. Let's see why that should be the case.

As we have seen, there are two main patterns in parliamentary governance: (1) either the Prime Minister safely controls a stable majority or (2) the Prime Minister heads a complex and shaky coalition of diverse parties. Each of these options illustrates the interdependence of parliamentary systems and the effect of the no-fixed-term situation on internal politics.

Prime Ministerial Control

In the first case, the prime minister dominates parliament. His supporters know that voting against this leader on any key matter could lead to the downfall of the government and a new election. We know the logic here: if the prime minister heads a government controlled by a dominant party or two strong, closely-aligned parties, the odds are good that she would call an election after losing a vote of no-confidence. Members of the legislative majority know this and shrink from ever voting against their leader on key issues.

If John McCain opposes President Bush on social security reform, what happens to John McCain? He might make some members of his party unhappy, but so what? He is still senator, and after all, you cannot please everyone all the time. And what happens to President Bush? He may lose on this issue, but you can't win 'em all—and he's still president.

Now what happens if Jerzy Blatzflyk votes against Prime Minister Schlossnik in East Ruratania? If Blatzflyk's action helps defeat Schlossnik on a key vote, Schlossnik might decide to call new elections. Remember that politicians do not relish elections. In addition to all the uncertainties and personal hardships they bring, things are even worse for the Blatzflyks of the political world. All faithful members of the majority will detest Jerzy for having caused this turn of events. Furthermore, the most powerful members of his party (the Prime Minister and cabinet) will be furious at him. Those hostile feelings will multiply if the election goes badly. Then, everyone in the previous majority will look at Blatzflyk and his associates as the people responsible for causing the downfall of "the rightful rulers of the nation."

In politics, people don't just get mad; they get even. The future of the Blatzflyk faction will be bleak. Members will never get top posts within the party; when the party regains power, they will get no appointments to high office; and it is entirely possible that they will be booted from the party altogether. After all, these "traitors" took us from a position of controlling the government to a position of helpless opposition. Their fates will not be pretty.

Given these facts, what would *you* do if you were a legislator inside the majority in a strongly-supported government? You'd obviously support every major government initiative. Few people like to commit professional suicide.

Besides, it is easy to rationalize this behavior. Even if you oppose a major government policy, and even if you are willing to sacrifice your own career, you know that you support *most* of this government's policies and like *almost none* of the opposition's. Why jeopardize everything the government stands for over just one issue? If you (and others) cause the government's downfall by forcing an election that the party loses, you go from getting 90 percent, say, of what you want to getting perhaps twenty percent (under the new government).

The result of this interdependence of government and legislature is to ensure straight-line party voting on all important matters. That in turn leads to straight-line party voting on almost everything. First, legislators get in the habit of voting with their leadership, and second, it is hard to tell which votes are "important" and which are not. If governments lose a string of votes on "minor" issues, it starts to look as if they are weak, don't have the country behind them, can't control their own supporters, and so forth. Each new "minor" vote starts to look "major"; it is part of an ongoing set of indicators of government support. In the end, it's simpler and becomes the pattern just to vote with the government *all* the time, rather than be seen as someone who's helped to weaken your party's control over the levers of power.

Parliamentary Control

There is a second major pattern in parliamentary governance. It occurs when parties are many, coalitions are shaky, and governments are weak. Now the tables are turned. When governments are weak, legislators know that any threat of dissolving parliament is an empty one.

As we have already seen, prime ministers who head a relatively small party and are riding herd on a fractious governing coalition simply cannot call for new elections. They would lose those elections and destroy their own career in the bargain. Since everyone knows these facts, *the Prime Minister in this situation is the captive of the legislature.* His term is now entirely dependent on his ability to please the members of his coalition on all important issues.

Remember that crucial parliamentary norm: governments must resign or call new elections if they lose parliament's confidence, and the loss of a key vote is one definition of losing parliament's confidence. Again, we see the effect of the no-fixed-term aspect of this system. Americans too have known weak presidents or presidents with little popular support. Harry Truman, Jerry Ford, and Jimmy Carter come to mind, as do certain periods in the presidencies of the first President Bush and Bill Clinton. Still, no matter how weak presidents might become, they never become Congress's spokesperson. They always retain a good deal of independent authority and power. In the end, they retain much freedom of action because, very simply, Congress can't fire them. In a parliamentary system, legislators do have that power, and they're much more likely to exercise it in an unstable coalition situation.

We know that legislators hesitate to overturn a prime minister whose party might win the next election. But when prime ministers are unlikely to come out of a new election in good shape, they are much more likely to resign than dissolve parliament. That's just fine with the legislators who are thinking of defecting from the governing coalition.

The reasons why legislators might vote against a government they currently support are many. These range from personal ambition to fury over a government policy. All legislators everywhere want, at one time or another, to vote against a given government policy. In a checks-and-balances, fixed-term system, many will do that and suffer few consequences. In a parliamentary system with a strong majority-supported government, few (to none) will do that for fear of dooming both the government and their own careers. But in a parliamentary system with a multi-party, shaky coalition, many will consider this option. Defection is always part of the system and can be used as a lever in the bargaining game. Since it is always possible, it is bound to occur from time to time, making clear to everyone that this outcome is not just plausible, but even likely.

The result is that the legislature now controls its leadership. Prime ministers of weak governments will pay extremely close attention to legislators' desires—or demands. Leaders know that legislators control their jobs. Lose a key vote, and they must resign. Hence, they'll pay close attention to what members of parliament want.

We now see clearly the three patterns of polyarchal governance.

1. Under the fixed-term system, *independent bargaining* occurs among relatively equal actors who don't control each other's immediate fates.

2. Under the parliamentary system with a strong majority, *executive dominance* is the rule.

3. And under the parliamentary system with a weak majority, one finds *legislative dominance*.

It is clear that in a parliamentary system, the lack of a fixed term, along with the need of governments to win all key votes, concentrates power. Whether it concentrates that power in legislators or in executives depends on the strength of the dominant party in government. If that party can hope for majority support at the polls in any future election, the executive leadership will dominate politics. If not, legislators will dominate the system. In either case, there is no question of individuals with independent bases of power confronting each other with varying degrees of potential influence. Power is either quite clearly in the hands of one set of actors or another.

As an aside, it's worth stating that whether the legislature or the executive controls power in parliament, we're not talking about dictatorial power. Prime ministers, even strong ones, can retain their majority only by a continual process of consultation and persuasion. In any case, the next election is never far away. Voters will ultimately pass judgment on the substance and style of any government.

Effect of the Parliamentary System on Party Loyalty

It is now clear that this external, structural, environmental variable (presidential or parliamentary system) seriously affects behavior. Most dramatically, parliamentary systems produce much greater party loyalty than occurs under presidentialism. Remember that in a parliamentary system no one knows the date of the next election. Everyone does know, however, that the odds of an election rise when Prime Ministers lose a key vote. Even if the Prime Minister does not call for new elections after a no-confidence vote, he or she will have to resign, the party will lose its power to govern, and many members of the party will lose a variety of perks.

No one wants any of this. It is simpler just to vote with the party at all times. For that reason, party-line votes become the absolute rule in parliamentary systems.

Americans are often startled at this strict party-voting norm. They wonder why foreign legislators cannot "think for themselves," the way American lawmakers supposedly do. Note, however, that people in the same party, in whatever nation, usually share the same values and policy preferences. Consequently, they will vote the same way on most bills that come before them. Even in the American Congress, party is the most significant predictor of voting behavior. No other variable (state, region, age, income, gender) comes close to this one in predicting how a member of Congress will vote on any given bill.

So politicians everywhere vote with their party—hardly a surprise. Party-line voting is stronger in parliamentary than in presidential systems, however, because the consequences for disloyalty differ significantly. In a parliamentary system, deviations from party loyalty can lead to disastrous consequences for one's party—and for one's own career. In a presidential system, deviations might make some people temporarily unhappy, but they do not destroy your party's hold on power, and they do not necessarily hurt your own career chances either.

So far, we have explained only why politicians in the *governing* party (or coalition) vote together loyally. The same logic drives those in the minority. What is the best chance for minority party members to become the majority (and thereby gain access to control of policy, status, and favors)? Naturally, it's to defeat the government in a key vote, thereby forcing the government's resignation. After that,

there'd either be a new government, perhaps with your party now in charge, or a new election, which your party might win. In all events, your future hopes depend entirely on defeating the current government. Thus, you will vote in a bloc against them at every opportunity.

Conclusion

The parliamentary environment goes a long way toward explaining the high degree of party discipline in most polyarchies outside the USA. The English and the French and the Italians are not more conformist than Americans. Far from it! They just happen to operate in an environment that demands party loyalty. If Americans adopted a parliamentary system, our legislators would soon be acting the same way. They'd be voting with their party 99.9 percent of the time—once they saw the disastrous consequences of *disloyalty* to their career chances and to their party's hold on power.

People often ask: which of these systems is "better?" There is, of course, no right or wrong when it comes to political structures. It is just a question of which behavior each structure encourages and which behavior one prefers. In any case, once a pattern becomes common in a society, it becomes the "expected" one, and anything else seems odd and deviant.

Americans are used to a system with many independent bases of power and no one dominant. Compromises and clashes among political actors are all worked out in a very public way. It is confusing, even infuriating, to the mass of citizens. They are especially unhappy at never knowing who to blame (or less frequently, reward) for a given policy. Is it the Democrats (who control some power centers) or the Republicans (who control others)? Still, American culture would almost certainly rebel at a system that concentrated power in one institution (and almost surely in one person—a Prime Minister with majority control of the legislature).

On the other hand, parliaments seem entirely rational for the rest of the polyarchal world. When voters speak, is it not reasonable that they should get their way? Should there really be some other power centers blocking their will? No, say backers of parliamentarism. With all power concentrated in the dominant house of the legislature, whoever emerges with a majority there *should* get to rule for the next few years. Let them carry on without obstruction. At least, we will know who is responsible for national policies. If we do not like the results, we will kick them out at the next election.

So, depending on whether you like power fractured, complex and murky, or concentrated and responsible, you will prefer either a presidential or a parliamentary system. Of course, most people never have to choose one or the other. We are simply used to "our" system and imagine that any other way of operating makes no sense. Government structures become part of our cultural expectations. Embedded in the consciousness of a nation's citizens, they develop a lengthy and deeply-entrenched life of their own.

Questions for Discussion

1. What if the USA adopted a parliamentary system? How would that change the American political process? Would there be any support for this change in the American public?

2. Do you think American politicians would be able to make coalition governments work?

3. Within parliamentary systems, the time that leaders stay in office varies a good deal—7 years in Germany and Canada, 2.5 years in Italy and Japan (Table 11.1.) What do you think accounts for these variations? Since they all use the same system, why don't leaders stay in power for about the same length of time?

4. Can you think of any situation in which a prime minister who heads a diverse, multi-party coalition could exercise strong leadership?

5. The author argues that the ties of party loyalty are strong everywhere. In your experience, does that generalization apply to American politics?

Notes

1. For a good summary of this perspective, see Fred W. Riggs, "Presidentialism vs. Parliamentarism: Implications for Representativeness and Legitimacy," *International Political Science Review* 18:3 (1997), pp. 253–278.

2. For a recent presentation of this argument, see José Antonio Cheibub, *Presidentialism, Parliamentarism, and Democracy* (Cambridge: Cambridge University Press, 2007).

3. See discussion of this point on pp. 215–220.

4. Variations exist. The norm in most parliamentary systems is a legislature with two houses (one popularly-elected and dominant, one weak—or at least weaker—and chosen in some way *other* than through direct popular election). But this norm is not universal. Sweden has abolished its second house and now has just one, while Italy has two nearly-equal houses that are both popularly-elected.

5. This situation is changing rapidly, as courts in many countries have recently gained (and are using) powers to slap down legislative actions. See the discussion of courts in Ch. 12.

6. As usual, there are exceptions to this general description of the typical parliamentary system. In Germany, the second house (the Bundesrat) must give its consent to any legislation that concerns *länder* (provincial) matters; it can therefore block the dominant house (the Bundestag) on

provincial issues, if it chooses to do so. France (and some of the newer, less-stable polyarchies like Poland and the Czech Republic) have "mixed" parliamentary-presidential systems, where directly-elected presidents and the dominant house of parliament often clash with each other (and can check each other in various ways). Italy is perhaps the clearest exception to the one-house-dominant rule in parliamentary systems. It has two legislative bodies, a Chamber of Deputies and a Senate, that are essentially co-equal (as in the American system). Both are directly elected by the mass electorate, and governments (Prime Ministers) must have majorities in both houses to continue in office.

7. Most countries have this second, weaker, non-popularly-elected house. In Canada, members of the Senate are appointed by the Prime Minister. In Britain, members of the House of Lords are either appointed by the Prime Minister or inherit a family seat that was bestowed on an ancestor earlier in history. In France, every 3 years, one-third of the members of the Senate are chosen for 9-year terms by groups of local and regional officials in a complex election process. These second, weaker houses of parliament have varying powers, depending on the country, but most can eventually be over-ridden by the stronger house, if push comes to shove. As mentioned earlier, some countries (like Sweden) have dispensed with a weak second house altogether.

8. Different countries have different names for the top executive official (Chancellor in Germany, Taoiseach in Ireland, etc.), but "Prime Minister" is most common and will be used throughout this text.

9. Other possibilities exist. Occasionally, a minority government is formed, but it tends to be short-lived. Occasionally, too (for various reasons), it is not the leader of the largest party who's named Prime Minister. We concentrate here on the most common outcomes after elections in parliamentary systems. For detail on all the possibilities, see Gallagher, Laver, and Mair, *Representative Government in Modern Europe*, 4th edn. (New York: McGraw Hill, 2005, pp. 381–421).

10. Union pour la Démocratie Française. The UDF split during the presidential and parliamentary elections of May and June, 2007, and its future is currently uncertain.

11. Of course, Prime Ministers do resign for reasons of health or other personal matters, and some have died in office, but those are chance events that can happen in all systems. We are dealing here with *political* reasons for a government changeover.

12. Parliaments can express their loss of confidence in the government in two ways: (1) through a formal vote of no-confidence and (2) through a negative vote on a major policy of the government. As an example of the second possibility, if the government's overall budget is defeated, or if it loses a vote on one of its central initiatives, it has effectively been told that parliament has lost confidence in it. It must then resign—unless it decides to call for new elections. [...]

13. Chamberlain's downfall was inevitable after the collapse of his appeasement policy toward Hitler. When war came, despite his futile efforts to avoid it, he had little choice but to resign. Luckily for his Conservative Party, they held a strong majority in the House of Commons and could easily replace him with Churchill, thus avoiding the need to dissolve parliament and face new elections.

14. Sweden used to elect parliaments every 3 years, but changed to 4-year terms in 1994.

CHAPTER 9

The Presidency

KEY TERMS

Electoral College

White House Staff

National Security Advisor

Veto Power

The Cabinet

Executive Office of the President

New Deal

National Security Council Staff

Executive Agreements

DISCUSSION QUESTIONS

1. Discuss how the growth of the Executive Office of the President has allowed presidents to enact a more activist agenda.

2. Discuss how presidents' role as chief of state gives them influence in enacting an agenda.

3. Discuss the importance of the presidential veto on the legislative role of the presidency.

4. Discuss the significance of the president's power to appoint federal judges.

EARLY INTERPRETATIONS OF THE PRESIDENCY

At the beginning of the republic, it was clear that the presidency was seen by the founders as being a caretaker and administrator, not the primary branch of government. The Constitution clearly gives the legislative branch primacy in policy making. There was a great deal of debate at the Constitutional Convention as to the role of the president, presidential election, and presidential terms.

At the Constitution Convention, both the Virginia and Connecticut plans called for the indirect election of the president by Congress. This set up a conflict between the larger and smaller states. This was one of the reasons why the Connecticut Plan was developed, as if the legislature were dominated by the larger states, they would also control the election of the president.

One of the compromises at the Constitutional Convention was the creation of the **electoral college**, which survives today. This is an indirect means of electing the president. Initially, the electors were chosen by state legislatures, and they were autonomous. They did not have to vote for the candidate who won the popular vote in their respective states. With the development of political parties they now put up a slate of electors in each state. The popular vote in a state determines which party's slate of electors will cast the respective state's electoral votes. As a result, the president of the United States is elected independently of Congress. This has contributed to the autonomy of the presidency.

THE GROWTH OF THE EXECUTIVE OFFICE OF THE PRESIDENT

At the beginning of the republic, the president had no staff. He frequently had an assistant to help in letter writing and appointments which he paid out of his own pocket. Usually, this was a relative. Eventually, in 1857, Congress approved the president having an assistant paid by the federal government.

EXECUTIVE OFFICE OF THE PRESIDENT

As the federal government has taken on more responsibilities over the course of the nineteenth and twentieth centuries, the government has grown, and the staff has increased. This has been especially true regarding the US presidency. The Executive Office of the President expanded as the presidency evolved from a caretaker administrator to having an activist legislative agenda. The Executive Office of the President was created in 1939. It is housed in the West Wing of the White House and has about 4,000 employees. The growth of the presidential staff has allowed some presidents to craft a very activist domestic and foreign policy agenda. Franklin Roosevelt, who was president when the Executive Office of the President was created, crafted the **New Deal**. This remains one of the most ambitious series of policies dealing with economic regulation of the economy.

THE ROLES OF THE PRESIDENT

- Chief administrator
- Chief of state
- Party chief
- Chief legislator
- Chief diplomat
- Commander in chief
- Chief judge

Chief Administrator
The president is in charge of the executive branch. The role of the administrator is to ensure that laws are being carried out and programs are functioning. Both the executive and congressional branches of government have the function of overseeing the bureaucracy. Presidents appoint the top layer of the bureaucracy subject to the advice and consent of the Senate. In addition to the 16 cabinet secretaries are the undersecretaries and assistant secretaries. In addition, presidents appoint the head of federal agencies, such as the Federal Bureau of Investigation (FBI) and the Environmental Protection Agency.

Chief of State
The president is the ceremonial head of the US government. In most of the other major industrial democracies, there is a separation between the head of state and the head of government. For example, in Germany and Italy, there is a president, elected by the Parliament, who has little political power but presides over ceremonial occasions while real power is vested in the prime minister

who is the leader of the dominant party or coalition in Parliament. In the United Kingdom the sovereign, Queen Elizabeth II, is head of state. She is also head of state for the commonwealth countries, such as Canada and the Bahamas. Real political and administrative power is held by the prime minister and the cabinet.

As a result, the US president has to spend a great deal of time in photo ops and presiding over ceremonial occasions, such as the annual White House Easter Egg Roll. Presidents often attempt to use these events to cultivate a good public image and for their reelection efforts. The State of the Union Address is an event in which the president uses the symbolism of head of state and head of government. This allows the president to use the symbols of office to put forth policy goals for the coming year.

Party Chief

This is one of the more informal roles of the president. The president does not have an administrative title as the head of a respective political party. Because the president is the top official in the United States, the president is essentially the face of their political party. This means that presidential popularity is very important. If the president is popular, then he/she can influence the election of other members of his/her party to Congress, governorships, and state legislators. Presidential popularity can also influence the passage of legislation and make it easier for the president to maintain the support of his/her party in Congress while winning votes from other members of Congress who are not in the president's party.

Chief Legislator

The president, because of the **veto power**, is able to be active in legislation. While Congress is the legislative branch, the Constitution does give the veto to the president. It is very difficult to override a presidential veto. It is necessary to gain a two-thirds vote in both houses of Congress to do so. Also, because much of the legislation passed in a given congressional term is done at the end, the president has ten days to decide on a bill. If Congress adjourns within the ten-day period, then the president can do nothing, and the bill does not become a law. This is known as a pocket veto. Even more important is the threat of a veto. As the bill is moving through Congress, the president can exert leverage in getting the language changed in a bill by threatening a veto. The authors of the bill realize how hard it is to override a veto and thus can often be persuaded to amend the language in a bill to gain presidential support.

An even more powerful component of the veto is the line-item veto. Most state governors have this power in which they can veto components of a bill instead of the bill in its entirety. President Bill Clinton briefly had the line-item veto, but it was challenged in the courts, and the Supreme Court ruled it unconstitutional.

Chief Diplomat

Because the president has the authority to conclude treaties, name ambassadors, and meet with foreign leaders, the president is considered the chief diplomat of the United States. This also ties into the chief of state role, as the president represents the United States for the rest of the world. There are constraints on this role, as ambassadors have to be confirmed by the Senate, and treaties need two-thirds support of the Senate. Presidents get around this through the use of **executive agreements**. They have the force of a treaty but do not need Senate confirmation. This is essentially an agreement between the president and another head of government, usually for simple issues, such as mail delivery. However, at times, it has been used for more important issues. When the Strategic Arms Limitation Treaty II was withdrawn from Senate consideration after the Soviets invaded Afghanistan in 1979, its terms were still adhered to by the United States and Soviet Union through an executive agreement first under President Carter and then carried on under President Reagan.

Commander in Chief

The president is first general and first admiral of the United States. The president is in overall command of the day-to-day armed forces. This power has increased over time because of the changing nature of warfare. The Constitution made the president commander in chief, while Congress has the power to declare war. However, because of the changing nature of warfare, wars do not get declared anymore. The last declared war for the United States was World War II. This gives the president a great deal of authority in committing US forces overseas. Politically, it is very difficult to challenge the president in this action, at least initially. Presidents also have the entire weight of the US national security establishment at their disposal to justify intervention. The president is also able to dominate media time to justify the case for intervention. There was an attempt to curb the ability of the president's ability to commit troops overseas in the aftermath of the Vietnam War with the War Powers Act. The act established that the president has to inform the leaders of Congress when troops are being committed to a war zone. After 60 days, Congress can authorize their withdrawal, and the president will have another 30 days to withdraw the troops. The president cannot veto this. It has never been invoked, and there are some experts who doubt it is constitutional as it essentially gives a legislative veto. Also, politically, it is very difficult for Congress to order a withdrawal once American troops have been committed.

Chief Judge

This is probably the foremost power of the presidency. Presidents appoint all federal judges subject to Senate confirmation. Federal judges have lifetime appointments. As a result, presidents have the ability to influence the interpretation of law well after they have left the White House. The check on this is in addition to Senate confirmation, once confirmed, judges have the freedom to rule according to their own judicial philosophies. President Eisenhower was against using federal troops to desegregate Little Rock Central High School. He attempted to lobby members of the Supreme Court whom he had appointed to influence their decision. However, the court ruled that the federal troops had to enforce the desegregation order. President Eisenhower grudgingly consented to federal troops escorting students to class.

EVOLUTION OF THE CABINET

In 1791, as Washington left the capital, he authorized his advisors; the vice president; secretaries of state, war, and treasury; and the chief justice to consult with each other on government matters. Unlike in parliamentary systems, **the cabinet** in the American presidential system is generally not a group decision-making body. Cabinet meetings are, for the most part, for show, not a source of collective decision making. Cabinet appointees for departments dealing with national security have more access to the president than those who deal more with domestic affairs. Cabinet appointees have to run departments, and this frequently becomes their frame of reference. Secretaries have become advocates for departments.

EXECUTIVE OFFICE OF THE PRESIDENT

The **Executive Office of the President** was established in 1939. It assists the president in performing policy tasks. The process of the expansion of the presidential staff had very humble beginnings. In the first 70 years of the republic, Congress did not provide the president with any secretarial support. Aides were relatives of the president and paid out of his own pocket. The 1857 Congress authorized an aide to assist the president. The president's staff went from being housed directly in the White House to having other offices nearby. President Roosevelt further expanded the staff to include aides budgeted to other departments doing White House work.

President Roosevelt emphasized more personal control to enact comprehensive New Deal programs. The Harry S. Truman and Dwight D. Eisenhower staffs were organized more uniformly. President Eisenhower created the chief of staff position. From the 1960s onward, more institutional power shifted to the Executive Office of the President.

REPERCUSSIONS OF THE GROWTH OF WHITE HOUSE STAFF FOR THE PRESIDENT POLITICALLY

- Allowed the president to claim credit for policy initiatives
- Enabled presidents to formulate policies independent of the bureaucracy
- Shifted power from the cabinet to White House advisors

This created rivalries between cabinet officials and **White House staff**. This is particularly the case regarding the secretary of state and the national security advisor. While the secretary of state is the chief public diplomat and foreign policy advisor to the president, the **national security advisor** has an office in the West Wing of the White House, sees the president every day, and travels with the president. During the Ronald Reagan administration, there was a clash between Secretary of State Alexander Haig and National Security Advisor Richard Allen. Haig was a former general and supreme military commander of NATO. Richard Allen had worked on the Reagan campaign. Alexander Haig felt he was not involved in major administrative decisions and eventually resigned. During the Jimmy Carter administration, a similar dynamic occurred between Secretary of State Cyrus Vance and National Security Advisor Zbigniew Brzezinski. Vance was an attorney and had served in the Lyndon B. Johnson administration. Brzezinski was an academic active in the Democratic Party; he was the son of a former pre-World War II Polish diplomat who could not return to Poland after the Communist takeover post-World War II. As a result, he was very conservative when it came to Cold War politics. Vance and Brzezinski clashed repeatedly over foreign policy issues. They had a fundamental disagreement on the attempt to rescue the hostages in Iran. Secretary of State Vance resigned as a result.

The national security advisor is one of the most important of the president's personal advisors. The national security advisor coordinates the **National Security Council staff**. The National Security Council was created by the National Security Act of 1947. The members are the president, vice president, and secretaries of state and defense. The director of the Central Intelligence Agency (CIA) and chairman of the Joint Chiefs of Staff are associate members. In recent years, the National Security Council staff has functioned as a second State Department. As a result, functions overlap, and this is a source of tension.

A problem for presidents is they are dependent on their staff. Aides serve at the pleasure of the president, and they are dependent on the goodwill of the president. They often hesitate to disagree with the president and be the bearers of bad news. Many times, presidential advisors tell the president what they think the president wants to hear. The president controls the executive branch and, like Louis XIV, is often treated as a kind of "Sun King." The executive branch rises and falls on the president. This is unlike a parliamentary system where the prime minister is the first among equals and has to take into account the preferences of the cabinet.

PRESIDENTIAL POWER AND ITS DILEMMAS
John P. Burke

This book examines the issues and theories of *presidential power,* that is, the ability of a president to attain political and policy goals. Examining presidential power is central to understanding the presidency, which is important because for better or worse, intentional or not, the American presidency has emerged as the central focus of our system of government. Starting in the twentieth century, especially since Franklin D. Roosevelt's presidency and his efforts to grapple with the Great Depression and World War II, we have turned to the presidency to solve national and international problems. What traditionally might have been regarded as largely local or state-level problems—or even matters of personal choice and responsibility—are seen today as presidential issues, calling for executive response and action. A few examples include the quality of education in local public schools, the costs of college and university education, gun violence and gun control, racial tensions in communities, health care, and environmental quality and conservation issues. If you are surprised that these were not always regarded as matters of clear presidential response and action, then that is all the more telling.

Policies that we take for granted today were not seen as presidential issues, much less the responsibility of the federal government, in eras past. Housing for the poor and the indigent? Until federal housing projects began in the 1930s under Roosevelt, the local "poorhouse" was the only option for those without

housing. Financial support for retired seniors? Social Security started during FDR's second term, but before that retirement income was entirely the responsibility of individuals. This was the same case for medical care, though local charity hospitals were sometimes available to those who could not pay. For seniors, government-assisted medical care started to be seriously discussed only after World War II, during Harry Truman's presidency, and it took until 1965, during Lyndon Johnson's administration, for Medicare to become law. And before Dwight D. Eisenhower's successful effort in 1956 to create interstate highways, states and locales created their own turnpikes, parkways, or freeways, but often they were not connected. In each of these cases, the president took the initiative to bring these issues under federal jurisdiction.

Of course, not all public policy originates with the president; much can percolate through Congress on its own and become law. Although this book focuses on how presidents secure their policy ends and goals, Congress is still obviously central to attaining presidential initiatives, especially if legislation is required, and the president must convince Congress to take action. How do presidents influence Congress? Is it just through traditional, direct bargaining? What about alternative strategies such as approaching Congress indirectly through third parties or using presidential appeals to the public to exert pressure on their congressional representatives? Presidents also often attempt to achieve their ends acting on their

John P. Burke, "Introduction: Presidential Power and Its Dilemmas," *Presidential Power: Theories and Dilemmas*, pp. 1–10. Copyright © 2016 by Taylor & Francis Group. Reprinted with permission.

own through a variety of executive actions such as executive orders, proclamations, and declarations. This invites certain questions of power: Does the president legitimately possess those powers? Is the president powerful enough to successfully assert these claims? Congress plays a role here as well in recognizing, and often legislatively authorizing, presidential claims to power but also sometimes denying them. Given this, presidents often exercise caution with executive actions when Congress is assertive and act bolder when it is not.

[…] The Supreme Court has had final say on a number of important constitutional issues in this area. Sometimes the president wins, and at other times the president loses. These tactics are all part of the presidential power toolkit, and as we shall explore throughout this book, presidents often need to employ some combination of these methods to achieve their goals. Depending on the situation and the context, some work better than others.

A Digression Back in Time: Early and Enduring Dilemmas

To begin framing our analysis of the issues and challenges concerning presidential power and its dilemmas, let us go back in time to a president of a different era, Rutherford B. Hayes. He served as the nineteenth president from 1877 to early 1881, and he kept extensive diaries of his life. On March 18, 1878, he records a typical day as president:

> I rise at about 7 a.m.; write until breakfast, about 8:30 a.m. After breakfast, prayers—i.e., the reading of a chapter in the Bible, each one present reading a verse in turn, and all kneeling repeat the Lord's Prayer; then, usually, [I] write and arrange business until 10 a.m. From 10 to 12 in the Cabinet Room, the Members of Congress having the preference of all visitors except Cabinet ministers. Callers "to pay respects" are usually permitted to come in to shake hands whenever the number reaches about a half dozen waiting. Twelve to 2 p.m., on Tuesdays and Fridays, are Cabinet hours. On other days that time is given to miscellaneous business callers. At 2 p.m., lunch. I commonly invite to that—cup of tea and biscuit and butter with cold meat—any gentleman I wish to have more conference with than

is practicable in hours given to miscellaneous business. After lunch the correspondence of the day, well briefed, and each letter in an envelope, is examined. By this time it is 3:30 p.m., and I then drive an hour and a half. Returning I glance over the business and correspondence again, take a fifteen or twenty minutes' nap, and get ready to dine at 6 p.m.[1]

There are a number of revealing items here. The president's cabinet mattered more than it does today, and Hayes met with them regularly as a group. Members of Congress might stop by to visit, but these calls were not necessarily scheduled. The White House at the time was an open, public building. As Hayes notes, "presentable" folks could actually enter and "pay respects" to the president. Most notably, the president's day ended at three thirty in the afternoon, much earlier than it does today, and dinner followed promptly at six o'clock. (No alcohol was served, by the way, in the Hayes White House. A popular nickname for his wife was "Lemonade Lucy," and the joke at the time was that at a Hayes White House formal dinner water flowed like wine.) Hayes was hardly overburdened by his official duties. Sunday was even more leisurely: "I have gone to church at least once every Sunday since I became President. Sunday after lunch I ride regularly with Secretary [of Treasury John] Sherman two to three hours. We talk over affairs and visit the finest drives and scenes near Washington."[2]

The most important takeaway is that things have changed considerably since Hayes's day. The contemporary presidency looks much different. For example, today's Congress members do not simply "drop by" or visit unless scheduled. Meetings of the full cabinet are rare, and good luck to citizens who want to enter the White House and pay their respects to the president. There is no mention in Hayes's diary of the press, of presidential speeches and travel, or of the White House staff. In fact the latter was quite small, fewer than ten in number. Hayes's longtime friend William King Rogers and then the president's own son, Webb Hayes, each served as personal secretary to the president (what was then the chief of staff position). But it was a vastly different job compared to that of the president's chief aides today. Neither was a substantive policy or strategic political adviser. They provided familiar comfort to Hayes, organized his letters and correspondence, took notes at meetings, and arranged his schedule. Today, the White House staff numbers over twenty-five hundred (and this is a conservative estimate).

However—and this is a very important point—Hayes still had to reckon with a core dilemma of presidential power: how to exert influence and work with the other two branches of government to achieve his legislative agenda. High on his list were returning the former states of the Confederacy to home rule while preserving the rights of African Americans and encouraging civil service reform. He often vetoed legislation, especially attempts to weaken the gold standard, to curtail federal monitoring of elections in the South, and to remove the federal government's power to deal with the Ku Klux Klan. Hayes used his executive powers to send troops to stop a national railroad strike and to pursue Mexican bandits across the border. He also issued an executive order that prevented federal employees from being required to make campaign contributions. Although not the broad agenda of a contemporary president, Hayes still needed to exert power and influence to achieve his goals. In this, Hayes struggled: his civil rights policies and efforts at civil service reform met with great resistance.

Hayes also serves as an example of the impact of political and historical context on a president's power, an issue we explore in this book. In Hayes's case, as a Republican, he had to deal with a Democratic majority in the House. This was not the progressive Democratic Party of today. Rather, it was a party that gained control of the House as southern states returned to home rule and white southerners, opposed to post–Civil War Reconstruction and civil rights for African Americans, rose to political power once again. Hayes did not always have an easy time with his own party either. The Republican Party's old guard, the "Stalwart" wing, clung to political patronage and fought against Hayes's efforts for civil service reform. In addition, Hayes was president during an era of congressional dominance, and his position was somewhat weakened because of this. Moreover, it was an era when party leaders and political bosses essentially determined the party's candidate for the presidency.

Hayes's presidency also helps illustrate the issue I refer to as the "internal time" of the presidency. What are the opportunities and constraints on power in each year of a president's first term? And what about the remaining four if there is a second term? Hayes became president in 1876 after a contested election, one in which he lost the popular vote but won the Electoral College by one vote after an improvised commission awarded him electoral votes in several southern states. It was not unlike the Bush-Gore election in 2000 but more weakening to the president in the way that it was resolved. Hayes's opponents quickly labeled him "President Rutherfraud" and "His Fraudulency." He also pledged not to run for reelection. Neither was helpful to Hayes's attempts to exercise presidential power during his time in office.

Greater Expectations Magnify The Dilemmas Of Presidential Power

If Hayes encountered difficulty and often considerable opposition in achieving his goals, think about the situation contemporary presidents face. The presidency has more of an impact on policy; the reach of policy initiatives is substantially broader; the daily activity of the White House is much more frenetic; and the twenty-four-hour media cycle (and Internet) is ever watchful. The role of the president and our expectations of the presidency have grown and heightened over time.

We now expect the president to be the chief proposer of domestic policies in response to the issues of the day. This ranges across a number of policy domains that would have been unfathomable not only to Hayes but also to a later president such as Franklin D. Roosevelt, including mandated health care, immigration reform, gay and lesbian rights, climate change, abortion policy, and gun control regulations, to list but a few. We also expect the president to be the guardian of our economic well-being. If there is a recession, if inflation and unemployment rates rise, or if stock markets drift downward, we turn to the White House for action.

In terms of foreign affairs, we expect the president to immediately have a strategy for dealing with any international crisis that develops. Should American force be needed, we expect the president to be a skilled commander in chief who is knowledgeable about military affairs and adept at crafting a successful response (hopefully one with a quick resolution). We expect the president to also manage crises in the domestic arena. If a school shooting occurs, we expect the president to address it and to propose remedies to minimize chances of it happening again. If a hurricane or a flood strikes, we expect an appropriate presidential response and immediate action. We expect the president to always be a skilled public communicator, one who is never caught off guard, always reassuring at times of crisis but also able to contextualize the issues and put forth the right policy initiatives. We shall explore the demands of this "public presidency" also in this book.

Finally, in the aftermath of September 11 and during the continuing war on terror, we expect the president to be ever vigilant in protecting homeland security and to take steps against those who threaten it. This is a relatively new presidential assignment and perhaps the most difficult of all. There is some history here in terms of presidents claiming inherent national security powers, and as we shall explore, the Supreme Court has ruled in a number of cases that presidents can go only so far with those claims. And as recent presidents have also experienced, excessive claims to power and the actions stemming from such claims can sometimes boomerang and hurt them.

All of these expectations can be summed up as our desire for the president to be a successful head of government. But there is an added major assignment. We also expect the president to be a successful head of state, respected by other world leaders, and the symbol and spokesperson of America's role in world affairs. In many political systems, these two roles are separated: the latter is represented by a monarch or a president, and the former by a prime minister or chancellor. This is how it is done in most of Europe, Russia, Japan, India, Israel, and Iraq, to name but a few. In the United States, both roles are filled by one person. Pardon the pun, but this is surely a "heady"— and difficult—assignment. In short, for contemporary presidents, the scope of power is vastly different and more challenging than ever. Thus, the enduring dilemmas of presidential power even from the days of Rutherford B. Hayes, including how to work with the other two branches to achieve presidential goals and how to contend with the specific challenges presented by political and historical context, are magnified for contemporary presidents. With ever-growing expectations for leadership in a greater number of areas, it is imperative for contemporary presidents to utilize every tool of presidential power available to them, from bargaining and public appeals to executive actions, to achieve a successful presidency.

Plan of The Book

So, what should presidents do to manage and resolve the public's expectations and the power they must wield to accomplish their goals? There are no easy, simple answers. However, broad lessons and conclusions about presidential power, based upon practical, presidential experience as well as scholarly insight, can be drawn. The job description for contemporary presidents has expanded significantly since the days of the Framers of our Constitution, but presidents are still constrained by the blueprint of "separate but shared powers" as laid out in the Constitution. In this book, I examine the various tools of power available to presidents and the historical and political circumstances in which they must exercise power, hopefully in an understandable way for readers who are learning about the presidency.

Chapter 1 begins with the creation of the presidency during the Constitutional Convention of 1787, laying the foundation for the book's discussions of why the issue of presidential power is so crucial. The chapter is called "The Madisonian Dilemma" to reflect James Madison's key role at the convention, which earned him the title of "architect of the Constitution." Madison believed that although a national executive was needed, "checks" on too much executive power were also required. His solution was that each branch of the federal government should share in some of the powers of the others, contesting for power and thus preventing any one branch from becoming too dominant. Unfortunately, there was little guidance in how that contest might be properly resolved. Nor, I might add, was there much anticipation that, in future times, we might expect more leadership on the president's part and thus more empowerment, not less. Control rather than empowerment is embedded in Madison's constitutional legacy, and that is the crux of the major dilemma of presidential power. This chapter also explores how George Washington immediately had to create a new presidency when he took office but with imperfect guidance in Article II (which directly addresses the presidency) to rely upon. It also explores the quick rise of political parties, and how that put a major wrench in the Framers' ideas on how selection of a president should work and how Congress and the presidency should operate and interact.

Chapter 2, "Neustadt and the Modern Conception of Presidential Power," moves us forward into the modern presidency and introduces what remains one of the most important works on this topic: Richard E. Neustadt's classic, *Presidential Power: The Politics of Leadership*. The first edition was published in 1960, followed by several others and with the final one covering the Reagan presidency. This chapter explicates and unpacks Neustadt's work and explores some of its difficulties and challenges. However, we also begin to examine alternatives to Neustadt's theory. Although his point about recognizing that power is at stake and exercising influence through bargaining remains important, the process of attaining presidential goals is a complex one. And as we shall see, there are other paths to attaining presidential ends beyond what Neustadt lays out.

In Chapter 3, "The Executive's Prerogative: Inherent Constitutional Powers," we explore why the exercise of constitutional powers remains important to presidents. Neustadt argues that use of constitutional "commands" does not do a president much good and that presidents who just stick to the Constitution are mere "clerks." However, the issue is more complex: because much is left unstated in the Constitution, it requires interpretation. In particular, this chapter focuses on what has been termed the exercise of a president's inherent and prerogative powers—those not clearly given to the president, but those that might be interpreted as present in the office based on several clauses in Article II. Such powers were anticipated but left broadly undetermined by the Framers of the Constitution, and today they have become a key

part of post-9/11 executive action. Using presidential prerogative, Neustadt's "clerks" can still claim great power, depending on the circumstances. At the same time, we must bear in mind that this is contested terrain. Although the Supreme Court is often reluctant to intervene in cases involving the powers of the other two branches, it does so on occasion. We shall explore the major patterns in the court's reasoning, in its jurisprudence, in these cases, because this is important to understanding the dilemmas in the exercise of the president's prerogative. Finally, we shall examine how claims—and often the exercise—of inherent powers became increasingly important for both Presidents George W. Bush and Barack Obama in the post-9/11 era.

Chapter 4, "Going Public and Presidential Power," focuses on public appeals and public support as a source of power. For Neustadt, what he calls "public prestige" is an ancillary resource, something that is only useful in bolstering bargaining power. However, though Neustadt may be correct about its impact on bargaining, his conception of the impact of public appeals may be too limited. In this chapter, we explore the idea that direct appeals to the public for support are often seen by presidents as a tool of power in its own right. A number of scholars, Samuel Kernell most notably, have argued that going public is now a central component of presidential power. Others, such as George C. Edwards III, have argued that it is overrated: little public opinion is actually moved and politically activated by presidential appeals. Presidents may not positively profit as much as they might think from going public. Finally, this chapter looks at how the ever-changing media pose significant challenges to presidents. In short, presidents must go public in ways that recognize the media technology of the times—they suffer when they don't.

In Chapter 5, "Presidential Power and Historical Time, Variously Interpreted," we discuss the historical factors that might affect the exercise and analysis of presidential power. The point in time a president occupies office may present both challenges and opportunities that are different had he or she become president earlier or later. As we shall see, scholars differ on the historical factors that most affect the successes or failures of a presidency. Is it the broader political regime or political coalition in which presidents finds themselves located, as Stephen Skowronek argues? Others argue that the interjection of new policy ideas, shifts in political ideology, or swings in public mood are of greater significance, and we consider all of these forms of historical change in this chapter. Furthermore, we examine whether and how presidents are able to understand the historical place they occupy. Can they understand the specific opportunities and challenges facing them and take appropriate steps during their time in office? Or is historical context simply something that helps us form a fuller understanding of a president's exercise of power as we study it in hindsight?

In Chapter 6, we turn inward and consider the internal rhythms of a president's first (and sometimes only) term. In short, we consider how the individual years of a term matter in different ways, and the different challenges presidents face in each year. This chapter begins with what we have learned as presidential scholars about the changing power situation within a presidential term—for example, that successful transitions greatly matter. It is crucial for presidents to use their transition periods to get personnel in place, organize the White House staff, and develop an early set of policy initiatives. Failure here likely proves problematic, whereas success bolsters presidential power. The remainder of the first term presents other challenges. Almost every president is dealt a blow when the first midterm congressional elections occur. After that, opportunities to secure proposals might surface in the pipeline, but they are often diminished by a decline in congressional support. And not long after the midterms, attention shifts to reelection.

Chapter 7 focuses on the internal rhythms of the second term, when presidents often seem to be especially bedeviled and politically weakened. This chapter explores some of those dynamics and how they differ from aspects of the first term. Recent reelections have been largely won based on the challenger's shortcomings, not the positive presentation of a prospective agenda. Given this, how do presidents build support for a second-term agenda? Most presidents suffer from a "sixth-year itch" on the part of the electorate, and party support in Congress suffers; thus, many have turned to foreign policy to secure their legacy in the second term. Has this worked? The question of presidential power in the second term is further complicated by the almost certain loss of congressional seats in the midterm and by waning focus on the president's agenda during the final two years of the second term as attention quickly turns to the election of a successor.

It is clear, even from this introduction, that contemporary presidents face a great number of tasks and challenges and that there are no easy answers or simple theories on how to best exercise presidential power. Given all they face, presidents today cannot rely on a single method of exercising power, nor can they ignore how historical context and the internal rhythms of their first and second terms can influence their presidencies. In the book's conclusion, I attempt to deduce broad lessons based on what we have learned of the benefits and limitations of each tool of power as well as what we have come to understand about the opportunities and challenges of historical time and internal time. I lay out a blueprint for how contemporary presidents might exercise power to address problems and achieve their goals.

Notes

1. Charles R. Williams, ed., *The Diary and Letters of Rutherford B. Hayes, Nineteenth President of the United States,* vol. 3 (Columbus: Ohio State Archeological and Historical Society, 1922), 469, http://apps.ohiohistory.org/hayes/browse/chapterxxxvi.html.
2. Ibid.

CHAPTER 10

The Federal Judiciary

KEY TERMS

Common Law

Stare Decisis

Judicial Activism

Judicial Restraint

Attorney General

Amicus Curiae

Judicial Precedent

Plessy v. Ferguson

Marbury v. Madison, 1803

McCulloch v. Maryland, 1819

Dred Scott

Miranda v. Arizona

Mapp v. Ohio

Roe v. Wade

Citizens United

Brown v. Board of Education

DISCUSSION QUESTIONS

1. Discuss the sources and evolution of American law.

2. Discuss the importance of judicial review. Address the significance of *Marbury v. Madison*.

3. Discuss the political process of appointing and confirming judges. Does this lead to good jurisprudence or partisan politics?

4. Identify the ramifications of judicial constraint and judicial activism.

STRUCTURE

The federal court system in the United States is three-tiered.

At the lowest level, there are 91 federal district courts, 89 are in the 50 states and territories. There is one for the District of Columbia and one for Puerto Rico.

Their jurisdiction consists of federal questions.

They hear cases concerning the following:

- Federal law
- US Constitution
- Treaties

In addition to the district courts, other specialty courts exist:

- US court of claims
- Court of international trade

- Tax court
- Court of military appeals

Above the district courts there are 13 federal appeals courts:

- Eleven are courts of Appeal: Each is at least composed of five district courts and three state courts. They consist of panels of judges hearing an appeal of a particular case. The number of judges on a particular appeals court varies in size: the first circuit has four judges, the ninth circuit has 23
- One District of Columbia: Hears appeals involving administrative agencies
- One US Court of Federal Claims

Above the courts of appeals is the US Supreme Court, which consists of nine judges. The Supreme Court of the United States is the highest court of appeals and hears cases from the highest state courts. Because it is the only court of its kind, it is very difficult to argue a case before the court. For a case to get on the docket, a writ of certiorari is needed. Four justices need to agree to hear the case. This is referred to as the rule of four.

The Supreme Court Also Has Original Jurisdiction in Other Cases
- Ambassadors
- Other public ministers and consuls
- Cases that involve a state or states

SOURCES OF AMERICAN LAW

- Common Law: **Common law** is composed of judicial decisions based on precedent—legal principles decided in previous cases.
- Stare Decisis: **Stare decisis** obligates judges to follow the precedents of their own or higher courts. This is also known as **judicial precedent**.
- Constitutions: Constitutions set forth the general organization of government, its powers, and its limits.
- Statutes: Statues are written laws, such as legislative acts, as well as rules and regulations established by administrative agencies.
- Case Law: Case law includes judicial interpretation of common law principles and doctrines, as well as interpretations of the types of law.

IMPORTANCE OF JUDICIAL REVIEW

The main power of the federal courts is to overrule legislation or executive acts. Judicial review is never mentioned in the Constitution; it came about as a result of precedent.

The Constitution initially was very vague regarding the courts. In the next sentence delete It and replace with Article III. It states that there should be a Supreme Court and other inferior courts, and discusses a definition of treason. It does not go into a great deal of detail about the structure of the court or its jurisdictions. It does not even set the number of judges on the Supreme Court. This is still the case today. A court of nine justices has become a consensus number. President Roosevelt attempted to pack the court during his second term. A Supreme Court that was predominantly made up of judges appointed by his Republican predecessors had been striking down New Deal legislation. A plan was put forth in Congress to increase the number of judges on the Supreme Court by adding a new justice for every justice that was over 70 years of age. The justification for this was to lighten the workload of the older justices. This was a very transparent attempt to pack the court with judges favorable to the New Deal. Not only were Republicans opposed but also many Democrats. They viewed this as a naked attempt by one branch of government to dominate another. In the end, this plan was dropped. Shortly thereafter several justices retired. President Roosevelt was able to appoint new judges who were supportive of his New Deal programs.

The first important case the Supreme Court heard that established the case of judicial review was **Marbury v. Madison** in 1803. This case revolved around the election of 1800 in which Thomas Jefferson defeated John Adams for the presidency. This was the first transition of power between rival political groups in US history. The Federalists, led by Adams, were defeated by the Democratic-Republicans led by Jefferson. Before the Adams administration left office, it attempted to appoint as many Federalists as possible to government positions. When the Jefferson administration came into office it was confronted with appointment letters that were not delivered.

The Jefferson Administration

James Madison was the secretary of state who was charged with delivering appointment letters, and he did not want to convey these appointments. Several of the office seekers sued the federal government, asking for a writ of mandamus. This is a legal term that forces the government to do some sort of action. The granting of writs of mandamus was given to the Supreme Court by the Federal Judiciary Act of 1789. This law established the federal court system of the United States. The Supreme Court was in a political quandary regarding the case. Most of the justices identified with the Federalist Party. Chief Justice John Marshall had been Adams's secretary of state. The court wanted to side with Marbury, but it had no way of forcing the Jefferson administration to comply with the decision. Ultimately, the justices decided that they were not able to rule on the merits of the case because the granting of writs of mandamus by the Federal Judiciary Act was unconstitutional because it gave the Supreme Court power that was not granted to it in the Constitution. The Jefferson administration was satisfied because it did not have to deal with Marbury or the other office seekers. However, what the Supreme Court did was the beginning of the establishment of judicial review: the ability to strike down a law, portion of a law, or executive act as unconstitutional. This was by far the greater power.

The Expansion of the Necessary and Proper Clause

The second prominent case heard by the Supreme Court was **McCulloch v. Maryland** in 1819. This case was an attempt by the state of Maryland to tax the Bank of the United States. The Supreme Court ruled in favor of a broad interpretation of the necessary and proper clause, Article I, Section 8 of the Constitution. The justification for this decision was that since Congress had the power to tax and regulate interstate commerce, a national bank was constitutional. Essentially, with this decision the Supreme Court established a broad interpretation of "necessary" to mean "desirable".

In the mid-1800s, as the civil war loomed, another significant decision of the Supreme Court was the Dred Scott decision in 1857. **Dred Scott** was a slave who lived in a free state before returning with his master to Missouri. He brought a case arguing that since he had lived in a state where slavery was illegal he should be given his freedom. The Supreme Court ruled that he had no standing before the court. The case heightened tensions between North and South and enflamed opinion of pro-slavery and abolitionist opinions.

SELECTION OF JUDGES

All federal judges are appointed by the president, subject to approval by the Senate.

Role of the American Bar Association
The American Bar Association evaluates potential appointees and assigns the following rankings:

- Exceptionally well qualified
- Well qualified
- Qualified
- Not qualified

The endorsement of the American Bar Association is important for any federal judicial nominee.

Politics Involved in the Selection of Judges
The president appoints all federal judges, who are subject to confirmation by the Senate. They serve for life. This is one of the most important powers of the modern presidency. The appointment of federal judges allows presidents to have influence over law, and the interpretation of law, for many years after they have left office.

Judicial appointments, especially to the Supreme Court, are very political. Presidents attempt to select the most qualified individuals whom they think mirror their own views on the law. Individual Senators can accept or reject a nominee for any reason. Nominations can also be held up by the Senate for political reasons.

For example, after the death of Judge Antonin Scalia in January of 2016, the Republican-controlled Senate, led by Senate Majority Leader Mitch McConnell (R-KY) refused to schedule confirmation hearings for President Barack Obama's nominee, Judge Merrick Garland.

The Republican leadership argued that because it was an election year and President Obama would be leaving office in January 2017, the new president should choose the nominee. They were clearly hoping that a Republican would win the election and a more conservative nominee would be appointed. They were successful, as with the election of President Donald Trump, and Neil Gorsuch became the nominee to the court. Judge Gorsuch was confirmed by the Senate.

SELECTION VARIABLES FOR ALL FEDERAL JUDGES

- Professional qualifications
- Political party considerations
- The approval of Senators (courtesy): Senators of the president's party have approval over federal judges appointed in their states (senatorial courtesy)
- Policy and ideological outlook

JUDICIAL RESTRAINT VERSUS JUDICIAL ACTIVISM

- Judicial Restraint: **Judicial restraint** places emphasis on the courts following a strict reading of the Constitution.
- Judicial Activism: **Judicial activism** is a belief that the courts can promote reform and advocate a broad reading/interpretation of the Constitution.

THE EXECUTIVE BRANCH AND THE COURTS

Courts are dependent on the executive branch to enforce their decisions. At times in American history, the executive branch has been unwilling to enforce court decisions. In 1955, Arkansas governor Orval Faubus refused to implement the federal court's decision to integrate Central High School in Little Rock. This led to President Eisenhower federalizing the Arkansas National Guard and sending troops to enforce the Court's decision.

While the courts are dependent on executive authority to get their decisions enforced, they are also dependent on the legislative branch, as many decisions need some funding to be implemented, which would require legislative approval at either the federal or state level.

A legislative body can also amend or change laws which the courts have previously ruled on.

PUBLIC OPINION

Public opinion can also lead to limitations on the Court's decisions. Many states and localities did not go along with the Supreme Court's ruling against prayer in schools. This goes back to the dependency of the courts on other branches of government to enforce their decisions.

JUSTICE DEPARTMENT

The chief officer of the Justice Department is the **attorney general**.

Solicitor General
The solicitor-general argues the case for the government before the Supreme Court.

Supreme Court Decisions
Decisions are made by the majority. Judicial opinions are important because they illustrate the basis of the ruling. Dissenting opinions are also important because they often serve as the basis for future courts overturning a precedent in another case.

Amicus Curiae
An **amicus curiae** is a friend of the court brief. Interested parties file briefs on a case. An example of this was the Bakke case, which dealt with reverse discrimination in higher education. Fifty-eight briefs were filed in this case.

Concept of Precedent

Courts look at previous decisions when making their rulings. Once precedents are established, they usually change very slowly, but they can change. Courts can overrule themselves. The following are several important cases in American history.

Plessy v. Ferguson (1896)

This case dealt with the issue of public accommodations. Homer Plessy, having purchased a first-class train ticket, was denied access to the first-class carriage because of his race. The court concluded that separate but equal was constitutional.

Brown v. Board of Education (1954)

This case dealt with a lawsuit against the Board of Education of Topeka, Kansas. The plaintiffs argued that education facilities for African Americans were inferior. The court ruled that separate but equal was unconstitutional. The court also ruled that, historically, the emphasis was more on maintaining separate facilities along racial lines than making them equal. Future Supreme Court justice Thurgood Marshall was the lead attorney for the National Association of the Advancement of Colored People on the case.

Mapp v. Ohio (1961)

This case was based on the fourth amendment to the Constitution, which prevents illegal searches and seizures. The Supreme Court concluded that evidence obtained as a result of an illegal search was not admissible in court. This is known as the exclusionary rule.

Miranda v. Arizona (1966)

In this case the Supreme Court ruled that a defendant's statement is inadmissible unless they have been informed of their rights against self-incrimination and the right to have an attorney present.

Roe v. Wade (1973)

The Supreme Court affirmed the right to have an abortion. It was considered within the right of privacy protected by the fourteenth amendment. States were allowed to regulate abortions in the second and third trimesters.

Citizens United (2010)

The Supreme Court ruled that corporations, unions, and nonprofits could spend unlimited amounts of money on political campaigns. This drastically increased the amount of money contributed to major party candidates. This added even further to the amounts of money spent in elections, especially in presidential elections.

JUDICIAL REVIEW, LOCAL VALUES, AND PLURALISM
Richard W. Garnett

I.

"It is," the Twenty-Seventh Annual National Federalist Society Student Symposium program reports, "a basic assumption of federalism that individual communities can be different; they may have different values, and they will certainly have different laws."[1] This is true. Notwithstanding *American Idol,* Starbucks, *USA Today,* and chain restaurants, individual communities not only *can be* different, they *are* different. They often sit on opposite sides of what commentator David Brooks has called the "meatloaf line," which divides places with "sun-dried-tomato concoctions on restaurant menus" from those with "meatloaf platters."[2] Even before the 2000 election, and the explosion of "Red-versus-Blue"-themed social commentary,[3] it should not have been controversial to note that the communities of San Francisco and Provo "have different values"—not entirely different, of course, but still different. And, if the legal enterprise involves, among other things, an effort to order our lives together in a way that reflects and promotes our understandings of human flourishing, then we should not be surprised that communities' "different values" often translate into "different laws."

The question presented to this panel was: Does pervasive judicial review threaten to destroy local identity by homogenizing community norms?[4] The short and correct, even if too quick, answer to this question is "yes." That is, *pervasive* judicial review certainly does *threaten* local identity. It does so, in part, because judicial review can homogenize community norms, either by dragging them into conformity with national, constitutional standards or, more controversially, by subordinating them to the reviewers' own commitments.

To say this is neither to criticize judicial review nor to celebrate excessively local identity; it is to identify neither the point at which judicial review becomes pervasive nor the point at which possibilities become threats. If we aspire to more than stating the obvious, we should reach for clarity about what are and are not the problems with and risks of judicial review, and also about what is and is not important about respecting community norms and protecting them from homogenization. We need to ask, for example, how much room the Constitution leaves for legal experiments that reflect local values.[5] When must legal expressions of local values give way to legal expressions of national ones? And who decides?

---

1   *See* Posting of Richard W. Garnett to PrawfsBlawg, http://prawfsblawg.blogs.com/prawfsblawg/2008/03/the-fed-soc-sym.html (Mar. 10, 2008, 10:13 EDT) ("The claims presented for the panel's consideration were, first, that 'it is a basic assumption of federalism that individual communities can be different'; second, that 'it is a benefit of federalism that free people can "vote with their feet" and migrate to communities that share their values'; and, third, that 'pervasive judicial review' can undermine this benefit, and this assumption, and 'destroy local identity by homogenizing community norms.'").

2   *See* David Brooks, *One Nation, Slightly Divisible,* Atl. Monthly, Dec. 2001, at 54, *available at* http://www.theatlantic.com/issues/2001/12/brooks.htm.

3   *See* Paul Farhi, *Elephants are Red, Donkeys are Blue,* Wash. Post, Nov. 2, 2004, at C1.

4   *See* Garnett, *supra* note 1.

5   *See* New State Ice Co. v. Liebmann, 285 U.S. 262, 311 (1932) (Brandeis, J., dissenting) ("It is one of the happy incidents of the federal system that a single courageous State may, if its citizens choose, serve as a laboratory; and try novel social and economic experiments without risk to the rest of the country. This Court has the power to prevent an experiment.").

It is true that an important feature of our federalism is local variation in laws and values. It is also true, however, that some values have been homogenized, not by judicial review, pervasive or otherwise, but by the ratification of the Constitution, which is the "supreme Law of the land … any Thing in the Constitution or Laws of any State to the Contrary notwithstanding."[6] Our federalism proceeds from the premise that individual communities can be different, but it also reflects a vision of national citizenship, some fundamental moral commitments, and a common project. It is a basic assumption of federalism that local communities may have different values. But it is also a basic assumption of federalism that the national Union is committed to *some* shared values, that separate communities are bound by *some* shared laws, and that there were and are *reasons* for America's distinct communities to come together and form, in the words of the Preamble, a "more perfect Union."[7] Our various local communities and political subdivisions are not merely next to each other in space; they do not simply share a continent and currency. They are meaningfully "united."

Of course, to gesture toward the Supremacy Clause and our nation's name is hardly to answer the hard and interesting questions that the panel's topic prompts. Still, even this gesture is enough to remind us that the text, history, structure, and theoretical premises of the Constitution point toward the importance of *both* diverse local "laboratories of democracy"[8]*and* a larger, national community—a Union constituted by "We the People."[9] Vindicating the values and aims of this national community will sometimes require constraining, revising, or rejecting some laboratories' experiments and some expressions in law of local majorities' values.

Americans often talk and think about the potential conflict between judicial review and local values in terms common to the discussion of dual sovereignty. That is, we ask, "Which government's policy choice, the federal government's or the state's, wins out here?" in a way that invites an answer couched in a states' rights idiom. The Constitution's liberty-protecting structural features should, instead, be understood more in terms of limited and enumerated powers than in terms of states' rights.[10] The Constitution appreciates, reflects, and incorporates pluralism and local values in a *particular way,* namely, by stating clearly that the national government and its various branches have only those powers that are "delegated to the United States by the Constitution."[11] And so, federal courts have the power—the "judicial Power of the United States"—to decide cases "arising under [the] Constitution."[12] They do *not* have the power to survey the national scene looking for local values and community norms in need of revision or homogenization, or to discover abstract rights and liberties in need of vindication.[13] That said, sometimes in the context of doing what it is authorized and supposed to do, a federal court will, and should, refuse to enforce a law that reflects the norms and values of a particular community. Such a refusal admittedly can appear to be a judicial interference with community values and will, in some cases, result in or aim toward the homogenizing of norms. But again, the Constitution itself makes *some* such judicial interference unavoidable because its text and structure both permit and call for it. The questions, then, are

---

6 U.S. Const. art. VI, cl. 2.

7 U.S. Const. pmbl.

8 *See New State Ice Co.,* 285 U.S. at 311 (Brandeis, J., dissenting).

9 U.S. Const. pmbl.

10 *See* Richard W. Garnett, *The New Federalism, the Spending Power, and Federal Criminal Law,* 89 Cornell L. Rev. 1 (2003).

11 U.S. Const. amend. X.

12 U.S. Const. art. III, §§ 1, 2.

13 *Cf.* Kermit Roosevelt III & Richard W. Garnett, *Judicial Activism and Its Critics,* 155 U. Pa. L. Rev. PENNumbra 112,126–27 (2006) ("Professor Roosevelt and I agree that, generally speaking, the job of 'weighing competing policies' is best 'left to the representative branches for reasons of democratic accountability.' I would also want to consider, though, the possibility that—putting aside concerns about competence and 'accountability'—the Court might not always be constitutionally authorized to take up the balancing task.").

not so much *whether* federal courts may or should interfere with community values, but *when* and *how* they should do so.

Both the Constitution and sound political theory counsel deference and restraint on the part of federal judges.[14] It is, however, easy to imagine exasperation on the part of those scholars and commentators who insist that words like "deference," "restraint," and "activism" are not uncontested, and who warn that these terms can be, and sometimes are, misused in discussions about the Court and the Constitution.[15] This is true enough. The political use of "judicial activism" rhetoric is often, as Professor Kermit Roosevelt and others have argued, "excessive and unhelpful."[16] Even if one wants to hold on to the view that the term is not *entirely* empty of content, and even if one is not ready to conclude that judicial activism (properly understood) is a myth, one can and should agree that the term today often serves as little more than a slogan or epithet. For present purposes, though, we can bracket the challenge of making the case that judicial activism is not merely code for "decisions with which I disagree." To say that federal judges can and should refuse to give effect to local laws and values that conflict with constitutional guarantees or that exceed constitutional limits is not to say that they should do so lightly, quickly, or too often. The Constitution commits us, as a national community, to certain values, which are reflected in and protected by certain specific provisions of that document. At the same time, an appreciation for the values associated with localism, and an appropriate humility when it comes to second-guessing political outcomes, will inspire wise judges to be cautious and to hesitate before declaring that a particular expression of local values must give way. Professor

H. Jefferson Powell put it well in his Walter F. Murphy Lecture, *Constitutional Virtues*, in which he defined the virtue of "humility" as

> the habit of doubting that the Constitution resolves divisive political or social issues as opposed to requiring them to be thrashed out through the processes of ordinary, revisable politics. … The virtue manifests itself in the continuing recognition that the Constitution is primarily a framework for political argument and decision and not a tool for the elimination of debate.[17]

That is a good start.

II.

So, how do we get it right? How should the conscientious federal judge, or American citizen, go about trying to find the place where responsible exercise of the judicial power of the United States ends and unwarranted, offensive, intrusive, homogenizing overreaching begins? The task is not easy. Certainly, the line will not always be clear, and there is no point in pretending otherwise. Certainly, it is not enough to merely attach "activist" or "restrained" to decisions one likes or dislikes. Certainly, the effort cannot be separated from the larger project of figuring out the on-the-merits answers to questions of the Constitution's meaning. All that said, the judicial philosophy of my former boss, the late Chief Justice William Rehnquist, is relevant and helpful here.

As the confirmation hearings for Chief Justice Roberts and Justice Alito reminded us, tracking down nominees' judicial philosophies is tiring, tricky work.[18] Senate staffers, pundits, journalists, and bloggers scour an ever-expanding range of sources,

---

14   *See id.* at 118 ("Clearly, appellate courts do and should 'defer' to lower courts and non-judicial officials all the time.").

15   *See, e.g., id.* (challenging Professor Roosevelt's definitions of deference).

16   *Id.* at 112.

17   H. Jefferson Powell, *Constitutional Virtues*, 9 Green Bag 2d 379, 388 (2006).

18   *See, e.g.,* Mike Allen & R. Jeffrey Smith, *Judges Should Have 'Limited' Role, Roberts Says: Statement to Panel Cites Need for Restraint on Bench; Prior Documents Question 'Right to Privacy,'* Wash. Post, Aug. 3, 2005, at A5 ("Roberts echoed the views of President Bush in describing his judicial philosophy. Roberts said that he views the role of judges as 'limited' and that they 'do not have a commission to solve society's problems, as they see them, but simply to decide cases before them according to the rule of law.'"); Senator Charles Schumer, Remarks of the Nomination of Samuel Alito to the Supreme Court (Oct. 31, 2005), *available at* http://www.washingtonpost.

including college research papers, job applications, appellate briefs and opinions, and even thank-you notes[19] looking for clues (or smoking guns). As it happens, though, Chief Justice (then Justice) Rehnquist provided a reflective and revealing sketch of his philosophy just a few years after joining the Court in a short essay called *The Notion of a Living Constitution*.[20] This notion, often associated with Justice William Brennan,[21] was, in Chief Justice Rehnquist's view, to be resisted—but not out of pious reverence for the Founders' insight into the moral, economic, and social challenges facing late-twentieth-century society.[22] Nor did his critique purport to be the product of a tight deduction from premises relating to the very nature of a written constitution. He was not, to use Professor Sunstein's term, a "fundamentalist,"[23] or even a thoroughgoing, principled originalist. He did not fail to observe and absorb the obvious fact that ours is a very different world from the Framers'.

Chief Justice Rehnquist's aim in critiquing the notion of a living Constitution, and in so doing, appearing to assume the unenviable "necrophil[iac]" position of playing partisan for a "dead" Constitution,[24] was to insist and ensure that "We the People," the "ultimate source of authority in this Nation,"[25] acting through our politically accountable representatives, retain the right to serve (or not) as the agents of and vehicles for constitutional change. What animates the essay is not so much a misplaced attachment to *stasis,* or a slavish adherence to ideological formulae, but a clear-eyed appreciation for the tension that can exist between the "antidemocratic and antimajoritarian facets" of judicial review and the "political theory basic to democratic society."[26]

And so, Chief Justice Rehnquist contended, it is one thing to note that the Constitution is, in many places, "not a specifically worded document"; it is

---

com/wp-dyn/content/article/2005/10/31/AR2005103100707.html ("A preliminary review of his record raises real questions about Judge Alito's judicial philosophy and his commitment to civil rights, workers' rights, women's rights, and the rights of average Americans which the courts have always looked out for.").

19   *See* Charles Babington, *Miers Hit on Letters and the Law,* Wash. Post, Oct. 15, 2005, at A7.

20   William H. Rehnquist, *The Notion of a Living Constitution,* 54 Tex. L. Rev. 693 (1976), *reprinted in* 29 Harv. J.L. & Pub. Pol'y 401, 410 (2006).

21   *See, e.g.,* Marsh v. Chambers, 463 U.S. 783, 816 (1983) (Brennan, J., dissenting) ("[T]he Constitution is not a static document whose meaning on every detail is fixed for all time by the life experience of the Framers."); William J. Brennan, Jr., *Construing the Constitution,* 19 U.C. Davis L. Rev. 2, 7 (1985) ("[T]he genius of the Constitution rests not in any static meaning it might have had in a world that is dead and gone, but in the adaptability of its great principles to cope with current problems and current needs.").

22   *See, e.g.,* Rehnquist, *supra* note 20, at 699 ("It seems to me that it is almost impossible … to conclude that [the Founders] intended the Constitution itself to suggest answers to the manifold problems that they knew would confront succeeding generations."); *cf.* Carey v. Population Servs. Int'l, 431 U.S. 678, 717 (1977) (Rehnquist, J., dissenting) ("Those who valiantly but vainly defended the heights of Bunker Hill in 1775 made it possible that men such as James Madison might later sit in the first Congress and draft the Bill of Rights to the Constitution. The post-Civil War Congresses which drafted the Civil War Amendments to the Constitution could not have accomplished their task without the blood of brave men on both sides which was shed at Shiloh, Gettysburg, and Cold Harbor. If those responsible for these Amendments, by feats of valor or efforts of draftsmanship, could have lived to know that their efforts had enshrined in the Constitution the right of commercial vendors of contraceptives to peddle them to unmarried minors through such means as window displays and vending machines located in the men's room of truck stops, notwithstanding the considered judgment of the New York Legislature to the contrary, it is not difficult to imagine their reaction.").

23   Cass R. Sunstein, Radicals in Robes: Why Extreme Right-Wing Courts Are Wrong for America 119–20 (2005) (discussing Chief Justice Rehnquist's "fundamentalist" views regarding the right to marry).

24   Rehnquist, *supra* note 20, at 693 ("At first blush it seems certain that a *living* Constitution is better than what must be its counterpart, a *dead* Constitution.").

25   *Id.* at 696.

26   *Id.* at 705. For a recent, powerful exploration of this tension, see Jeremy Waldron, *The Core of the Case Against Judicial Review,* 115 Yale L.J. 1346 (2006).

one thing to concede that "[t]here is ... wide room for honest difference of opinion over the meaning of general phrases in the Constitution."[27] It is another, however, to authorize "nonelected members of the federal judiciary"—functioning as "the voice and conscience of contemporary society" and "as the measure of the modern conception of human dignity"[28]—to serve as a "council of revision"[29]armed "with a roving commission to second-guess Congress, state legislatures, and state and federal administrative officers concerning what is best for the country."[30]

Chief Justice Rehnquist's big-picture view of the Constitution, the government that it constitutes, and the task of federal judges that it authorizes can be well and efficiently captured through two short quotations from his opinions. First, from his opinion for the Court in *United States v. Lopez:*

> The Constitution creates a Federal Government of enumerated powers. As James Madison wrote: "The powers delegated by the proposed Constitution to the federal government are few and defined. Those which are to remain in the State governments are numerous and indefinite." This constitutionally mandated division of authority "was adopted by the Framers to ensure protection of our fundamental liberties. Just as the separation and independence of the coordinate branches of the Federal Government serve to prevent the accumulation of excessive power in any one branch, a healthy balance of power between the States and the Federal Government will reduce the risk of tyranny and abuse from either front."[31]

Second, is this passage from his dissent in *Texas v. Johnson:*

The Court's role as the final expositor of the Constitution is well established, but its role as a Platonic guardian admonishing those responsible to public opinion as if they were truant schoolchildren has no similar place in our system of government.[32]

These two passages go a long way in presenting the vision or, at least, the disposition that plausibly can be said to have animated Chief Justice Rehnquist's work and career on the Court, and that could also be of some use, even comfort, to federal judges wrestling with the questions presented by this Symposium.

Chief Justice Rehnquist was a federalist, in the Madisonian sense, and, within limits, a conservative majoritarian. He believed that "We the People," through our Constitution, had authorized our federal courts, legislators, and administrators to do many things, but not everything. The nation's powers are vast where they exist, but they are also divided, separated, "few and defined."[33] As a result, the national government may not pursue every good idea, smart policy, or worthy end, nor are local governments forbidden to enact all foolish or immoral ones. The point of this arrangement is not so much to hamstring good government as to "ensure the protection of our fundamental liberties"[34] by dividing, enumerating, and structuring powers. The Constitution's freedom-facilitating structural features, Chief Justice Rehnquist believed, should not be left entirely to the care of those branches that might not have, or might not perceive clearly, an interest in their health. The structure of government, as he emphasized in *Lopez,* matters to the well-being and flourishing of persons, and it is appropriate for courts of law to enforce the boundaries inherent or involved in those structural features.[35]

27 Rehnquist, *supra* note 20, at 697.

28 *Id.* at 695.

29 *Id.* at 698.

30 *Id.; cf.* Trimble v. Gordon, 430 U.S. 762, 777 (1977) (Rehnquist, J., dissenting) ("[T]his Court seems to regard the Equal Protection Clause as a cat-o'-nine-tails to be kept in the judicial closet as a threat to legislatures which may, in the view of the judiciary, get out of hand and pass 'arbitrary,' 'illogical,' or 'unreasonable' laws.").

31 514 U.S. 549, 552 (1995) (citations omitted).

32 491 U.S. 397, 435 (1989) (Rehnquist, C.J., dissenting).

33 THE FEDERALIST No. 45, at 137 (James Madison) (Roy P. Fairfield ed., 1981).

34 Gregory v. Ashcroft, 501 U.S. 452, 458 (1991) (internal quotation marks omitted).

35 *Lopez,* 514 U.S. at 552.

The *Texas v. Johnson* dissent underscores a companion commitment to judicial modesty with respect to moral controversies and debatable policies.[36] True, many regard Chief Justice Rehnquist's "Platonic guardian" line,[37] along with similar calls for judicial modesty, restraint, and deference, as little more than *a* disingenuous cover for his own conservative brand of activism. But this charge is misplaced. It is neither arrogant nor illegitimate for a judge to enforce the Constitution's structural features, nor is it disingenuous for such a judge to believe that federal courts should only rarely employ judicial review as an "end run around popular government."[38] Running through Chief Justice Rehnquist's opinions in cases involving a broad spectrum of policy questions is not opportunistic conservative activism but reasonably consistent fidelity to the idea that our Constitution leaves many important, difficult, and even divisive decisions to the People or, for our purposes, to local communities. It is possible and reasonable to distinguish between votes to invalidate the policy choices of state legislatures as inconsistent with the Constitution's substantive individual-rights provisions, on the one hand, and votes to invalidate regulatory measures enacted by Congress as outside Congress's enumerated powers, on the other. It is one thing to invalidate federal laws for reasons having to do with the distribution of power; it is another to strike down local laws as misuses of power.

To be sure, the Constitution has countermajoritarian features. It effectively removes certain questions (such as "Should we criminalize seditious libel?"[39] or "Should Congress select the Russian Orthodox Archbishop of New York?"[40]) from the political arena. At the same time, it is a document that reflects strong commitments to popular sovereignty and that relies at least as much on constitutional structure and institutional design as on judicial review to constrain majorities' resolutions of challenging moral questions.[41]

III.

This panel's focus has been on the homogenizing threat that judicial review can pose to local communities' distinctive values and legal experiments. We have been considering the worry that when federal judges second-guess local-values-reflecting policies, it can be difficult to hold the line between enforcing the Constitution's trumping commitments—*our* shared commitments—and imposing their own preferences. This worry is not frivolous, but there is no easy way to soothe it.

Although judicial review of local legislation *does* threaten to undermine local identity by homogenizing community norms, such review is both helpful and necessary to the task of protecting the institutions, groups, associations, and communities that generate, nurture, test, express, and advocate for those norms. In a case like *Romer v. Evans*,[42] for example, the Supreme Court's exercise of judicial review can be seen as homogenizing local norms by subordinating

---

36 *See* 491 U.S. at 430–31 (Rehnquist, C.J., dissenting).

37 *Id.* at 435.

38 Rehnquist, *supra* note 20, at 706; *see* Washington v. Glucksberg, 521 U.S. 702, 735 (1997) (observing that "[t]hroughout the Nation, Americans are engaged in an earnest and profound debate about the morality, legality, and practicality of physician-assisted suicide. Our holding permits this debate to continue, as it should in a democratic society.").

39 *See* U.S. CONST. amend. I; N.Y. Times Co. v. Sullivan, 376 U.S. 254, 276 (1964) (discussing the unconstitutionality of criminalizing seditious libel).

40 *See* U.S. CONST. amend. I; *cf.* Kedroff v. St. Nicholas Cathedral, 344 U.S. 94 (1952) (striking down New York law purporting to transfer control of Russian Orthodox churches from the governing hierarchy of the Russian Orthodox Church to the governing authorities of the Russian Church in America).

41 It is incorrect to conclude, as Professor Chemerinsky does, that Chief Justice Rehnquist's willingness and ability to enforce the Constitution's structural features represents a departure from, or is in tension with, his "majoritarianism." *See* Erwin Chemerinsky, *Understanding the Rehnquist Court*, 47 ST. LOUIS U. L.J. 659, 662–63 (2003).

42 517 U.S. 620 (1996).

their expression in local ordinances to the requirements of the Equal Protection Clause.[43] In a decision like *Boy Scouts of America v. Dale*,[44] on the other hand, the Court's invalidation of a law reflecting local values can perhaps be seen as protecting the existence and independence of competing and diverse sources of meaning.[45] Put simply, to the extent that one cares about values-pluralism, judicial review can be a friend as well as a foe.

As it happens, this point also finds support in the work and views of Chief Justice Rehnquist. As Professor John McGinnis has explored in some detail,[46] a powerful and pervasive theme in the Rehnquist Court's decisions is recognition and even celebration of the place and function of mediating institutions in civil society.[47] The landscape that is created, regulated, and reflected by the Constitution includes more than a federal government and states, and more than persons and governments. The structural features of that charter both preserve and clear out the space of civil society in which associations and mediating institutions work to safeguard political liberty and constrain political authority. Associations, therefore, serve a number of critical purposes:

> [A]ssociations have a structural, as well as a vehicular, purpose. They hold back the bulk of government and are the "critical buffers between the individual and the power of the State." They are "laboratories of innovation" that clear out the civic space needed to "sustain the expression of the rich pluralism of American life." Associations are not only conduits for expression, they are the scaffolding around which civil society is constructed, in which personal freedoms are exercised, in which loyalties are formed and transmitted, and in which individuals flourish.[48]

The same judicial review that we might fear could impose unwelcome moral uniformity is, it turns out, sometimes necessary to preserve the freedoms of associations upon which a healthy moral conversation depends.

---

43 U.S. Const. amend. XIV, § 1.

44 530 U.S. 640 (2000).

45 *See generally* Garnett, *Henry Adams's Soul, supra* note*.

46 *See generally* John O. McGinnis, *Reviving Tocqueville's America: The Rehnquist Court's Jurisprudence of Social Discovery*, 90 Cal. L. Rev. 485 (2002).

47 *See, e.g., Boy Scouts*, 530 U.S. at 648 (noting that the freedom of association is "especially important in preserving political and cultural diversity and in shielding dissident expression from suppression by the majority" (internal quotation marks omitted) (quoting Roberts v. U.S. Jaycees, 468 U.S. 609, 622 (1984))).

48 Garnett, *Henry Adams's Soul, supra* note*, at 1853–54.

CHAPTER 11

Bureaucracy

KEY TERMS

Iron Triangle   Max Weber

Betsy DeVos   Lobbyists

Standard Operating Procedures   Qualities of Bureaucracy

DISCUSSION QUESTIONS

1. Identify and discuss the significance of iron triangles/subgovernments. Do they make for effective policy making? Why or why not?

2. What is the spoils system?

3. Discuss three reasons for the evolution of the modern bureaucracy.

4. Discuss four characteristics of bureaucracy as described by Max Weber.

THE ROLE OF BUREAUCRACY

Bureaucracy is the permanent government. It is the staff that implements public policy. The civil servants who staff all levels of government are in place from one election to another. At the county level, these are the folks who serve as sanitation workers, police officers, firefighters, public school teachers, parks department employees, etc. At the state level, these are officials who staff parks, serve on the highway patrol, work at public universities, etc. Federally, these are the employees who work for the cabinet-level departments and agencies, such as NASA, the FBI, the CIA, and the Energy Department. At the federal level, the top administrators change with the different administrations, but the rank-and-file employees stay the same.

This is a process that developed over time. When the government was small and had only certain assigned functions, there were few employees. Those who did work in government owed their jobs to their political affiliations. This was known as the "spoils system," a reference to the phrase "To the victor goes the spoils." In American politics, this is largely attributed to President Andrew Jackson. However, as the United States became a global power and advanced economically, the government took on more of a role for defense and directing the economy by promoting key sectors. In addition, the gradual increase of the voting franchise led people who did not own property to have the vote. As a result, they put more demands on the government, and politicians wanted to curry favor with these voters, so they advocated greater spending on government programs. This led to an increase in government employment and expenditures.

The German sociologist **Max Weber** did extensive research on bureaucracies. In 1922, in his essay on bureaucracy, he developed a number of **qualities of bureaucracy**:

- Hierarchical organization
- Formal lines of authority
- Specific areas of activity
- Division of labor
- Regular assigned tasks
- All decisions and powers are regulated

This also led to a need to establish a system to hire people to staff these positions. The need for this was sparked by the assassination of James Garfield by a disgruntled job seeker in 1881.

This helped to lead to the establishment of the Pendleton Act in 1883, which began the process of developing a modern civil service. Employment for various positions would be based on qualifications, skills, and competitive examinations.

CHARACTERISTICS OF MODERN BUREAUCRACIES

The Development of Standard Operating Procedures
Standard operating procedures represent how things get done in a certain way and according to various rules and regulations that have been developed over time and that are occasionally revised. This may seem inflexible and harsh to the casual observer, but it develops uniform standards, and at least in theory, everyone is treated equally.

Specialization
Specialization translates into members of a bureaucracy undergoing specific training to master skills and to develop a culture of specialists.

Bureaucracies Are Not Interchangeable
As a result of their training, bureaucracies serve a unique function. For example, to deal with crime or urban violence, the politically popular thing to advocate may be to call out the National Guard or army. However, the training and orientation members of the armed forces get is very different from the training police officers receive, and the tactics that they use in dealing with a crisis are different. Part of the problem the United States is experiencing regarding police violence, especially against minorities, is that many police forces in the United States are becoming militarized.

The Control of Information
Because bureaucracies deal with the same issues every day, they become experts in those issues. As a result, they are able to control information on an issue and control the debate over it. This at times can be detrimental to public policy making, as the public and other sectors of government do not get full disclosure of information on an issue.

Success Is Measured by Increased Funding and Responsibility
In these times of shrinking budgets, bureaucracies are in competition with each other for funding. In areas where bureaucracies overlap, there is often conflict, as each sector wants to protect its

territory. We see this sometimes with conflicting jurisdictions in law enforcement at the federal, state, and local levels. In the military, this is also seen in bureaucratic conflicts between the armed services. The air force wants to procure jet fighter aircraft and long-range bombers central to what it feels is its mission of attacking potential adversaries of the United States. It is not very interested in procuring cargo aircraft to transport troops and equipment to battlefields.

Bureaucracies are components of what political scientists label iron triangles or subgovernments. These are narrow groups of decision makers focused on specific issues. In addition to members of the bureaucracy, it consists of members of Congress and their staffs, as well as the private sector, which can include interest groups and academia. It is referred to as an **iron triangle** because the three axes of the triangle are the bureaucracy, interest groups, and Congress. Within the triangle, money, information, and personnel flow.

Typically, interest groups lobby Congress to change a law or program to benefit them. When this is done, they have oversight over the bureaucracy to ensure that these rules are adhered to. The way the bureaucracy applies these rules affects interest groups. Interest groups provide campaign contributions to members of Congress for their reelection campaigns. Congress, in turn, appropriates money to the bureaucracy. The way the bureaucracy enforces the law or program affects the financial well-being of individuals or companies that are represented by the interest groups. People often move from one part of the triangle to another throughout their careers. Members of an interest group may be nominated to lead a bureaucracy at the cabinet or subcabinet level. They could also run for office themselves and get elected to a legislative body. Individuals who retire from the bureaucracy or Congress may end up working as **lobbyists** for private-sector interest groups. This is very common among military officers who can retire after 20 years of service when they are middle-aged. They can then have a second career either in government service as a civilian or with the private sector. They will frequently interact with the institutions and individuals they knew in the military.

Betsy DeVos: Secretary of Education

Before becoming secretary of education, **Betsy DeVos** was an advocate of charter schools and vouchers. She was promoting alternatives to traditional public education. She was very active politically in the Michigan Republican Party.

THE CONQUERING BUREAUCRACY

A New History of The FDA Shows How Regulators Entrenched and Extended Their Own Power
Keith E. Whittington

After spending months in the Amazon sometime in the early 1960s, a young pharmaceutical salesman just wanted to cross an airstrip and board a plane to begin his long journey home. But a Brazilian soldier had a different idea: "You can't come in."

The salesman pleaded, "I gotta come in!" The soldier pointed his rifle at the young American, unlocked the safety, and repeated, "You can't come in." The drug rep relented: "Oh, now I got it. I can't go in there."

In 1985 that salesman, G. Kirk Raab, was named the president of Genentech, which has since become one of the leaders of the modern biotech industry. But early in Raab's tenure Genentech was dealt an almost crippling blow at a critical stage of its development by the formidable Food and Drug Administration (FDA). In the spring of 1987, a mere suggestion that an advisory panel to the FDA was entertaining doubts about approving Genentech's first blockbuster drug was enough to send the company's stock plummeting, wiping out a quarter of its value overnight. When talking about the incident and its implications, Raab liked to recall his jungle encounter with state power. "The FDA is standing there with a machine gun against the pharmaceutical industry, so you better be their friend rather than their enemy. They are the boss. ... They own you body and soul."

> Dr. Massengill's Elixir Sulfanilamide included the essential ingredient in antifreeze, and more than 100 people died from drinking it. The FDA quickly stepped in to deal with the crisis, grab the spotlight, and set the agenda going forward.

The FDA is one of the oldest and most powerful regulatory agencies in the United States. In his massive, magisterial *Reputation and Power: Organizational Image and Pharmaceutical Regulation at the FDA,* the Harvard political scientist Daniel Carpenter provides both a history of the agency and an analysis of how it gained and flexed its most important regulatory power, the ability to keep new drugs off the market. Carpenter carefully documents the ways FDA bureaucrats have worked to exploit opportunities to expand their influence and reshape how the drug industry and the medical profession operate.

The precursor to the FDA was launched in 1906, when the Pure Food and Drugs Act bestowed limited regulatory powers on the Department of Agriculture's Bureau of Chemistry, mostly in the identification and removal of impure or misbranded food and drugs used in interstate commerce. Though pressure for the law had been triggered by muckraking accounts of the food industry, such as Upton Sinclair's best-selling novel *The Jungle,* the government's chemists were more concerned in those early years with the accuracy of material printed on drug labels.

Back then, "patent" or "proprietary" medicines—direct-to-consumer products heavy on curative claims and light on detailed chemical information—were a major force in American medicine, raking in hundreds of millions of dollars in annual sales and advertising heavily in mass-circulation newspapers and medical journals. Patent medicine manufacturers could be charged with fraud or "misbranding" under the new law, and many were, but that was easy to avoid. As long as the labels did not contain false information about the ingredients or make demonstrably false claims about their effects, the Bureau of Chemistry had no power over them.

So how could people distinguish between quack medicine and quality pharmaceuticals? The American Medical Association (AMA) and the Council on Pharmacy and Chemistry offered some nongovernmental solutions. In 1905, the AMA created the council to evaluate the validity of the claims made on behalf of patent medicines, awarding a "seal of approval" to any drug it regarded as safe and effective. Drugs it deemed unsafe were barred from advertising in the influential *Journal of the American Medical Association.* The council also published a separate journal that listed and described the new drugs that had won its approval. Regulators at the time often relied on the council for their own analysis.

By the time the Depression hit, officials at the Bureau of Chemistry (which was re-christened the Food and Drug Administration in 1930) were waging an active public relations campaign against patent medicines and lobbying for tougher regulations of drug labels and advertising. The League of Women Voters—a leading consumer advocate of the day—joined the push for broadened regulatory authority. Sympathetic lawmakers came close to passing a bill during Franklin Roosevelt's first term, but drug regulation was not a New Deal priority, and drug makers and self-medication advocates lobbied successfully against the legislation.

Then Dr. Massengill's Elixir Sulfanilamide hit the market in the fall of 1937. Massengill's potion included the essential ingredient in antifreeze, and more than 100 people died from drinking it. The AMA broke the story of the poisonings, but the FDA quickly stepped in to deal with the crisis, grab the spotlight, and set the agenda going forward. FDA officials were soon featured in a "nationwide race with death" as they flew across the country with reporters in tow to seize bottles of Dr. Massengill's evil Elixir.

Initially, the story had been downplayed by the press as a case of southern blacks using a deadly treatment for venereal disease. That was not particularly accurate, since the medicine had been distributed nationally, was marketed as suitable for a wide variety of ailments and patients (especially children, since it was in liquid form), and had claimed a wide range of victims. But the patent medicine industry was particularly strong in the South, and initial reports from both the AMA and Massengill attempted to limit the scope of the problem by emphasizing that one group of patients had been seeing a "Negro" doctor.

That all changed when Secretary of Agriculture Henry A. Wallace distributed photos of a 6-year-old white girl who had died after her mother gave her Dr. Massengill's Elixir to treat strep throat. FDA officials used the occasion to argue that a "governmental licensing system" was needed before any new drug could be distributed. All medications should be brought under the same regulatory umbrella, and no drug should be put on the store shelf or into the medicine cabinet until it had been vetted for safety by the federal government. Congress quickly agreed, and modern drug regulation was born.

The Food, Drugs, and Cosmetics Act of 1938 gave the FDA gatekeeping power over new pharmaceuticals, as well as expanded authority over drug labels and carte blanche to prohibit drugs it deemed dangerous. Agency officials have been using these powers ever since to dictate how the drug industry operates and what modern medicine looks like, not only in the United States but across the globe.

The 1938 statute empowered the FDA to evaluate whether new drugs were safe to use before being released to the public. But what did that mean? Working with a favored set of university professors and drug company researchers, the regulators developed a new system for evaluating drugs. Large, controlled studies displaced doctor testimonials. The AMA ceased being the leading source of information on drug safety, and eventually abandoned its seal-of-approval program altogether.

The FDA distrusted medical professionals, leading regulators to aggressively expand their control over drug labels through bureaucratic rulemaking in the 1950s. In addition to examining the words on packages, the FDA required regulators to preapprove all inserts and even marketing brochures before they could be distributed to doctors. Drug manufacturers bristled when field investigators from the FDA began insisting they had the power to review personnel policies at factories, or when regulators required an entirely new approval process (with clinical trials) for lower-dosage versions of already-approved drugs.

Perhaps the most controversial issue arising from the 1938 statute came after the FDA decided to create and apply a cost-benefit test to each drug, rather than merely prohibiting poison. The question was no longer whether you would drop dead from taking a single dose of bad patent medicine. It was whether the positive effects of a drug at a given dosage and over a given course of treatment outweighed the negative effects. This test then opened the door to asking whether a drug under review performed better than placebos or existing drugs on the market. Opponents to this approach argued that drug efficacy, which they distinguished from drug safety, was a case-by-case medical decision outside the scope of the FDA's statutory authority.

But then another scandal struck. In the late 1950s and early '60s, Western Europe was rocked by birth defects caused by the sedative drug thalidomide. The FDA had blocked thalidomide from coming onto the U.S. market out of concern for its safety. The agency was able to exploit that success to win statutory support in 1962 for new powers, including the explicit authority to consider efficacy when reviewing new drugs.

The FDA's entrenched power to keep drugs off the market often operates off the public radar, though interest groups and the media sporadically focus attention on the issue. The *Wall Street Journal* editorial page has voiced concerns that the agency is too conservative in evaluating new medications. AIDS and cancer patient groups have lobbied for less delay in releasing drugs for treating critical patients.

On one hand, the FDA's approach to pharmacology has created and enforced a culture of research and development that slows the infusion of new drugs into the market. On the other hand, as Carpenter documents, the FDA's review process is sensitive to politics. When Congress or national newspapers take an interest in the fate of a particular drug or class of drugs, they tend to move through the review process more quickly. The FDA worries about damaging its reputation by approving drugs that ultimately prove unsafe or ineffective (as with the popular painkiller Vioxx, which was pulled from the market in 2004 after it was shown to significantly increase the risk of heart attacks and strokes), but administrators also worry about taking heat for delaying the release of promising new cancer drugs. The agency's power and reputation turn on how effectively bureaucrats balance those competing pressures.

One common approach to thinking about bureaucracies and regulatory policy is through "capture theory." Pioneered by political scientists such as Marver Bernstein and economists such as the Nobel laureate George Stigler, capture theory argues that regulatory agencies and policies often end up benefiting most those who are being regulated. Large firms use regulation to put small firms at a competitive disadvantage.

Carpenter's perspective, by contrast, emphasizes the power of the bureaucrats over their domain. FDA officials developed their own ideas about good policy and cultivated a diverse and changing set of political allies to help them put those ideas into practice. The agency was not above taking advantage of (or stoking) public fears of the "doctor's trust" (the AMA) or "unscrupulous" big drug companies to enhance its own reputation and power. FDA Commissioner David Kessler's attempt to regulate cigarettes as a drug in the 1990s without any new statutory authority was thoroughly consistent with the agency's history.

Still, there are limits to the FDA's reach. Nutritional supplements and herbal remedies have largely eluded the agency's grasp; in some ways they're the modern patent medicines. And the regulators have seen political and legal pushback on everything from Kessler's tobacco power grab to the approval pace of AIDS and cancer drugs. Nonetheless, the FDA has accumulated an immense amount of power since it was born. No account of that power—and of the growth of government in general—should neglect the influence of the bureaucrats themselves in extending their own reach.

CHAPTER 12

Political Socialization

KEY TERMS

Aristotle

Political Culture

Concentration of the Media

Presidential Press Conferences

Immanuel Kant

Agents of Political Socialization

Social Media

Kennedy-Nixon Debate

DISCUSSION QUESTIONS

1. Address four aspects of political socialization and their significance.

2. Discuss the significance of presidential press conferences.

3. Discuss the role of television in campaigning, particularly in presidential campaigns.

WHAT IS POLITICAL SOCIALIZATION?

Political socialization is how individuals learn about their society in a political context. Political socialization takes many forms, and it is something that people are constantly experiencing.

CITIZENSHIP

Citizenship is the right and the obligation to participate constructively in the ongoing enterprise of self-government.

ARISTOTLE AND ANCIENT ATHENS

Aristotle believed the measure of the political system is the kind of citizen it produces. He believed that free citizens needed to participate directly in affairs of state.

In ancient Athens however only a small percentage of the population were free citizens with full political rights.

TOTALITARIAN SYSTEM

In a totalitarian system, people are compelled to participate in the political system. This is done usually through a mass political party, appearances at rallies, and other events.

DEMOCRATIC SYSTEM

In a democracy, the essence of citizenship lies in individual rights and personal liberties. Modern democracies also safeguard the rights of the minority to freely articulate their points of view.

EIGHTEENTH-CENTURY EUROPE

- Citizenship meant those who could petition the government and had standing in court. Usually, this was white male property owners.
- Citizens versus subjects: Subjects are required to obey and show loyalty to the ruler. According to German philosopher **Immanuel Kant** (1724–1804), citizens have the right to obey laws that they have consented to through due process of a Republican form of government.

POLITICAL CULTURE

Political culture encompasses the moral attitudes, beliefs, and history of a society. Political culture is the collective memory of a society.

These perceptions are affected by factors such as the following.

- Geography/Terrain: Countries that share borders with powerful nations are going to be more concerned about defense and most likely have stronger centralized governments.
- Climate: Countries in a more temperate climate generally have better food security and are less dependent on food imports.
- Religion: A dominant religion can shape a society and certain political and social norms may be considered givens.

Examples

Russia versus the United States
Russia has a long history of strong centralized government for defense. Russian history features attacks and threats from hostile neighbors. The United States has a history of more limited government. For much of American history, the United States was geographically isolated and did not have to worry about foreign invasion.

Religion
Societies are shaped by religious influences. For example, Islam has shaped the political culture of many countries around the world. Judaism has shaped the dominant political culture of Israel. Taoism and Confucianism have shaped China politically, and Hinduism has done the same with India.

AGENTS OF POLITICAL SOCIALIZATION

Political socialization means learning those rules and ways of thinking deemed most important for the success and survival of the individual and society. It provides a link between past and future generations.

FACTORS THAT SHAPE PUBLIC OPINION AND POLITICAL SOCIALIZATION

Importance of the Family
Up until children start school, the family shapes children socially and politically. Statistics illustrate that when children grow up and begin to have political opinions and vote for the first time, they tend to mirror the political views of their parents.

Educational Influence
Public education, in part, was created as a socialization tool. The idea was to inculcate the history of the state and ensure loyalty. In countries that have large immigrant populations, such as the United Kingdom, Australia, Canada, and the United States, public education was a way to socialize diverse immigrant populations, as well as teaching them a working knowledge of English. Public education is also a way to unify countries. An example of this is Italy, which unified relatively late in 1871. It was made up of numerous provinces with language dialects that varied even within provinces. One of Mussolini's policies was the standardization of Italian and the mandating that the Italian spoken in the province of Tuscany would be the official Italian language. While linguistic dialects are still used, there is a standard Italian language spoken throughout the country.

Media Influence
The media shapes what we see and how we interpret the news. How the news is presented is important. What is being emphasized? What does not get covered? In the contemporary media climate, there is more of a bias slant toward news and commentary. CNN is more oriented toward Democrats and Fox News toward Republicans.

Peer Group Influence
People are influenced by their own age group in cultural tastes as well as politics.

Influence of Religion
People who participate in organized religion tend to be more conservative politically than the population average.

Economic Status and Occupation
Both economic status and occupation can often influence how people view politics. People who are more affluent and more involved in business tend to favor Republican positions. Blue-collar workers, such as factory workers and people in the building trades, tend to favor Democratic positions. However, this becomes complicated, as sometimes blue-collar workers are more socially conservative and feel more comfortable with conservative positions on social issues. Likewise, some wealthy individuals are more socially liberal and gravitate toward liberal positions.

Political Events
People are politically influenced by the times and events they live through. This is referred to as generational effects. People who experienced certain events, such as World War II or the Great Depression, generally have a more favorable view of government than people born later whose primary life experiences were affected by the Vietnam War and Watergate. These individuals tend to be more skeptical of the government's intentions.

Influence of Opinion Leaders

Leaders' opinions are important at all levels. At the national level, people often pay attention when celebrities get involved in causes or support political candidates. At the local level, those who aspire to office try to get the support of activists in their communities. Frequently, these people are listened too by others.

Influence of Race and Gender

Identity politics are important. Certain racial and ethnic groups tend to support a particular political party. Sometimes this changes over time. For example, after the Civil War, when African Americans could vote, they voted overwhelmingly Republican as that was the party of Lincoln. The 1932 election realigned US politics in many ways. The Democrats become the dominant party, and their modern-day electoral coalition was forged. Because of the various New Deal programs, African Americans began to vote Democrat in large numbers, in particular outside of the South. In modern times, women tend to vote more Democratic than men.

MEDIA

Traditionally, most people received their news from newspapers. Newspapers and political magazines appeared in a big way in the 1800s. Newspapers prior to 1800 tended to be very political, as they supported a political party or a specific faction. Radio became important in the 1920s and 1930s. Television emerged as the most popular medium in the 1950s. The internet, and most recently **social media**, has become the dominant medium from which people receive news.

Initially, TV was seen more as entertainment, but very quickly, people began to be exposed to the news. The format was simply reading the news. Networks covered the news in 30 minutes and emphasized visual images. Television provided more immediate coverage.

Newspapers are more thorough, and people tend to remember something they have read. Television, particularly with the expansion of cable news, and the internet allow people to get their news around the clock.

Concentration of the Media

Journalism is a big business. Most media outlets are part of larger corporations. For example, AOL® bought Time Warner® in 2000; more recently, Disney® purchased 20th Century Fox®.

Facebook®, Twitter®, Instagram®, and other social media platforms have changed how people connect with each other, as well as get their news and entertainment. Social media has also changed political campaigning. Now virtually every campaign, in addition to having a website, has Facebook, Twitter, and Instagram accounts.

Importance of Television in Campaigning

Candidates frequently announce their candidacy on television. TV talk shows have become an important aspect of campaigning for candidates running for president. This phenomenon began in the 1990s with then-candidate Bill Clinton going on the *Phil Donahue Show* and playing the saxophone on the *Arsenio Hall Show*. Al Gore and George W. Bush followed up by appearing on the *Oprah Winfrey Show* in 2000. These shows give politicians access to new audiences that do not regularly follow traditional news shows. They allow politicians to get involved in a format that is primarily entertainment. A similar phenomenon occurred in radio.

Presidential Press Conferences

Politicians and media are in a symbiotic relationship and adversarial at the same time. Reporters need information and commentary for their stories. Politicians can give them this and help them with their stories. Press secretaries' primary goal is to work with the media.

Teddy Roosevelt started **presidential press conferences**. They began as informal sessions while he shaved. Subsequent presidents offered few press conferences and demanded the questions in advance.

The growth of media has contributed to the decline of party leadership. Candidates can appeal directly to the public and bypass party leaders. The media also publicizes information about candidates, and as a result, voters are less dependent on party organizations.

Media also has enabled the emergence of nontraditional candidates. These are candidates who moved from other careers into high political office without going through an apprenticeship. President Trump is a good example of this as he moved from the business world to show business and used his media presence to contest the Republican nomination for the presidency. He was able to use his name recognition to become the front-runner in a crowded Republican field.

Presidential Elections and Debates

Media affects the outcomes of elections. Media coverage can convey the title of front-runner on a candidate, which has benefits and liabilities. Expanded media coverage is important in attracting support and financial contributions. Money in campaigning tends to go toward the front-runner.

Liabilities Can Include Overdramatizing Errors and Flubs

Televised debates are very important in campaigning, in particular in presidential elections. They provide viewers with a visual image. The first televised debate was the **Kennedy-Nixon debate** in the 1960 election. Kennedy was able to present himself as the more youthful and energetic of the candidates. The visual image made a big impression and is credited with his narrow electoral victory in 1960.

POLITICAL SOCIALIZATION AND PUBLIC OPINION
Cal Jillson

Political Socialization: Where Our Ideas About Politics Come From

How are the broad ideas of the American political culture taught by one generation of Americans and learned by the next? Political scientist Fred Greenstein described political socialization as the study of "(1) who (2) learns what (3) from whom (4) under what circumstances (5) with what effects."[6] Greenstein's fundamental interest was in how young children acquire their first impressions of politics and political leaders. More recently scholars have asked how easily early political learning is modified as people move through the life cycle. Do people change their political views as they experience school, work, marriage, family, retirement, and old age? Do poor children who get rich in adult life change political assumptions and beliefs?

Political engagement involves a desire and a willingness to be involved in the political world—to follow political news and events, to join in political discussions, perhaps to work to advance one set of political ideas or issues over others, and to

Q2 Where do individual Americans get their opinions about politics, and what are the forces that shape those opinions?

Cal Jillson, Selection from "Political Socialization and Public Opinion," American Government: Political Development and Institutional Change, pp. 94–106, 117–118, 541–543. Copyright © 2018 by Taylor & Francis Group. Reprinted with permission.

vote and maybe even to stand for election. Students of political engagement study how people feel about politics, how interested they are in politics, how much they actually know about politicians, politics, and public policy, and how and how much they engage in politics. As we shall see, scholars find that political engagement varies by age, education, income, race, region, and much more.[7]

Agents of Socialization

How does it happen that the vast majority of Americans come to believe that market competition is the best way to organize an economy, that elections are the best way to pick political leaders, and that the flag, the White House, the Lincoln memorial, and the Capitol dome represent a political heritage and culture worth passing on, worth defending, even worth dying for? As we shall see, while political socialization is a powerful process, much of it takes place informally, below the radar screen, almost automatically. Neither those who teach nor those who learn are much aware that they are doing it.

agents of socialization The persons, such as parents and teachers, and settings, such as families and schools, that carry out the political socialization process.

Agents of socialization are the persons by whom and the settings in which the process of political socialization is accomplished. Persons include parents, family, friends, teachers, coworkers, and associates of various kinds, as well as those whose views are transmitted through the media and online. Settings include homes, churches, schools, workplaces, clubs, union halls, and professional associations.

Agents of socialization are also categorized by the timing, scope, and intensity of their influence. Students of political socialization distinguish between primary groups and secondary groups. **Primary groups** are face-to-face groups with whom the individual has regular, often frequent, contact. These include close personal associations like family,

primary groups Face-to-face groups, such as families and friends, with whom an individual has regular, often continuous, contact.

friends, and coworkers. Primary groups are usually made up of persons of similar background (income, education, race, religion) engaged in frequent conversation on a wide range of topics including politics.

Secondary groups are broader and more diffuse. Examples include churches, unions, the military, and clubs and professional associations such as the Sierra Club, the National Rifle Association, and the Chamber of Commerce. Their members come from a variety of income, educational, racial, and religious backgrounds. Moreover, secondary groups usually have a substantive focus—that is, they are environmentalists, business owners, or gun owners. Their influence is limited to a distinctive set of issues to which the group is thought relevant.

secondary groups Broader and more diffuse than primary groups, secondary groups often serve a particular role or purpose in the life of the member, and often do not meet together as a full membership.

New technology, like the Internet and social media, and new uses of old technology, like talk radio, allow geographically disparate groups to form around and act on shared interests. Rush Limbaugh's "ditto heads" learn a coherent ideology and arguments supporting their positions by tuning in every day. Meetup.com, YouTube, and Facebook allow like-minded people to find each other and share enthusiasms, ideas, and plans. And where like-minded people do not find each other, pollsters, political strategists, and niche marketers work to identify people with shared values and interests so that they can target them with political information designed to mobilize them to political action.[8]

Family, School, and Work. Everyone agrees that the first and most important agent of political socialization is the family. Virtually all American families teach respect for democracy and capitalism, but they differ on the lessons they teach regarding participation, partisanship, politics, and public policy. Studies show that 80 to 90 percent of married couples share the same party affiliation. In such homes, children receive consistent messages from both parents. In Democratic households, children hear favorable comments about Democrats and unfavorable comments about Republicans as parents converse at the dinner table and as they respond to what they see and hear on the evening news. Parents rarely sit young children down and tell them that they are Democrats and not Republicans, or vice versa, but children learn just as effectively by overhearing their parents, observing their actions and reactions, and sensing their party affiliation.

Over the past half century, scholars have consistently shown that high school and college-age young people generally adopt their parents' partisan identification. If both parents share the same party affiliation, Democrat or Republican, 60 to 65 percent of young people adopt the family partisanship, about 30 percent abandon it for an independent stance, while only about 10 percent join the opposition party. Young people from those uncommon households where Mom is a Democrat and Dad is a Republican or vice versa scatter with remarkable uniformity across Democrat, Republican, and independent categories. In households where both parents are independents, the children choose independent status at least two-thirds of the time, while the remaining one-third divide equally between the Democrats and the Republicans.[9]

Schools also play an important role in early political socialization. School curricula lay down layer after layer of American history, civics, and social studies. Students learn patriotic songs and rituals (who has not been either a Pilgrim or an Indian in a Thanksgiving day pageant?), they learn about political heroes such as Washington ("I cannot tell a lie") and Lincoln (reading law books by candlelight), and they cast their first presidential straw ballots. Moreover, schools, even elementary schools, offer a broader horizon than the family. Respect for diversity, equality, fair play, toleration, majority rule, and minority rights are required for the first time in a setting where people actually differ.

Fred Greenstein's seminal work with schoolchildren in New Haven in the late 1950s and early 1960s remains fascinating even today. Greenstein found that children begin to learn about politics in their elementary school years. Second graders can name the president. Over the remainder of the grade school years, children become aware of

other branches of government and other levels of government. Initially, children see Congress as the president's "helpers." By eighth grade, they know that Congress can differ with the president and that this is how the system is supposed to work. A half century of subsequent scholarly work, best summarized by Robert Erikson and Kent Tedin in their classic *American Public Opinion*, affirms "the primacy principle" that early learning has staying power. Still early views are not set in stone. Students begin their college careers somewhat more liberal than the adult population and become somewhat more liberal still by their senior year. Scholars attribute this to education challenging stereotypes and prejudices and to the diversity of the college environment. Later life may roll back some of these changes, but, as some parents worry, college tends to be a liberalizing experience.[10] Childhood political socialization can be deepened or partially reshaped during "the impressionable years" of 17 to 29.[11] Socialization continues after early adulthood, but early foundations are deeply set.

Work has both general and specific effects on political socialization. In fact, employment, quite apart from the nature of the job, has a profound effect on a person's political outlook. Having a job is one's ticket to participate in a whole range of social and political processes. Having a good job teaches confidence that carries over into political activity. Unemployment, particularly chronic unemployment, takes away the status, time, opportunity, and confidence that political participation requires. Having a bad job, where you put in long hours at low pay, saps confidence and discourages political activity. Not surprisingly, studies show that higher income people are more aware of politics, issues, and candidates than are lower income people. The wealthy are socialized to a more active political life than are the poor.[12]

The Media. The media, like the schools, provide pervasive and continuous support to effective political socialization simply by routinely reporting political and economic events. The president's latest statements, the work of the Congress, and the latest Supreme Court decisions are all reported on the evening news and in the morning paper. Trade figures, corporate profits, and the rise and fall of the stock market are reported in ways that assume the fundamental legitimacy of democratic capitalism. Even talk radio and the Internet offer few hints that politics or economics might be organized differently. [...]

The Impacts of Transformative Events and Personalities. Political socialization is the process by which families, schools, and the media transmit the American political culture to young people and newcomers, but that broad process of cultural teaching and learning, of memory and renewal, can be disrupted. Some events including wars, economic upheavals, social turmoil, and political scandal can transform the way people see and understand their society. Depending upon how these challenges are handled by political leaders, the nation's faith in its political culture, its confidence in its basic ideals and institutions, is renewed and strengthened or called into doubt and weakened. Leadership interacts with crisis to convince people that society and government are or are not up to the task of confronting the major issues of the day.

Abraham Lincoln held the nation together through a terrible Civil War, and Franklin Delano Roosevelt did the same through a dozen years of economic depression and world war. Both gave the Americans who witnessed their virtuoso political performances the confidence to confront their world forcefully and for the most part successfully. Alternatively, leaders that misperceive or mismanage the major threats of their time, as Herbert Hoover misperceived the threat posed by the Great Depression of the 1930s, may raise doubts about the viability of the nation's most basic political assumptions. Leaders facing crises must respond effectively to challenges and do so in ways that protect and strengthen the nation's basic principles. President Bush believed that his War on Terror would bring the nation and the world through to a safer, more peaceful, and democratic future. Critics contend that his policies failed and the means that he used to pursue them undercut U.S. rights and liberties and weakened national security. President Obama retained some Bush initiatives, such as intensive surveillance, and rejected others, like enhanced interrogation and Guantanamo. History will judge both men on how well they protected the nation's ideals, institutions, and citizens.

The Nature of Public Opinion in The United States

The agents of socialization discussed above, although they all work within a general American political culture revolving around capitalism and democracy, do not teach the same lessons to all members of society. The poor and the wealthy are socialized to different roles; minorities are socialized differently from whites, and women are socialized differently from men. Hence, public opinion varies across a wide range of social group characteristics.[13] Public opinion, in its most general formulation, is simply the current distribution of citizen opinion on matters of public concern or interest.

Before we can discuss public opinion in detail, we must address a prior question. How do we measure public opinion and how confident should we be in those measurements? Once we understand how public opinion is measured, we can ask how attitudes and opinions vary within the American public by class, race, ethnicity, and gender.

History of Public Opinion Polling

Citizens have always wondered how others see the leading candidates and major issues of the day. Informal preference polls for the leading presidential candidates in the election of 1824 were reported in the press. In fact, the partisan press of the nineteenth century regularly reported on rallies, straw polls, and citizen reports of voter attitudes in their area. (See Table 12.1 for a summary of the ways public opinion has been expressed and assessed through history.) As late as 1916, a prominent national magazine called the *Literary Digest* simply asked its readers to send in whatever information they had from their areas about the presidential contest between Democrat Woodrow Wilson and Republican Charles Evans Hughes. Over the next two decades, the *Literary Digest* conducted huge and reasonably accurate surveys in the presidential elections of 1920 through 1932. However, the famous failure of its survey in 1936 helped usher in a new era in the history of polling.

In 1936, the *Literary Digest* mailed 10 million ballots to citizens—whose names were compiled from automobile registration lists, telephone directories, and magazine subscription lists—asking them to choose between the Democrat, Franklin Roosevelt, and the Republican, Alf Landon. The 2 million ballots that were returned suggested a big win for Landon; in fact, Roosevelt won in a landslide, carrying the popular vote 57 percent to 43 percent and the Electoral College 523 to 8. Analysts concluded that the *Literary Digest* poll results were so far off because the magazine's subscribers were mostly wealthy, those who owned cars, had phones, and subscribed to literary magazines. The poll missed less wealthy voters, who did not own cars or subscribe to literary magazines, and who were more likely to vote for Roosevelt.[14]

Scientific Polling. In the same year that *Literary Digest*, with its 2 million responses, was completely wrong about the election outcome, George Gallup, with a much smaller but scientifically selected sample of voter opinion, predicted the outcome correctly. Gallup and his competitors—Louis Harris, Elmo Roper, and others—gauged citizen opinion on public issues and political candidates with "quota samples" of the broader electorate. The new scientific pollsters did well in the 1940 and 1944 elections as well, but then disaster struck again in 1948.

Quota samples were supposed to defend against the skewed sampling that had undermined the *Literary Digest* poll, but more subtle biases became evident in 1948. Pollsters might fill their quotas, securing the right number of men, women, blacks, Catholics, rich, poor, etc., but they might avoid a dangerous or hard to reach neighborhood. As a result, even a quota sample might be skewed. In 1948, all of the supposedly scientific polling firms projected that the Republican Thomas Dewey would defeat the incumbent Democratic President Harry Truman. Truman won and subsequent inquiries concluded that quota samples should be replaced by more dependable "probability samples." They also concluded that pollsters, lulled into overconfidence by Dewey's stable lead, stopped polling too early and missed Truman's late surge.[15]

Probability sampling is based on a statistical model in which every person in the target population has an equal or known chance of being selected for the sample to be polled. In a simple probability sample, all members of the population have an equal chance of being selected. In a stratified probability sample, the population is first divided by some theoretically relevant characteristic—like gender, income, or likelihood of voting—and then the population is randomly sampled within each category. Pollsters have understood for more than half a century that a well-constructed national sample of just 1,000 persons produces results that have a sampling error of +/–3 percent with a confidence interval of 95 percent. What do these ominous phrases, sampling error and confidence interval, actually mean?[16]

Assume we had a well-designed poll of 1,000 adults telling us that 60 percent of them approved a certain policy. Remember, we have not asked all American adults whether they support the policy, just a carefully selected sample of them, so we know that our 60 percent result is unlikely to be precise. The 3 percent sampling error is the pollster's admission, or at least sampling theory's admission, that in a sample of 1,000 the results could be off as much as 3 percent either way—so maybe not precisely 60 percent, but somewhere between 57 and 63 percent support the policy. The 95 percent confidence interval is another admission. It says that if you polled 100 similarly drawn samples, at least 95 of them would produce results in that 57 to 63 percent range; meaning that the remaining 5 might be off by more than 3 percent either way.[17] None of this means that polls are always wrong, just that even well-constructed polls can be off within a certain known range and should be interpreted appropriately.

On the other hand, consumers of polling information should also keep in mind that not all polls are trying to be accurate. Polls released by campaigns are often—surprise—intended to serve political purposes, to suggest momentum or to trigger positive news stories. Polling analyst Nate Silver of Five ThirtyEight.com has found that campaign polls tend to be about six points more favorable to their candidate than independent surveys.[18] As we shall see below, some polls strive for accuracy, some have other purposes. Sophisticated consumers of polls, as you are about to become, know how to tell the difference.

Kinds of Polls. Different kinds of polls and surveys are designed to produce different kinds of information. Polls play a large role in political campaigns, to gauge who is ahead and why, but they are also conducted between elections to determine what citizens think about the major issues of the day. The main kinds of polls are benchmark polls, preference polls, opinion surveys, focus groups, tracking polls, and exit polls.

A candidate considering a particular election or a group considering a particular issue campaign will often run a **benchmark poll** to see where they stand before undertaking the campaign. A benchmark poll might seek to determine a candidate's name recognition, how he or she is viewed by potential voters, critical issues in the district, and key demographic information on the district's voters. **Preference polls** offer respondents a list of candidates for a particular office such as the presidency and ask which candidate they prefer. Preference polls show whether a candidate enters a race from a position of strength or from way back in a crowded field.

Opinion surveys may be conducted within the context of a campaign, but they are much more broadly used by the media, civic and interest groups, marketers, and others who wish to know how opinion is distributed across particular questions and issues. Focus groups are not really polls, but they are often used in conjunction with polls and provide similar but richer information. A **focus group** is made up of ten to fifteen carefully selected people who are led through an in-depth discussion of their thoughts and reactions to particular policy issues, candidates, or campaign themes and arguments. Focus groups are meant to supplement surveys by uncovering why people think what they think.

TABLE 12.1   Historical Techniques for the Expression and Assessment of Public Opinion

Periods	Techniques
5th century B.C.	Oratory/Rhetoric
16th century	Printing
17th century	Crowds
Late-17th century	Petitions
18th century	Coffee houses and taverns
Late-18th century	Revolutionary movements
Early-19th century	Strikes, General elections, Straw polls
Mid-19th century	Modern newspapers, magazines, photography
1920s	Radio
1930s	Sample surveys
1940s	Television
1980s	Cable television
1990s	Internet, Web, E-mail
2000s	YouTube, Twitter, Tumblr
2010s	Snapchat, Periscope

Source: Susan Herbst, *Numbered Voices* (Chicago: University of Chicago Press, 1993), p. 48. Updated and expanded by the author.

A **tracking poll** provides constantly updated information on the rise and fall of support for a candidate or policy. Late in a presidential campaign, for example, tracking polls provide daily updates on the status of the race—is the gap narrowing, or does the leader seem to be widening his or her margin? Tracking polls interview several hundred new people a day and then average the samples for the last two or three days to create a continually updated picture of the race. An **exit poll** is taken after voters have cast their ballots; it is a survey of actual voters rather than of potential or even likely voters. Exit polls interview carefully selected samples of voters as they exit the polls to find out how they voted and why they voted that way. Exit polls are used by the media to "call" elections, sometimes even before the polls close.

probability sampling A sampling model in which every person in the target population has an identical chance of being selected for the sample to be polled.

Should Citizens Believe Polls? Many Americans are skeptical about polls and there are some good reasons to be skeptical. Doubts about polls were deepened when virtually every major national poll forecast a two- to five-point Hillary Clinton win anchored by a blue wall of traditionally Democratic states in the upper Midwest. On election night, though Clinton narrowly prevailed in the popular vote, Trump took Florida, Pennsylvania, Wisconsin, and Michigan—all states in which the polls had Clinton leading. How could the pollsters have gotten it so wrong?

Polls are not easy to conduct well, and the increasing use of answering machines, caller identification devices, cell phones, and the general unwillingness of citizens to respond to surveys make it more difficult. The Romney campaign "turnout model," meaning the campaign's best estimate as to how many whites, blacks, Hispanics, etc. would turn out on election day, was off. They estimated more whites and fewer minorities than actually showed up on election day—and they lost. Political pros also know that poll results can be shaped and manipulated by the order in which questions are asked and by the way that they are phrased.[19]

Moreover, every election cycle includes reports of **push polls**. Push polls are pseudo polls, not really intended to gather information about the respondent's opinions, but to use negative and often false information to push the respondent away from a particular candidate. Push polling is among the dark arts of politics. In the guise of a simple question, such as, "Would you be more or less likely to vote for Candidate X if you knew he tortured kittens?" Candidate X may love kittens, he may even contribute to the local Humane Society, but a push poll, employed late in a campaign when no effective response is possible, can do real damage. Concern about push polls deepens public skepticism about all polls.

Still, skepticism should be directed toward some polls more than others. As a general rule, citizens can trust polls from organizations that have reputational incentives to be accurate—major polling organizations like Gallup, major news outlets like ABC and the *New York Times*, and major research organizations like the Pew Charitable Trusts. Citizens might well mistrust polls from groups that pop up in the middle of a campaign or that have a dog in the fight—an advocacy group, candidate, Super PAC, or political party.

Variations in Socialization by Class, Race, and Gender

What then do reputable polls tell us about how citizens differ in regard to politics and public opinion by class, race, ethnicity, and gender? Broadly, the more thoroughly and comfortably integrated a person is into the community and society, the more likely he or she is to be politically active. Wealthy, well educated, professionals tend to be engaged in lots of ways, and not just voting, while those for whom life is more difficult tend to be less active politically.

Class. Poor children enter school with fewer skills than wealthy children and less is expected of them. Children from lower-class backgrounds have less information about politics than children

benchmark poll A poll conducted early in a campaign to gauge the name recognition, public image, and electoral prospects of a candidate.

from upper-class backgrounds. Extensive research, summarized by Chris Garcia and Gabriel Sanchez, reports that schools serving children of the working class and poor "are less involved in preparing future leaders, and instead emphasize the importance of becoming good law-abiding citizens, paying taxes, serving one's country, and similar 'subject' rather than participant … styles."[20] Many studies have shown that these early differences in knowledge and confidence can translate into differences in political participation that last a lifetime.

preference poll A poll that offers respondents a list of candidates for a particular office and asks which is preferred.

The most recent National Election Study found that poor adults were only about half as likely as the wealthy, 22 percent to 38 percent, to say that they paid attention to public affairs "most of the time." But they were 14 points more likely, 52 percent to 38 percent, to agree with the statement that "people don't have a say in what government does." The poor believe, rightly in many cases, that society and government do not move to their commands. They also know that they are not expected to lead, perhaps not even to participate, and so many times they do neither.

opinion survey Poll or survey used by political campaigns, the media, civic organizations, and marketers to gauge opinion on particular questions or issues.

focus group A small but carefully selected group of ten to fifteen persons led through an in-depth discussion of a political issue or campaign to delve behind opinions in search of their root causes.

Race. An important new book, entitled *Black Politics Today*, by political scientist Theodore J. Davis, argues that blacks have not fully embraced the dominant political culture because it has not rejected and moved to dismantle cultural and

tracking poll Frequent polling using overlapping samples to provide daily updates of the status of a race.

institutional racism in the country. The cultural gulf has produced deep and systematic divisions between white and black opinion across a wide range of issues. Davis reports that 81 percent of blacks felt that society had not dealt fairly with their racial group (only 15 percent of whites agreed), 76 percent thought government should spend more to improve conditions among blacks (only 27 percent of whites agreed), and 55 percent felt that there still was a fair amount of discrimination against blacks (only 28 percent of whites agreed).[21]

exit poll A poll taken after voters have cast their ballots to get an early sense of who won and why.

In the 2012 presidential election, a remarkable 93 percent of blacks voted for Obama, as did 71 percent of Hispanics, but just 39 percent of whites. Moreover, blacks and whites have tended to differ on a broad range of policy issues, sometimes quite dramatically. Blacks are more supportive of government spending on health care, education, and job training than whites and less supportive of spending for defense and corporate subsidies. For example, over the last three decades, blacks have been 20 to 30 points more favorable than whites toward busing to achieve desegregation of public schools and 30 to 40 points more favorable than whites to the idea that government should guarantee fair treatment in jobs. Scholars explain the cohesion in black opinion by positing a "linked-fate" hypothesis in which blacks stand uniformly against racial discrimination because each individual knows that if it occurs he or she will be impacted by it.

Finally, in both foreign and domestic policy, blacks are much less comfortable than whites with the use of force. A *New York Times* poll taken in late March 2003 as war with Iraq loomed, found that 82 percent of whites and only 44 percent of blacks supported military action to oust Saddam Hussein. At home, the 2014 General Social Survey asked respondents whether they could approve police officers hitting people. Seventy

push poll A push poll is not a real poll; instead it is designed to influence voters by providing negative, often, false information.

percent of whites, but only 42 percent of blacks, said they could imagine a situation in which they could approve police striking an adult male.[22]

Ethnicity. Political scientists Chris Garcia and Gabriel Sanchez, in *Hispanics in the U.S. Political System*, contend that, "most Latinos would grow up in a subcultural environment, that is, a cultural environment that is different from the majority mainstream environment in some ways." They describe the traditional Latino family as more controlled, gender defined, and patriarchal than the dominant cultural model of the family.[23]

Until recently, Hispanic Americans were less likely than blacks to feel that discrimination was a major problem for their community. In a 2002 Pew Hispanic Center poll, 47 percent of Hispanics claimed that discrimination was a major problem. But by 2010, after several years of public debate about immigration and border control, 61 percent believed that it was and another 24 percent believed it was at least a minor problem.[24]

Hispanics favor special efforts to remedy past discrimination and help minorities get ahead by 76 percent to 14 percent and favor a bigger government offering a wider array of services by 75 percent to 16 percent. On the other hand, Hispanics favor tax cuts over deficit reduction by a margin of two to one, 59 percent to 30 percent, and are twice as likely as non-Hispanics, 44 percent compared to 22 percent, to think that abortion should be illegal.[25] Hispanic public opinion is often said to reflect an "in-between" community, with life experiences and attitudes in-between those of blacks and whites.

Asian-Americans, after Hispanics, are the fastest growing racial and ethnic minority in the nation. Asians currently make up about 5 percent of the population. In a recent major survey, 32 percent of Asians claimed a Democratic party affiliation, 12 percent claimed a Republican affiliation, 19 percent were Independent, and 35 percent were non-partisan. Chinese, Filipino, Indians, Japanese, and Koreans tend to lean Democratic, while Vietnamese tend to lean Republican.

An interesting difference among Asian-Americans showed up in regard to Iraq policy. While a majority of Asian-Americans supported withdrawing from Iraq, only 15 percent of Vietnamese-Americans did. Vietnamese-Americans obviously remember the Vietnam War of the 1960s and 1970s where U.S. withdrawal led to the fall of South Vietnam. These figures also remind us that no broad racial or ethnic group is monolithic.[26]

Gender. Similar differences, although not so large and across a narrower set of issues, exist between men and women. Women have consistently been more supportive than men of gun control, stern punishments for drunk driving, and spending on education and health care, and less supportive of capital punishment at home and the use of force abroad. Women oppose force at home and abroad about 10 percent more than men and favor the "moralistic" position on domestic issues about 3 or 4 percent more consistently than men.[27]

The terrorist attacks of September 11, 2001 and the subsequent conflicts with Al-Queda, Afghanistan, and Iraq put these historical differences between men and women on stark display. In early September 2001, just prior to the attacks, 41 percent of men, but only 24 percent of women, favored additional defense spending. In the immediate wake of the 9/11 attacks, support for increased defense spending among men increased to 53 percent, but among women it nearly doubled to 47 percent, still 6 points below men. Nonetheless, only a year and a half later, as war with Iraq loomed in late February 2003, women were about 10 percent less willing than men to consider the potential costs in troops and treasure acceptable.[28] And in late 2011, as the last troops were being withdrawn from Iraq and the Afghan War ground on, men remained 17 points more supportive of the war than women, 43 percent to 26 percent.[29]

[...]

Suggested Readings

Asher, Herbert. *Polling and the Public: What Every Citizen Should Know.* 8th ed. Washington, D.C.: CQ Press, 2010. Asher seeks to make citizens better consumers of polls by describing their design, methodological issues, and interpretation.

Bejarano, Christina E. *The Latina Gender Gap in U.S. Politics.* New York: Routledge, 2014. Latinos are rising in U.S. politics, but Bejarano notes that female Latinos, Latinas, are more involved politically than their male counterparts.

Ellis, Christopher and James A. Stimson. *Ideology in America.* New York: Cambridge University Press, 2012. This book explains why so many Americans call themselves conservatives but still support active government and oppose spending cuts.

Erikson, Robert S. and Kent L. Tedin. *American Public Opinion.* 9th ed. New York: Longman, 2015. The leading general text on American public opinion.

Hetherington, Marc J. and Thomas J. Randolph. *Why Washington Won't Work.* Chicago: University of Chicago Press, 2015. The authors present theory and data to support the view that a decline in political trust is a prime cause of polarization and stalemate in Washington.

Sunstein, Cass. "Polarization and Cybercascades," from chapter 3 of *Republic 2.0.* Princeton, NJ: Princeton University Press, 2007. Sunstein argues that the Internet has strengths and weaknesses as a forum for sharing political information.

Verba, Sidney. "The Citizen as Respondent: Sample Surveys and American Democracy," *American Political Science Review,* vol. 90, no. 1, March 1995, 1–7. Verba's address as president of the American Political Science Association highlights the importance of good polling to democratic politics.

Web Resources

For practice quizzes, key term flashcards, videos, links, and other study tools, visit the *American Government* website: www.routledge.com/cw/jillson.

1. **www.cnn.com/politics/**
   This Time Warner website is operated by CNN and is dedicated to providing news and features concerning politics. It provides up-to-date political information.

2. **www.fair.org**
   Official home page of Fairness and Accuracy in Reporting. This organization is a media watchdog group that reports on the performance of media outlets.

3. **www.electionstudies.org/nesguide/nesguide.htm**
   The major academic survey of voting behavior in U.S. national election is done by the National Election Studies (NES). The site gives online access to tables and graphs that reveal the trends in public opinion.

4. **www.gallup.com**
   The Gallup organization website affords use of an enormous number of polls and analyses, both current and archived.

5. **typology.people-press.org/**
   This is the website for the Pew Research Center for the People and the Press. Take the survey to see where you fit in the political typology.

6. **www.charneyresearch.com/resources/the-top-10-ways-to-get-misleading-poll-results/.**
   Excellent list, with examples, of ten ways in which polls can be misleading. Reputable pollsters guard against these errors, but the intelligent consumer of polls—you—should be aware of them.

Political Socialization and Public Opinion

1. See, for example, Donald J. Devine, *Political Culture of the United States* (Boston, MA: Little, Brown, 1972); and Herbert McClosky and John Zaller, *The American Ethos: Public Attitudes toward Capitalism and Democracy* (Cambridge, MA: Harvard University Press, 1984), 17.

2. Fred I. Greenstein, *Children and Politics*, rev. ed. (New Haven, CT: Yale University Press, 1969), 157–158. See also David Easton and Jack Dennis, *Children in the Political System* (New York: McGraw-Hill, 1969).

3. Louis Hartz, *The Founding of New Societies* (New York: Harcourt, Brace & World, 1964).

4. Gunnar Myrdal, *An American Dilemma: The Negro Problem and Modern Democracy* (New York: Harper and Brothers, 1944), I: 4, 8.

5. Samuel P. Huntington, *American Politics: The Politics of Disharmony* (Cambridge, MA: Harvard University Press, 1981), 14–15; Seymour Martin Lipset, *American Exceptionalism: A Double-Edged Sword* (New York: Norton, 1996), 19.

6. Greenstein, *Children and Politics*, 12.

7. Lawrence R. Jacobs, Fay Lomax Cook and Michael X. Delli Carpini, *Talking Together: Public Deliberation and Public Participation in America* (Chicago: University of Chicago Press, 2009).

8. Jeffrey M. Berry and Sarah Sobieraj, *The Outrage Industry: Political Opinion Media and the New Incivility* (New York: Oxford University Press, 2014).

9. Frank J. Sorauf, *Party Politics in America*, 2nd ed. (Boston, MA: Little, Brown, 1972), 144. See also M. Kent Jennings and Richard G. Niemi, *Generations and Politics: A Panel Study of Young Adults and Their Parents* (Princeton, NJ:

Princeton University Press, 1981), especially chapter 4. More recently, see M. Kent Jennings, Laura Stoker, and Jake Bowers, "Politics across Generations: Family Transmission Reexamined," *Journal of Politics*, vol. 71, No. 3, July 2009, 782–799.

10. Robert S. Erikson and Kent L. Tedin, *American Public Opinion*, 9th ed. (New York: Longman, 2015), 135.

11. Erikson and Tedin. *American Public Opinion*, 123–125.

12. Jan E. Leighley and Jonathan Nagler, *Who Votes Now? Demographics, Issues, Inequality and Turnout in the United States* (Princeton, NJ: Princeton University Press, 2014), 128, 135. Michele Lamont and Mario Small, *Culture and Inequality* (New York: W.W. Norton, 2008).

13. Deborah J. Schildkraut, "Defining American Identity in the Twenty-First Century: How Much 'There' Is There?" *Journal of Politics*, vol. 69, no. 3 (August 2007): 597–615.

14. Amy Fried, *Pathways to Polling: Crisis, Cooperation, and the Making of Public Opinion Professions* (New York: Routledge, 2012), 9, 30.

15. Fried, *Pathways to Polling*, 89–97.

16. Erikson and Tedin, *American Public Opinion*, 28–30.

17. Jack Rosenthal, "Precisely False vs. Approximately False: A Reader's Guide to Polls," *New York Times*, August 7, 2006, Wk 10.

18. Nate Silver, "Spin and Bias Are the Norm in Campaigns' Internal Polling," *New York Times*, December 3, 2012, A17.

19. Cliff Zukin, "What's the Matter with Polling," *New York Times*, June 21, 2015, SR3.

20. F. Chris Garcia and Gabriel R. Sanchez, *Hispanics and the U.S. Political System: Moving into the Mainstream* (Upper Saddle River, NJ: Pearson, 2008), 107.

21. Theodore J. Davis, Jr., *Black Politics Today: The Era of Socioeconomic Transition* (New York: Routledge, 2012), 35, 40, 72. See also Andrew Romano and Allison Samuels, "Is Obama Making It Worse," *Newsweek*, April 16, 2012, 40–42.

22. Jesse Holland, "Most Whites Back Police Hitting," *Associated Press*, April 14, 2015.

23. Garcia and Sanchez, *Hispanics and the U.S. Political System*, 104–106.

24. Mark Hugo Lopez, Rich Morin, and Paul Taylor, "Illegal Immigration Backlash Worries, Divides Latinos," Pew Hispanic Center, October 28, 2010.

25. Simon Romero and Janet Elder, "Hispanics Optimistic About Life, Poll Finds," *Dallas Morning News*, March 6, 2003, 9A. Adam Nagourney and Janet Elder, "Hispanics Back Big Government and Bush, Too," *New York Times*, August 3, 2003, Yt 1, 14.

26. See the 2008 National Asian-American Survey at http://www.naasurvey.com. See also Zoltan L. Hajnal and Taeku Lee, *Why Americans Don't Join the Party: Race, Immigration and the Failure (of Political Parties) to Engage the Electorate* (Princeton, NJ: Princeton University Press, 2011), 151, 168.

27. Adam J. Berinsky, *In Time of War: Understanding American Public Opinion from World War II to Iraq* (Chicago: University of Chicago Press, 2009).

28. Pew Research Center for the People and the Press and the Council on Foreign Relations, Calendar and Correspondence, December 2001, 14. New York Times/CBS News poll, *New York Times*, February 23, 2003, Wk 5.

29. CNN/ORC Poll, October 28, 2011, Question 15 at http://iz.cdn.turner.com/cnn/2011/images/10/28/rel17h.pdf.

30. James A. Stimson, *Tides of Consent: How Opinion Movements Shape American Politics* (New York: Cambridge University Press, 2004).

31. Erikson and Tedin, *American Public Opinion*, 58–59.

32. Marcus Prior and Arthur Lupia, "Money, Time, and Political Knowledge," *American Journal of Political Science*, vol. 52, no. 1 (January 2008): 169–183.

33. Erikson and Tedin, *American Public Opinion*, 59.

34. James M. Prothro and Charles M. Grigg, "Fundamental Principles of Democracy: Bases of Agreement and Disagreement," *Journal of Politics*, vol. 22, no. 2 (May 1960): 276–294.

35. Darren Davis and Brian Silver, "Civil Liberties versus Security," *American Journal of Political Science*, 48: 47–61.

36. Richard J. Niemi, John Mueller, and Tom W. Smith, *Trends in Public Opinion: A Compendium of Survey Data* (New York: Greenwood Press, 1989), 22–23, 180.

37. The Gallup Organization, "In U.S. Socialist Presidential Candidates Least Appealing," June 22, 2015.

38. Ibid.

39. http:www.pollingreport.com/abortion.htm. See also the poll archive at http:// www.youdebate.com/abortion.htm.

40. Erikson and Tedin, *American Public Opinion*, 42.

41. John R. Zaller, *The Nature and Origins of Mass Opinion* (New York: Cambridge University Press, 1992).

42. Philip E. Converse, "The Nature of Belief Systems in Mass Publics," in David E. Apter, ed., *Ideology and Discontent* (New York: Free Press, 1964), 215–218.

43. Michael S. Lewis-Beck, William G. Jacoby, Helmut Norpoth, and Herbert F. Weisberg, *The American Voter Revisited* (Ann Arbor, MI: University of Michigan Press, 2008), 241–247, 258–291.

44. Tom Raum, "Study: We Talk of Austerity, Want New Spending," *Dallas Morning News*, March 9, 2013, A11.

45. Christopher Ellis and James A. Stimson, *Ideology in America* (New York: Cambridge University Press, 2012). See also Robert S. Erikson, Michael B. Mackuen, and James A. Stimson, *The Macro Polity* (New York: Cambridge University Press, 2002), 223–230.

46. William S. Maddox and Stuart A. Lilie, *Beyond Liberal and Conservative: Reassessing the Political Spectrum* (Washington, D.C.: Cato Institute, 1984), 59.

CHAPTER 13

Interest Groups

KEY TERMS

Lobbying

Soft Money

Indirect Techniques of Interest Group Lobbying

Elite

Political Action Committees

Citizens United Case

Pluralists

DISCUSSION QUESTIONS

1. Discuss the role of interest groups in a republican form of government.

2. Compare and contrast the direct versus indirect tactics that interest groups use to influence decision makers and the public.

3. Compare and contrast the pluralist and elite perspectives of interest groups.

DEFINITION OF INTEREST GROUPS

Interest groups are composed of individuals who organize collectively to advance particular goals. They share common objectives and actively attempt to influence policy makers using both direct and indirect methods.

Interest groups can vary in size, characteristics, and organization. They can be based on ethnicity, racial, religious, occupational, economic, or social and political issues. Certain groups are much easier to organize; they tend to have a disproportionate amount of power than their numbers warrant. Government policy is thus biased in favor of producers and the affluent and educated.

LOBBYING

Lobbying is the attempt by organizations or individuals to influence the passage, defeat, or contents of legislation and administrative decisions. This can be done through a variety of venues.

Private Meetings

Private meetings are held with elected officials as well as members of their staffs. They can also include meeting with bureaucrats.

Testifying Before Congressional Committees

Providing congressional testimony is usually done publicly unless it involves national security. Members of interest groups convey information to committees. This usually involves narrow policy issues. This action is part of the interaction between interest groups and elected officials in subgovernments/iron triangles.

Testifying Before Segments of the Bureaucracy
Testifying before the bureaucracy includes assisting in the drafting of legislation and providing legal advice.

This is especially important at the state and local levels, as most elected officials are part-time positions and have a limited number of staff members if any at all.

Running Social Occasions
Social gathering can include dinners, receptions, and events. These occasions allow lobbyists to interact with officials in a relaxed setting.

Furnishing Political Information to Legislators
Information can include polling data and other types of electoral support.

INDIRECT TECHNIQUES OF INTEREST GROUP LOBBYING

Generating Public Pressure
Generating public pressure involves using the media to shape public opinion. Interest groups often take out ads and members appear in the media to shape public opinion.

Using Constituents as Lobbyists
Using constituents in lobbying efforts can be effective if interest groups can get their members to meet with their representatives. This makes an impression on elected officials when voters they know are supporting a particular group and its goals.

Building Alliances with Other Interest Groups
Interest groups can pool resources and consolidate efforts if they have the same goals, although they may have different reasons for supporting these goals.

OTHER TYPES OF SUPPORT

Ratings
Interest groups often provide ratings to elected officials based on their voting behavior on the issues the groups are interested in. For example, the National Rifle Association rates legislators at the federal and state levels. This gives voters an indication of how to vote. Also, elected officials use ratings in their election media to promote themselves to various groups.

Interest Groups
Interests groups also provide campaign assistance to elected officials. This can include financial support through direct contributions to a candidate. They can encourage their members to contribute as individuals, and they can also campaign independently for candidates they favor. The latter tactic insulates the candidate from any negative or controversial advertisements interests groups may run. In addition, interest groups can provide volunteers to work on campaigns. In many big cities, getting the support of municipal unions is very important. Police, firefighter, and teacher unions are very good about turning out for candidates when their union leaders ask them to.

Importance of Political Action Committees
Political action committees are groups organized to raise campaign funds in support of or in opposition to specific candidates.

Soft Money
Soft money is funds donated to national parties that do not have to be reported to the Federal Election Commission as long as the funds do not benefit an individual candidate.

Citizens United Case 2010
The ruling in the **Citizens United case** stated that corporate campaign spending cannot be limited under the First Amendment. This gives corporations and unions the ability to contribute unlimited funds to candidates.

INTEREST GROUPS AND A REPUBLICAN DEMOCRACY

Pluralists
Pluralists argue that interest groups are the building blocks of democracy. People learn about politics by participating in interest groups. Often, elected officials started in politics because of their concern regarding a particular economic, political, or social issue. They acted politically on the issue and that drew them into, eventually, running for office. People learn about politics through their participation in an interest group.

Elite Theorists
Elite theorists argue that there is an upper-class bias of interest groups. Only those who are educated and have a certain socioeconomic status have the time to participate in interest groups. They also possess the knowledge to navigate the political system. They argue that all interest groups are composed of and benefit the wealthy.

MEASURING INTEREST GROUP ACTIVITY
Silke Friedrich*

Introduction

Special interest groups play an important role in the political systems of the developed world. Repeated accounts of this can be found in economics and political science literature, and also among journalists and policy makers. But measuring the influence of interest groups is both important and challenging.

There is little consensus among social scientists about the appropriate definition of "special interest group". Some authors use the term broadly for

* Ifo Institute for Economic Research at the University of Munich.

Silke Friedrich, "Measuring Interest Group Activity," DICE Report, vol. 8, no. 4, pp. 37–46. Copyright © 2010 by Ifo Institute. Reprinted with permission. Provided by ProQuest LLC. All rights reserved.

any subset of voters who have similar socio-demographic characteristics, or similar beliefs, interests and policy preferences.[1] Others define special interest groups as organizations that engage in political activities on behalf of their members. In the following we will focus on studies that employ the more narrow definition.

In order to analyze the influence of special interest groups on public policy making, measures of interest group influence have to be determined. This has shown to be a complicated task because there are at least three distinct problems: the existence of different channels of influence, the occurrence of counteractive lobbying and the fact that influence can be wielded at different stages of the policy process. The most basic challenge is to find measures that address the different channels of influence. This is crucial to be able to address the impact of different lobbying tactics on policy outcomes.

In order to promote their political objective, special interest groups engage in a variety of activities, which is why there is extensive theoretical literature on different channels of special interest group influence. Grossman and Helpman (2001), for example, give an overview of models that explain the effectiveness of special interest group tactics. They describe two main channels of influence of special interest groups, the dissemination of information and campaign contributions.

Interest groups inform policy makers, the public and their members. The reason for the dissemination of information is simply to inform and persuade policy makers of the wisdom of the groups' position. Special interest groups can be an important source of information for politicians because they are already familiar with the subject they are promoting and are willing to undertake research in the area. According to findings of extensive surveys conducted among interest groups in the US on the federal level, special interest groups spend a majority of their resources on informing policy makers.[2]

The other main tactic of special interest groups mentioned by Grossman and Helpman (2001), which may be unrelated to the groups' access to information, is the provision of resources to candidates and parties. Campaign contributions can buy access, credibility or simply influence for special interest groups. Of all forms of special interest activity, campaign contributions are the most broadly analyzed lobbying tactic.

While the theoretical approach to assessing interest group influence is essential to determine the mechanisms and channels used to exert influence, the evidence from surveys is very helpful to analyze the actions taken by special interest groups. But in order to analyze the influence of special interest groups on public policy making, measurable determinants of interest group influence are necessary. A first step in this direction is to register lobbying activity. The purpose of this study is to analyze the status quo of lobbying registration in the US and in Europe and to show how this data has been used to find measurable determinants of interest group activity.

Lobbying in The US

Registration of Lobbying

Data on all lobbying establishments in the US are available for recent years, i.e., since the Lobbying Disclosure Act of 1995 (LDA). The LDA requires organizations to register and report information on their special interest activities to the Senate Office of Public Records (SOPR) every six months. According to the Act, a lobbyist is any individual who (1) receives compensation of USD 5,000 or more per six-month period, or makes expenditures of USD 20,000 or more per six-month period for lobbying, (2) who makes more than one lobbying contact, and (3) who spends 20 percent or more of his or her time over a six-month period on lobbying activities for an organization or a particular client. According to this definition, two types of registrants are obliged

---

1   See for example Putnam (1994).

2   For surveys conducted, see, for instance, Baumgarner et al. (2009); Nownes and Freeman (1998); Heinz et al. (1993); Schlozman and Tierney (1986).

to report under the LDA, lobbying firms and organizations or firms that conduct in-house lobbying activities (self-filing organizations).[3] Lobbying firms are private firms who take on work for a number of different corporate and non-corporate clients. They have to declare their lobbying revenue. Self-filing organizations declare (a good faith estimate) of their spending on in-house lobbying efforts.

The following three figures summarize the information on lobbying activity in the US that is available as a result of the LDA.[4] The data for these figures is drawn from the Center for Responsive Politics (CRP), a Washington based non-profit organization for the promotion of political transparency.[5] Figure 13.1 shows how many registered businesses, labor unions and other organizations have lobbied the US Congress and federal agencies between 1998 and 2008. While the number of active lobbyists has increased only slightly during the last decade, Figure 13.2 shows that the lobbying expenditures in the US have more than doubled during that time. This increase in spending on lobbying has not been driven by a particular

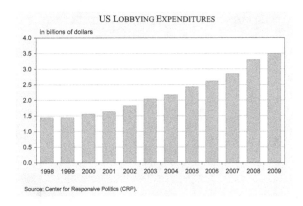

FIGURE 13.2

industry, as shown in Figure 13.3. This figure also highlights which sectors have spent most on lobbying during the last decade: the health sector, followed by the business sector and finance, insurance and real estate.

Contributions from Political Action Committees

Besides spending resources on informing policy makers, interest groups can give contributions to campaigns. There are two main types of campaign contributions, individual contributions and contributions by Political Action Committees (PACs). Since individual contributions are made by American citizens, and not by organized groups, we focus on PAC contributions here.[6] PACs are political committees organized for the purpose of raising and spending money to elect and defeat candidates. Most PACs represent business, labor or ideological interests. PACs can give USD 5,000 to a candidate committee per election (primary, general or special). They can also give up to USD 15,000 annually to any national party

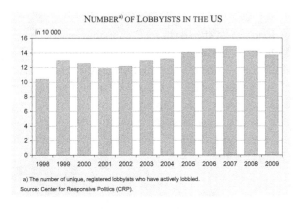

FIGURE 13.1

---

3   An example of a private lobby firm is Van Scoyoc Associates, who represent some of the largest corporations, as well as many universities, non-profit organizations and trade associations in Washington. Self-filing organizations include corporations such as Wal-Mart, who have their own lobby shop in Washington, as well as peak industry groups such as the American Medical Association.

4   The figures summarize lobbying activity on the federal level. Each US state has individual rules for monitoring and/or restricting lobbying activities.

5   http://www.opensecrets.org/(accessed November 2010).

6   It is important to note that individual contributions constitute a large share of campaign contributions and are essential to analyze the impact of such contributions on election outcomes. See Stratmann (2005). Data on individual contributions to campaign can be found at the Federal Election Commission (accessed October 2010).

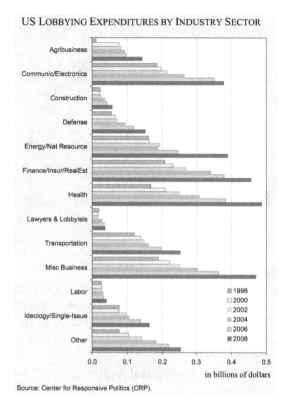

FIGURE 13.3

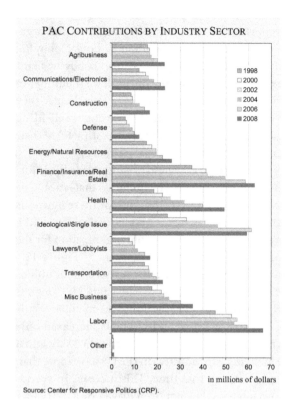

FIGURE 13.5

committee and USD 5,000 annually to any other PAC. PACs may receive up to USD 5,000 from any one individual, PAC or party committee per calendar year.

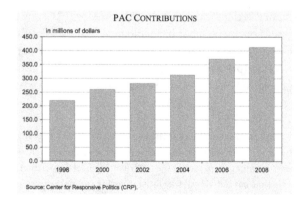

FIGURE 13.4

Figure 13.4 shows the PAC contributions between 1998 and 2008 as reported by CRP. Comparing the PAC contribution with the lobbying expenditures above shows that a fraction of resources spent by special interest groups is spent on PAC contributions. But the same sectors that have the highest lobbying expenditures spend most on PAC contributions (Figure 13.5).

Empirical Evidence of Interest Group Influence in The US

In general, studies that incorporate interest group activities other than donating to campaigns are rare. Moreover, there is limited empirical work linking the theory to the data.[7] The few studies that assess such influence generally estimate an equation in which the dependent variable represents a decision variable of the public sector which the interest group

---

7 See Potters and Sloof (1995) or de Figueiredo (2009) for summaries of the existing literature.

is hypothesized to influence. Roughly, two sets of dependent variables can be distinguished. One set concerns the behavior of individual political decision makers (i.e., voting records). The second set relates to policy outcomes. The LDA data has been used to analyze how much firms lobby and how they lobby.[8] Furthermore, the data has been used to quantify the effect of lobbying activities on policy outcomes in specific industries.[9]

Evidence from survey data show that a main value for lobbyists is their proximity to policy makers.[10] One important way to establish personal connections between lobbyists and politicians is to employ ex-government staffers in the industry or in lobbying firms, the so-called "revolving door" movement. Lobbying salaries are typical several times higher than public sector salaries, which suggests that there is the opportunity for former officials to cash in on their government connections. While there is a lot of anecdotal evidence of this practice, direct empirical evidence on the extent to which previous officials are able to convert political contacts in to lobbying revenue is scarce.[11] Blanes i Vidal et al. (2010) conducted one of the few studies that is able to quantify the value of direct connections between lobbyists and politicians. They analyze the relationship between previous government officials and the Congressional politician in whose office they had previously worked. The authors use data on the lobbying revenues of these ex-staffers and show how these revenues change once their previous employer leaves the Senate.

The only form of lobbying activity that has been recorded rigorously for a long time are campaign contributions. Hence, it is not surprising that PAC contribution have been extensively analyzed. The main question concerning PACs is a very sensitive one: What exactly do they buy? Stratmann (2005) surveys the existing literature on campaign contribution and summarizes different hypotheses about the purpose giving PACs. A main argument in the literature is that PACs buy influence. If this is the case, then incumbents who receive money from special interest groups cater to their wishes because they received campaign contributions. Many theoretical models predict that interest groups buy political favors with their contributions.[12] But the empirical evidence for this prediction appears mixed.[13] Other possible explanations for Political Action Committees to contribute to elections could be that, according to Stratmann (2005), special interest groups derive consumption value from PACs, or see them as investments in policy or as a means of gaining access to the legislator. But while it is relatively straightforward to examine the influence of PACs on election outcomes or policy choices, other hypotheses about the purpose of PACs are not as easily quantifiable.

Lobbying in Europe

Registration of Special Interest Groups

In the US, lobbying regulations, both in the form of registration and limitations, have been a matter of concern since World War II. In most European countries, special interest groups have been analyzed to a far lesser extent. Chari et al. (2010) give a comprehensive assessment of lobbying regulations around the globe. The term "regulations" for lobbyists, as it is used by Chari et al. (2010), means that political systems have established rules which lobby groups must follow when trying to influence government officials. The most basic rule is that lobbyists have to register with the state before contact is made with public officials. Other lobbying regulations that have been put into place are that special interest groups

---

8 See, for example, Schuler et al. (2002) and de Figueirdo and Kim (2004).

9 See, for example, Schuler (1996) for evidence from the US steel industry; Hedge and Mowery (2008) for evidence from the biomedial industry; and de Figueirdo and Silverman (2006) for lobbying in the education sector.

10 See, for example, Baumgartner et al. (2009).

11 See Dal Bo (2006) for a review on regulatory capture.

12 See, for example, Grossman and Helpman (2001).

13 See Stratmann (2005) for details.

TABLE 13.1   Lobbying Regulations in EU Countries and in EU Institutions

Country/Institution	Rules governing lobbyists as of 2009
Austria	No statutory rules
Belgium	No statutory rules
Denmark	No statutory rules
Estonia	No statutory rules
France	Indicated its aim to introduce a voluntary parliamentary run register—July 2009.
Germany	Regulation and registration through rules of procedure introduced by the Bundestag in 1951; later amended in 1975 and 1980.
Hungary	Regulation of lobbying activity since 2006.
Latvia	No statutory rules
Lithuania	Regulation since 2001.
Luxembourg	No statutory rules
Ireland	No statutory rules
Italy	No statutory rules at national level. Nevertheless, regional schemes have been introduced in the Consiglio regionale della Toscana in 2002 and Regione in 2004.
Malta	No statutory rules
Netherlands	No statutory rules
Poland	Regulations since 2005
Portugal	No statutory rules
Romania	No statutory rules
Slovakia	No statutory rules
Slovenia	No statutory rules
Spain	No statutory rules
Sweden	No statutory rules
United Kingdom	No statutory rules in either Commons or House of Lords.
EU: European Parliament	Regulated by Rule 9(2) of the Rules of Procedure, 1996.
EU: Commission	Before 2008, "self-regulation" was the model adopted by the Commission. However, as of 23 June, 2008, the Commission opened a *voluntary* register of interest representations.
EU: Council	No statutory rules

Source: Chari et al. (2010).

have to indicate which public actors they intend to influence, that they provide the state with individual/employer spending records or that there has to be a publicly available list with lobbyists. Another registration criterion is if revolving door practices are openly monitored.

Chari et al. (2010) show that lobbying regulations are relatively rare in liberal democracies and that the norm in most countries is that there are no lobbying rules. See Table 13.1 for an overview of lobbying regulations in the EU and in the US. In the EU, Germany is the only country with a long history of lobbying regulations (since 1951). In Italy, lobbying regulations exist at the regional level. Hungary, Poland and Lithuania have adopted special interest regulations after 2000.

Contributions to Political Parties and Campaigns

As in the US, campaign contributions are another way for special interest groups to influence public policy in European countries. Many governments regulate from where and how much funding candidates or parties can obtain from private organizations. The regulations concerning the disclosure of campaign contributions also differ from country to country.

Table 13.2 presents data from the CESifo Database for Institutional Comparisons in Europe (DICE) on Financing of Political Parties. The Table gives a summary of the political structure of the countries and the institutional framework in which campaign finance takes place, as well as laws limiting contributions and disclosure requirements. This summary shows that most countries have limitations to campaign contributions (with the exception of Austria, Sweden and the Netherlands). Additionally the source of campaign contributions has to be disclosed in all countries except in the Netherlands. But there is no reliable data source on campaign contributions in any of the countries mentioned in Table 13.2.[14]

Registration of Lobbying in the European Union

Besides the obvious lack of data on lobbying activity in European countries, there is another issue that makes the analysis of the influence of special interest groups within European countries almost impossible: the Europeanization of interest group activity.

Today, many laws and regulations concerning European Union (EU) member countries originate in Brussels. Töller (2010) estimates that 40 to 80 percent of German laws passed between 2002 and 2005 are at least influenced by European impulse.[15] With this shift in political power from national governments to EU institutions, one would expect interest groups to change their focus of attention towards Brussels. In the words of Mazey and Richardson (2006), one would expect interest groups to "shoot where the ducks are". This is why Coen describes this shift in interest group attention as the "Europeanization of interest groups".[16] The groups active in EU politics represent a large variety of interests, from countries within and outside of Europe. Hence, in order to measure the influence of lobby groups on political economic decision making processes in the EU countries as well as in Europe as a whole, it is important to understand the impact of special interest groups on decisions made in Brussels.

In contrast to the US, EU scholars have not had access to a single, systematic source of data on lobbying activities in the form of lobbying registration. Furthermore, the current absence of a comprehensive registration system in the EU makes it impossible to identify the universe of the lobbying community in Brussels. Available data on EU lobbying activities come from the European Parliament, the EU Commission and from Landmarks' commercial register.

In 1996, the European Parliament (EP) adopted a mandatory system of lobbyist registration. The EP accreditation registers all groups and their representatives that obtained the EP's special entry pass, which is needed for lobbyists to access the EP building and to interact with members of the EP. But the only information available from the interest groups active in the EP is the name of the organization.

In 2008, the European commission adopted a voluntary system of lobbyist registration which was initiated by the European Transparency Initiative. As a result, the CONECCS database (Consultation, European Commission and Civil Society) was replaced with the new Register of Interest Representatives.

---

14   A caveat of the data presented in Table 13.2 is that it relates mainly to the year 2000. Hence, even though the main regulations have remained in place, the data collection process might have changed since then.

15   Töller (2010) finds that the degree of Brussel's influence on German laws varies across fields and that 40 percent of the new laws in the fields of economics and transportation are at least influenced by decisions made in Brussels. These shares are higher in finance (42.6 percent), justice (42.2 percent), family and health (42.3 percent), agriculture (75 percent) and environmental policy (81.3 percent).

16   Coen (2007) talks about "the Europeanization of interest groups".

TABLE 13.2   Contributions to Political Parties

	Restrictions	Transparency
Austria	No limits on individual or corporate donations. No limits on expenditure. Political donations by interest groups are subject to an income tax surcharge to be paid by the recipient party. Donations in excess of EUR 7,730 must be disclosed (total amounts and type of donor, i.e., individual, interest group, corporation).	States do not require strict reporting and data provided by parties on the federal level thought to be incomprehensive for it covers only part of the parties' activities and financial dimensions.
France	No foreign donations. No donations from private or public-sector companies (since 1995). Individual donations may not exceed ca. EUR 7,575 per year and donations of more than ca. EUR 150 must be given by cheque, thereby disclosing the identity of the donor.	Legal status of parties is vague; data protected and not released to the public due to the constitutional freedom of action granted to parties. Available reports are incomplete: expenses for local activities are not detailed and links between parties and foundations remain unclear. Poor level of supervision by regulating authorities.
Germany	No limits on individual or corporate donations. Ban on tax benefits for corporate donors imposed by the Federal Constitutional Court. Donations in excess of ca. EUR 10,300 must be disclosed (names, addresses, and amounts). Ban of foreign donations except from EU citizens and EU corporations. No donations in excess of EUR 500 from anonymous individuals.	Reports and lists of donors are published in parliament material (Bundestagsdrucksache). Reports have a common format and are well documented. The total revenue of assessments remains unclear. For detailed info and statistics see: http://www.bundestag.de/datbk/finanz/ index.html; http://www2.spd.de/partei/finanzen/ausw_rechenschaftsbericht9 9.pdf
Italy	No limits on individual or corporate donations for routine activities (donations to candidates are limited to EUR 8,700). Donations by privately run businessses must be approved by its board of directors and disclosed in the company's annual report. No donations from public or semi-public entities. Donations in excess of ca. EUR 2,640 must be disclosed by party and donor.	Reports are published in *Gazzetta Ufficiale*, the official publication for laws and decrees. Reports contain few details: donors are not disclosed and income is only in itemized total amounts of money (i.e. membership fees, donations and public subsidies). Political routine has often not followed disclosure rules.
Netherlands		No common format for financial reports. "Dutch legislators are still rather inexperienced with regulation on the transparency of political finance." Nassmacher (IDEA Handbook).

Portugal	No donations from public or semi-public entities or from foreign governments and institutions. Private corporate donations limited to 1,000 monthly minimum wages, with a limit of 100 monthly wages per contributor. Private individual donations limited to 30 monthly minimum wages per contributor; annual total may not exceed 500 monthly minimum wages. Donations in excess of 10 times the monthly wage must be made by cheque, thereby disclosing the identity of the donor.	Reports are published in *Diario da Republica*. Unreliable data; although provided with account information, the Tribunal Constitucional has no authority to verify or investigate financial statements and transactions.
Spain	No donations from public or semi-public entities or from foreign governments and institutions. No limit on total amount of income from private donations (the total of anonymous donations may not exceed 5% of total income); private donations must be disclosed (name, address, and ID number). Private individual donations limited to ca. EUR 60,120 per year (est. 1987).	Reports are published in *Boletin Oficial del Estado*. Unreliable data; although provided with account information, the Tribunal de Cuentas has no authority to verify or investigate financial statements and transactions. In addition, disclosure is not strictly regulated or enforced: in recent years, accounts have gone unpublished.
Sweden	No formal limits on individual or corporate donations. No limits or regulation on expenditure or on the use of public subsidies. Although corporate donations are permitted and parties are not obliged to disclose information about donors, parties have voluntarily agreed not to accept corporate donations and to disclose donations from private organizations (amount and name). Under the agreement, individual donations are also disclosed, but only total income and number of donors must be reported.	No officially published reports; data on income and spending protected by a traditional privilege of privacy and different bookkeeping systems by the parties. Only data concerning public subsidies is reliable.
United Kingdom	No foreign donations. Limits on expenditure. No paid broadcast advertising. Donations in excess of EUR 8,210 (GBP 5,000) must be disclosed. No donations in excess of GBP from anonymous individuals or blind trusts.	
Note: This table is a condensed version of a table in the DICE Database: www.cesifo.de/DICE		

Main Source: Nassmacher (2001). Other sources consulted: Baran (2000) and Nassmacher (2003). The information relates mainly to 2000. Compilation: CESifo.

TABLE 13.3   Sources of the EU Interest Group Population Dataset 2007–2008

Dataset	Number of organizations
CONECCS	749
Landmarks directory[a)]	2,522
EP accreditation register	1,534
Total groups listed in any of the three sources	4,805
Minus duplicates	–1,105
Final Dataset	3,700

a) Landmarks' directory lists organizations in different categories (trade organizations, professional organizations, etc.). Some organizations are listed in more than one category. The figure 2,522 in the table refers to the number of unique organizations listed, after deleting duplicates.

Source: Baumgartner et al. (2010).

The former CONECCS database lists groups participating in commission committees or hearings on a voluntary basis. The aim of this database was to make the commission more transparent, to function as a venue for interest groups and to help the commission to find the appropriate mix of partners. The Register of Interest Representatives is continuing the data collection of CONECCS and requires additional information from the interest groups that choose to register. For example, in-house lobbyists who want to be listed in the register have to disclose their estimated lobbying expenditures per year in ranges of EUR 50,000, and lobbying firms have to disclose their annual income in ranges of EUR 50,000. Interest groups that choose to register also declare their compliance to an ethics code.

Another data source available to study interest group activity in the EU is Landmarks' European Public Affairs Directory. This is a commercial register of groups, firms, national and international institutions as well as regional actors active in EU politics in Brussels.

Berkhout and Lowery (2008) have compared these different datasets and found that there is surprisingly little overlap. Baumgartner et al. (2010) have

TABLE 13.4   Types of Organizations Registered to Lobby in the EU

Group Type	Frequency	Percent
1. Professional associations and interest groups	1,847	49.9
2. Corporations	492	13.3
3. Chamber of Commerce	36	1.0
4. Consultants	219	5.9
5. National employers' federations	58	1.6
6. International organizations	118	3.2
7. Law firms	124	3.4
8. National trade and professional organizations	252	6.8
9. Regions (incl. municipalities)	267	7.2
10. Think tanks and training	146	4.0
11. Labor unions	30	0.8
12. National associations of Chambers of Commerce	27	0.7
13. Political parties*	7	0.2
14. Other	7	0.2
Missing	70	1.9
Total	**3,700**	**100.1**

* Not a Landmarks' category.

Source: Baumgartner et al. (2010).

combined the data from CONECCS (now Register of Interest Representatives), the EP's accreditation register and Landmarks' European Public Affairs Directory. With the EU Interest Group Population Dataset 2007–2008, they have created the most inclusive and accurate list of lobbying organizations in the EU yet compiled.[17] But this new data set only lists lobbying organizations, without providing any information about the number of lobbyists working for each organization and without disclosing lobbying expenses of the organizations listed. Table 13.3 shows the size of the disaggregated data sets used by Baumgartner et al. (2010).

---

17   According to Baumgarner et al. (2010), the full dataset will be made freely available at http://sites.maxwell.syr.edu/ecpr/intereuro

It has been observed in earlier analyses of interest group populations in various national systems that professional associations and corporations, i.e., groups representing business interests, provide the largest share of groups mobilized for political action. Table 13.4 shows that the EU is no exception to this trend. The Table gives an overview of the type of organizations that are registered to lobby in the EU. 50 percent of the groups mobilized for political action are professional associations and interest groups. Combing the categories associated with business interests (e.g., all those except international organizations, regions, think tanks, political parties and other) shows that 82.5 percent of the lobbying organizations in the EU come from the business sector.

Analyzing the origins of the special interest groups active in the EU shows that representatives from large member states dominate the scene (Table 13.5). 43.7 percent of all registered special interest groups are based in Germany, France or the UK. The Benelux groups benefit from their geographical proximity to the EU capital Brussels. With 14.7 percent of all registered special interest groups in the EU, these countries are overrepresented given their relative size. Organizations from Eastern Europe so far seem hesitant to enter the Brussels scene. Only 4.5 percent of organizations registered to lobby in the EU are from new EU states.

Empirical Evidence of Special Interest Group Activity in Europe

Most economic studies that explain the impact of lobbying activities are based on evidence from the US. This is not surprising since the registration of lobbyists is most transparent in the US. But even in the US, empirical evidence on the impact of special interest groups on public policy is scarce.

In Europe, data on special interest group activity is simply non-existent in many countries. This explains why there is hardly any empirical evidence on the impact of special interest groups. Coen (2007) summarizes the empirical and theoretical studies on interest groups influence in the EU. He notes that there is an increasing amount of theoretical literature

TABLE 13.5   Country of Origin of Organizations Registered to Lobby in the EU

A. EU–15 states	Frequency	Percent
Germany	380	18.7
United Kingdom	285	14.0
France	274	13.4
Netherlands	150	7.4
Italy	139	6.8
Belgium	120	5.9
Spain	75	3.7
Austria	54	2.7
Sweden	41	2.0
Denmark	42	2.0
Finland	18	0.9
Portugal	15	0.7
Luxembourg	13	0.6
Ireland	13	0.6
Greece	5	0.3
B. New EU–27 states		
Poland	28	1.4
Czech Republic	16	0.8
Slovakia	12	0.6
Hungary	11	0.5
Romania	7	0.3
Latvia	4	0.2
Estonia	4	0.2
Lithuania	2	0.1
Slovenia	3	0.2
Cyprus	2	0.1
Malta	2	0.1
Bulgaria	2	0.1
C. Selected non–EU states		
USA	181	8.9
Switzerland	75	3.7

Note: The table lists the nation of origin for those organizations that report it. For non–EU states, we include only the two prominent home countries.

Source: Baumgartner et al. (2010).

explaining the Europeanization of interest groups. Most studies concerned with the impact of special interest groups tackle similar methodological and theoretical questions as their counterparts in the US.

However, Woll (2006) warns, for example, that before the replication of US models becomes the norm in Europe, it is important to investigate how applicable these concepts are to the EU public policy process and distinct EU institutions as well as to the national political systems in Europe. And while recognizing that Europeanization has occurred, it must not be forgotten that not all interest groups make use of the new EU opportunities and distinct national interest groups remain.[18]

The Challenge

Measuring the influence of interest groups is both important and challenging. Dür (2008) quotes Loomis (1983), who describes the attempt of measuring lobbying activity as "searching for a black cat in the coal bin at midnight". Baumgartner and Leech (1998) describe research on special interest groups as an area of "confusion" in the literature.

In order to assess the impact of interest groups it is crucial to know who exerts influence. As this study shows this in itself is a major challenge, since lobbying regulations are non-existent in many European countries.

Hence, a first step towards being able to measure the influence of special interest groups in Europe would be to register lobbyists and disclose their expenditures related to lobbying activities. In the EU, the EU Interest Group Population Dataset 2007–2008 is a first step in this direction. So is the European Transparency Initiative (EIT), which obtained the disclosure of lobbying expenditures for the interest groups who voluntarily register as lobbyists at the European Commission. But while registering lobbying activities at the EU level is important, it does not replace the need for lobbying regulations in the EU countries.

The disclosure of contributions to political parties and campaigns would be another important step towards more transparency of interest groups activities in Europe. Such data is available in most EU countries. But there is no equivalent to the US organizations – the Center for Responsive Politics or the Federal Election Commission – to publish the available records on campaign contributions.

In the literature concerned with the influence of special interest groups, the practice of revolving door lobbying is getting more and more attention. This practice is widespread in European countries and in the EU. Hence, the disclosure of former politicians who move on to the private sector would be necessary to address the impact of this practice.

The most elaborate analysis of interest group influence has been conducted in the US. One reason for this is certainly a political environment that makes it necessary to investigate who pulls which strings in politics.[19] Another reason is the availability of data.

But even in the US, empirical determinants of special interest group influence are scarce. The problems are that there are not only different channels of influence. Interest groups also affect each other, which has to be taken into account when measuring their impact on public policy. Furthermore, interest group influence can be wielded at different stages of the policy process and depends crucially on the political environment the interest group operates in.

But the recent changes in the rules on lobbying registration in the developed world are a step in the right direction. Even though the question of interest group influence is difficult to analyze, not only because of a lack of data, but also because of the many facets of the issue, it is too important to ignore.

References

Baumgartner F. R., J. Berkhout, C. Mahoney and A. Wonka (2010), "Measuring the Size and Scope of the EU Interest Group Population", *European Union Politics* 11(3), 463–76.

Baumgartner, F. R., J. M. Berry, M. Hojnacki, D. C. Kimball and B. L. Leech (2009), *Lobbying and Policy Change, Who wins, who looses, and why*, The University of Chicago Press, Chicago.

Baumgartner, F. R. and B. L. Leech (1998), *Basic Interests: The Importance of Groups in Politics and in Political Science*, Princeton University Press, Princeton.

---

18   See Beyers and Kerremans (2007).

19   Bertok (2009), for example, examines how lobbying regulations depend on political regimes.

Berkhout, J. and D. Lowery (2008), "Counting Organized Interests in the European Union: A Comparison of Data Sources", *Journal of European Public Policy* 15(4), 489–513.

Bertok, J. (2009), "Lobbyists, Government and Public Trust: Promoting Integrity by Self-regulation", *OECD Working Paper* GOV/PGC 9.

Beyers, J. and B. Kerrmanns (2007), "Critical Resource Dependencies and the Europeanization of Domestic Interest Groups", *Journal of European Public Policy* 14(3), 460–81.

Blanes I Vidal, J., M. Draca and C. Fons-Rosen (2010), "Revolving Door Lobbyists", *CEP Discussion Paper 993*, London School of Economics.

Baran, J.W. (2000), "Political Parties and Spending Limits", *Harvard Journal of Law and Public Policy* 24(1), 83–90.

Chari, R., J. Hogan and G. Murphy (2010), *Regulating Lobbying: A Global Comparison*, European Policy Research Unit Series, Manchester University Press, Manchester.

Coen, D. (2007), "Empirical and Theoretical Studies in EU Lobbying", *Journal of European Public Policy* 14(3), 333–45.

Dal Bo, E. (2006), "Regulatory Capture: A Review", *Oxford Review of Economic Policy* 22(2), 203–25.

de Figueiredo, J. M. (2009), "Integrated Political Strategy", *NBER Working Paper* 15053.

de Figueiredo, J. M. and B. S. Silverman (2006), "Academic Earmarks and the Returns to Lobbying", *Journal of Law and Economics* 49(2), 597–626.

de Figueiredo, J. M. and J. K. Kim (2004), "When Do Firms Hire Lobbyists? The Organization of Lobbying at the Federal Communications Commission", *Industrial and Corporate Change* 13(6), 883–900.

Dür, T. (2008), "How much Influence Do Interest Groups Have in the EU? Some Methodological Considerations", in B. Kohler-Koch, D. De Bièvre and W. Maloney, eds., *Opening EU Governance to Civil Society – Gains and Challenges*, CONNEX Report Series, vol. 5, 45–67.

Grossman, G.M. and E. Helpman (2001), *Special Interest Politics*, The MIT Press, Cambridge, Mass.

Hedge, D. and D. Mowery (2008), "Politics and Funding in the U.S. Biomedical Research System", *Science* 322(19), 1797–98.

Heinz, J. P., E. O. Lauman, R. L. Neelson and R. H. Salisbury (1993), *The Hollow Core: Private Interests in National Policymaking*, Harvard University Press, Cambridge, Mass.

Loomis, B. A. (1983), "A New Era: Groups and the Grassroutes", in A. J. Cigler and B.A. Loomis, eds., *Interest Group Politics*, CQ Press, Washington, 169–190.

Mazey, S. and J. Richardson (2006), "Interest Groups in the EU Policy-making: Organizational Logic and Venue Shopping", in J. Richardson, ed., *European Union: Power and Policy Making*, Routledge, London and New York, 247–65.

Nassmacher, K.-H., ed. (2001), *Foundations for Democracy*, Nomos Verlagsgesellschaft, Baden-Baden.

Nassmacher, K.-H. (2003), *International IDEA Handbook on Funding Parties and Election Campaigns*, Stockholm.

Nownes, A. J. and P. Freeman (1998), "Interest Activity in the States", *Journal of Politics* 60, 86-112.

Potters, J. and R. Sloof (1996), "Interest Groups: A Survey of Empirical Models that Try to Assess their Influence", *European Journal of Political Economy* 12, 403-442.

Putnam, R. D. (1994), *Making Democracy Work – Civic Transitions in Modern Italy*, Princeton University Press, Princeton.

Schlozman, K. L. and J. T. Thierney (1986), *Organized Interests and American Democracy*, Harper and Row, New York.

Schuler, D., K. Rehbein and R. Cramer (2002), "Pursuing Strategic Advantage through Political Means", *Academy of Management Journal* 45, 659-672.

Schuler, D. (1996), "Corporate Political Strategy and Foreign Competition: The Case of the Steel Industry", *Academy of Management Journal* 39, 720-737.

Stratman, T. (2005), "Some Talk; Money in Politics. A (Partial) Review of the Literature", *Public Choice* 124, 135-156.

Töller, A.E. (2010), "Measuring and Comparing the Europeanization of Public Policies", *Journal of Common Market Studies* 48(1), 413-440.

Woll, C. (2006), "Lobbying in the European Union. From sui generis to a Comparative Perspective", *Journal of European Public Policy* 13(3), 456-469.

CHAPTER 14

Political Parties and Elections

KEY TERMS

Functions of Political Parties
Dominant Party System
Multiparty System
Broker Party
Cadre Party
Winner-Take-All Electoral System
Single Transferable Vote

One-Party System
Two-Party System
Doctrinaire/Ideological Party
Revolutionary Party
Mass Party
Proportional Representation

DISCUSSION QUESTIONS

1. Address four functions of political parties.

2. Discuss the difference between political parties and interest groups.

3. Contrast a doctrinaire/ideological party with a broker party.

4. Contrast a winner-take-all electoral system verses a proportional representation electoral system.

5. What is a single transferable vote electoral system? Does it promote fairer, more accurate electoral outcomes?

THE BIRTH OF POLITICAL PARTIES

Political parties arose in response to demands of the working- and middle-class movements. A political party is any group, however loosely organized, seeking to elect government officeholders under a given label.

During the early years of the United States, political parties were viewed as fostering division. Many political scientists view political parties as being essential to the development of democracy.

Organized political parties developed in the late eighteenth and nineteenth centuries as the voting franchise was extended from just property owners to working-class white males.

POLITICAL PARTIES SERVE A NUMBER OF FUNCTIONS IN THE POLITICAL SYSTEM

- Political socialization: The process of educating people about politics.
- Recruitment/citizen participation: Getting people to participate in political events and encouraging them to vote.

- Recruitment of elites: Parties want to field attractive candidates so they attempt to recruit people who are respected and who others look to for leadership.
- Communication: Parties provide an avenue for political leaders to communicate with the electorate.
- Interest articulation: Interest groups and citizens turn to political parties to voice their demands.
- Interest aggregation, prioritization of demands: Political parties, in trying to craft their party platforms, sort through these various demands and adopt them as goals should they win election.
- Policy making: Political parties propose new policies or change policies already in existence as part of their campaign strategy.
- Policy Implementation: Once political parties are successful and their candidates are elected they attempt to implement the policies they advocated in the election.
- Adjudication of demands: Citizens make demands on the government; political parties seek to satisfy those demands in return for electoral support.

TYPES OF POLITICAL PARTY SYSTEMS

One-Party System
In the **one-party system**, only one political party is allowed, which happens in authoritarian and totalitarian states.

Dominant Party System
In a **dominant party system**, parties are free to compete in elections but one party historically wins all of the time. Examples of these types of party systems are the Institutional Revolutionary Party of Mexico and the Liberal Democratic Party of Japan.

Two-Party Systems
In the **two-party system**, two dominant political parties compete for control. Other parties are present, but their influence and electoral success are usually limited. The electoral system is usually characterized by a single-member winner taking all districts. A party needs to win a plurality of votes in a district.

Multiparty Systems
A **multiparty system** can have several large parties that compete for control. There are alternative parties that have more significance, as they are usually part of governing coalitions. They are helped by the electoral system, which usually incorporates some aspect of proportional representation. Voting is done by party, and seats are allocated in proportion to the electoral strengths of the parties.

DIFFERENCE BETWEEN POLITICAL PARTIES AND INTEREST GROUPS

Political parties have to have a position on a broad range of public policy issues. Interest groups focus on one or a small set of issues.

For the interest group, the implementation of policy is the primary objective. For the political party, policies are usually intermediate steps toward their primary objective of winning the next election.

TYPES OF PARTIES

Doctrinaire/Ideological Party
These parties support a distinct ideology. An example would be the Socialist Party.

Broker Party
A **broker party** mediates among diverse interest groups and avoids narrow ideological goals. These include large parties that incorporate many different groups that can go back and forth. Examples include the Democratic and Republican Parties in the United States.

Revolutionary Party
Revolutionary parties seek to undermine the existing political system. Examples include the Nazi Party in Germany and the Bolshevik/Communist Party of the Soviet Union.

Cadre Party
In **cadre parties**, small groups of notables are in control. Elites use this form of political party as a source of patronage.

Mass Party
In a **mass party**, members of the electorate are members of the party, although it is led by a small group of leaders. These parties form as a result of increases in political participation and the growth of middle-class and working-class involvement in political organizations.

ELECTIONS

- The purpose of elections is to decide who governs and to indirectly influence public policy by presenting voters with a choice of alternative candidates and differing approaches to public policy.
- Candidates hope that elections will give them a mandate to govern. A mandate is the perception of popular support for a program or policy based on the margin of electoral victory won by a candidate who proposed it during a campaign.

TYPES OF ELECTORAL SYSTEMS

Winner-Take-All Electoral Systems
Winner take all is also referred to as first past the post. A country is divided into single-member districts; winners need to get a plurality of the vote. In the United States, the US House of Representatives has 435 seats allocated among the 50 states. Each state is a single-member district. The successful candidate needs to gain a plurality (the most votes) to win. This system tends to favor large parties, as often those who support alternative parties tend to vote for the major

party they find the least objectionable. In the US Senate, there are two seats for every state, and senators are also elected by a plurality of the vote. Unlike proportional representation, there is no reward for coming in second place. As a result, this system encourages two large parties and discourages smaller parties.

Proportional Representation

Proportional representation is a system where seats in a legislature are allocated to each party based on its percentage of the popular vote.

Typically, the country is divided into multimember districts. Through the list system, parties rank their candidates, and seats are awarded based on popular vote. This electoral system encourages a multi-party political system as small parties can usually win seats in the legislature. It also gives smaller parties influence in government policy as they are often needed by larger parties to form a governing coalition. Countries that have this type of system include Germany and Israel.

List System

The following is an example of the list system in proportional representation: if there are ten seats in a district and a party wins 30 percent of the vote, then the top three on their list are awarded seats.

Single Transferable Vote

The **single transferable vote** system allows voters to indicate a second and perhaps third choice preference. If the must-have choice does not make the initial cut, then the vote is transferred to the second choice, and so on. Many scholars and political activists argue that this is the fairest system, as it eliminates what some argue are "wasted votes." Essentially, a voter can vote for the candidate (party) he/she really wants and indicate the major party he/she finds the least objectionable as a second choice. Candidates who do not reach a certain threshold are eliminated, and their votes are redistributed to other candidates. This goes on until one candidate has a majority of the votes cast. This system fosters a greater ideological diversity, which is reflected in the party system.

DO PARTY SYSTEMS MATTER?

Governance Through Modern Political Parties
Kenneth Janda

Kenneth Janda is Payson S. Wild Professor Emeritus at Northwestern University's Political Science Department and received his PhD from Indiana University. He is recipient of the "Lifetime Achievement" award from the American Political Science Association.

Do party systems matter? Funding agencies think so. In fact, they spend millions of dollars annually to create and cultivate democratic party systems in developing countries. They want competitive party systems with stable factions that avoid fragmentation. These party system traits—competitiveness,

Kenneth Janda, "Do Party Systems Matter? Governance Through Modern Political Parties," Harvard International Review, vol. 34, no. 4, pp. 58–62. Copyright © 2013 by Harvard International Relations Council. Reprinted with permission. Provided by ProQuest LLC. All rights reserved.

stability, and lack of fragmentation—are important in the world of party aid.

Thomas Carothers describes these funding efforts in *Confronting the Weakest Link: Aiding Political Parties in New Democracies*. International aid to parties blossomed in the 1970s, when German foundations aided democratic parties in Southern Europe and Latin America. In the mid-1980s, the United States created the National Endowment for Democracy, which funded the International Republican Institute (IRI) and the National Democratic Institute for International Affairs (NDI) to support party development in countries across the globe. Since then, foundations in other Western European countries developed and expanded their own programs of party aid.

International agencies, such as the Organization of American States, the Organization for Security and Cooperation in Europe, and the United Nations joined in funding party development in the context of democratic assistance. The UN Democratic Governance Group's *Handbook of Working with Political Parties* set forth the rationale, saying that "political parties are an essential part of the apparatus of governance." It cited many contributions of political parties: aggregating interests, mobilizing the electorate, shaping public policies, holding politicians accountable, and fostering future leaders.

Citizens across the world, however, do not share the UN's positive view of political parties. When the World Values Survey asked people in 55 countries "how much confidence" they had in their parties, almost 75 percent on average said either "not much" or "very little." Only in China, Vietnam, and Malaysia did a majority say they had "a great deal" or "quite a lot" of confidence in their parties.

Notwithstanding the public's negative views, most scholars agree with the UN Democratic Governance Group and regard parties as necessary to democratic government and value their contributions to governance. Assuming that political parties contribute to the quality of country governance, international organizations and non-governmental organizations have poured millions of dollars into party development under the framework of democratic assistance. Carothers offers a "very rough estimate" of US$200 million spent in 2005 on total worldwide party aid. By 2011, the AP reported that the IRI and NDI alone spent over US$100 million to support the democratic movement in Egypt. Agencies providing the funds assume that their spending has positive effects, but there is little measurable evidence.

Case studies in different countries show mixed results. African and Asian leaders and scholars have accused Western donors of pressing multiparty politics on skeptical publics that think parties represent corrupt elites, while ruling elites fear that party reforms threaten their hold on power. Carothers described these national concerns and problematic results anecdotally in *Confronting the Weakest Link*. He offers an "up-to-date analytic treatment of party aid," but he does not demonstrate that aiding political parties helps country governance in any measurable way.

Relying on a comprehensive cross-national survey of political parties and country governance in 212 countries, we addressed the underlying assumption of funding party aid in developing countries. In *Party Systems and Country Governance*, written with Korean scholar Jin-Young Kwak, we ask, "Does the quality of the party system affect the quality of governance?" We sought to explain variance in the World Bank's six 2007 Worldwide Governance Indicators for 212 countries by traits of their party systems.

Using data on parliamentary representation of political parties, we found party system traits that significantly improved the quality of country governance. Countries with political parties have better governance than countries without parties, and those with competitive and stable party systems have better governance than those with less competitive and less stable systems.

Measuring Governance

"Governance" is a loose term associated with a messy concept, so it means different things to different people. We define governance simply as the extent to which a state delivers to its citizens the desired benefits of government, at acceptable costs. Government benefits may reflect specific values—such as high literacy, good roads, clean water, sanitation—or abstract meta-values, such as Rule of Law, Government Effectiveness, Control of Corruption, Regulatory Quality, Voice and Accountability, and Political Stability. In fact, the Worldwide Governance Indicators (WGI) targeted precisely those six meta-values.

We used the 2007 WGI data for 212 countries, which included all 192 members of the United Nations, some non-member nations (such as Taiwan), and some entities (such as Guam and Hong Kong) not normally regarded as independent nations. The WGI measures were all significantly intercorrelated, most above $r = 0.70$. This article focuses on one indicator, the Rule of Law. According to the WGI's web site, "Rule of Law captures perceptions of the extent to which agents have confidence in and abide by the rules of society, and in particular the quality of contract enforcement, property rights, the police, and the courts, as well as the likelihood of crime and violence." It stands at the core of what many people regard as good governance. Relying on thirty-five sources from research organizations around the world, the WGI project scored 211 countries on Rule of Law (RL)—failing to do so only for Niue, an island nation in the South Pacific.

The histogram in Figure 1 illustrates the distribution of the WGI scores for RL, with selected countries identified to aid interpretation. Switzerland enjoyed the highest score and Somalia suffered the lowest. The United States also ranked relatively high, while South Korea was substantially above the mean of 0.0, and China and Russia somewhat below it.

The scores were normed to have a mean of 0 and a standard deviation of 1. Commonly called z-scores, they tell—in standard deviation units—where each country stands in relationship to all other countries.

Figure 1 helps us appreciate the variability of governance across countries. How much of this variance is due to their party systems? Governance

of varying quality occurs in both democratic and autocratic governments—under multiple political parties, single parties, and no parties. We attempted to explain variations in Rule of Law over all 211 countries by variations in the countries' party systems. In statistical terms, RL became the dependent variable, while aspects of the party systems were the independent variables.

Other Effects on Country Governance

In social research, no explanatory model includes all possible causes for the dependent variable. A complete explanation of country governance cannot be limited to the effects of party systems. Many other factors—certainly including intelligent, honest, courageous governmental leadership—affect the quality of governance. Studying the quality of government leadership was beyond our capabilities. We could not include that critical factor in our explanatory model, leaving it knowingly incomplete.

But we could and did control for two other factors that theory and data showed to explain country governance. One was country size, and the other country wealth. Early Greek and modem European philosophers believed that small countries, but not large ones, could maintain a democratic form of government. The effect of country wealth on country governance is even more obvious than that of country size: delivering the benefits of government costs money, so poor countries are inherently disadvantaged.

Variables for country size and wealth are included in our model as control variables: the larger the country (in either population or area), the more difficult to govern; and the poorer the country, the more difficult to govern. The statistical method of regression analysis adjusts for the effects of country size and wealth while assessing the effects of the party system variables.

To measure country size, we tried both population and land areas—expressed as logarithms to deal with the few very large countries that dwarfed the many small ones. To measure country wealth, we used the logarithm of GDP per capita—adjusting for the few very wealthy countries far richer than the very many poor ones. Variations in country size (land area log

Histogram of Rule of Law Scores

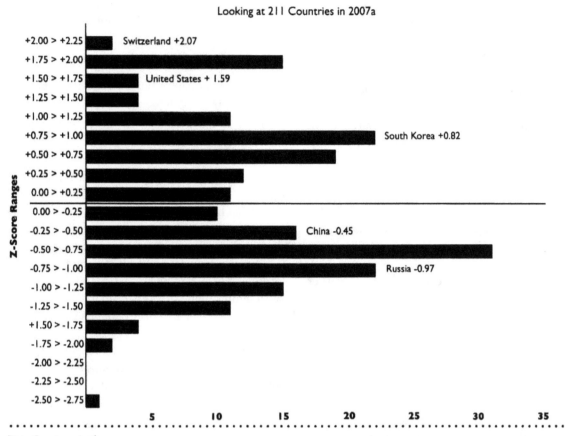

Looking at 211 Countries in 2007a

Data Courtesy Author

did better than population log) alone explained 16 percent of the variation in Rule of Law. Variation in GDP per capita (log) explained 61 percent of the variation. Entering both country size and wealth into the analysis explained 66 percent of the variance in the WGI measures of Rule of Law.

Effects of Party Systems

Space available for this article does not allow thorough description of our data on party systems. Two points must suffice: (1) We collected data only on the percentage of seats held by the three largest parties in the legislative body or parliament and the number of parties seated; and (2) the seat data represented two points in time: after a stimulus election prior to 2007 and after a referent election adjacent to the stimulus election. The stimulus election captured the party system that was positioned to affect governance in 2007 (measuring competitiveness), while seat differences between the stimulus and referent elections measured the party system's stability. The number of parties seated measured fragmentation.

The data in Table 1 on the status of parliamentary parties in 212 countries were derived mostly from the 2006 CIA World Factbook (available on the Internet), and they apply to unicameral parliaments or to the lower chambers of bicameral parliaments. The table cross-classifies countries by two criteria: do the deputies represent parties and were deputies popularly elected?

Column 1 shows that 185 of the parliaments in 2006 seated deputies by publicly identified political parties. Only 152 countries popularly elected all parliamentary seats. In another 28 most seats were elected, but some were indirectly elected or appointed, and in one country fewer than half were directly elected. Only 181 chose at least some of their deputies through popular elections—using the phrase generously to mean direct selection by voters, regardless of the quality of the process. Four countries did not select deputies through popular elections, yet seated them by parties.

Column 2 classifies 9 countries with "shadowy" parties (unofficial or underground) by which deputies were selected. Seat data was obtained for only four (identified in boldface). Column 3 shows 16 parliaments without party deputies, half of which (mostly small island nations) were elected through nonpartisan elections. Two nations in 2006 (Nepal and Myanmar) had no parliament or legislative council.

Given that country wealth and size together explain two-thirds of the variation in country ratings on Rule of Law, we should not expect variations in party systems to explain much more.

Data Analysis

We tested five theoretical propositions concerning the effects of party systems on Rule of Law as a key indicator of governance. The first two propositions should be separated from the other three, for they apply to a small subset of the countries.

1. Without parties and elections, the Rule of Law is lower.

2. Without parties but with elections, the Rule of Law is higher.

Only 26 countries had no parliamentary parties. Of these, 16 (e.g., Swaziland, Togo, Myanmar, Somalia) also had no elections, and two (Myanmar and Nepal) had no parliament. The other eight were mostly island nations (e.g., Tuvalu, American Samoa, Palau, Micronesia) that held nonpartisan elections. Controlling for country size and wealth, the regression analysis showed that these two groups of countries differed significantly compared with all 211 countries scored for Rule of Law. Having no parties and no elections had a significant negative effect on RL, while having no parties but nonpartisan elections had a significant positive effect on RL.

The analysis supported Propositions 1 and 2. The absence of both parties and elections depressed RL, but RL was enhanced if parliamentary deputies were popularly elected. At least in small island nations, popularly elected deputies need not represent political parties in order to promote the quality of governance.

Were Deputies Popularly Elected to Parliament?	Did Deputies Represent Political Parties?				
	Public Parties	**Shadowy Parties**	**No Parties**	**No Parliament**	**Total**
All Deputies were Popularly Elected	152	0	8	0	160
Most Were Popularly Elected	28	8 Iran, Kyrgystan, Jordan, Uganda (4)	1	0	37
Some Were Popularly Elected	1 Macao	1	1	0	3
None Were Popularly Elected	4 China, Congo (Kinshasa), Sudan, Eritrea	0	6	0	10
No Parliament Existed	0	0	0	2	2
Total	85	9	16	2	212

Data Courtesy Author

The next three propositions apply to most of the 212 countries that had parliamentary parties, regardless of whether the deputies were popularly elected.

3. The more competitive the party system, the greater the Rule of Law.

4. The more stable the party system, the greater the Rule of Law.

5. The more fragmented the party system, the lower the Rule of Law.

After trying out several measures of party system competition, volatility, and fragmentation, we settled on single measures for each. To measure party system competition, we used the strength of the largest opposition party, measured by the percentage of parliamentary seats held by the second largest party after the stimulus election. Controlling for country size and wealth, as well as the absence of political parties and nonpartisan elections, we found a significant positive effect for party system competition. The data supported Proposition 3. More competitive party systems had higher RL scores.

To measure party system volatility, we used a standard formula based on the percentage point differences in votes cast for all parties in two adjacent elections (we only had data for the three largest parties, but they accounted for almost 80 percent of the seats after the stimulus and referent elections). Because one-party systems, like China, emerged as the most stable party systems, we tested proposition 4 for only the 137 nations that qualified as "electoral democracies" according to Freedom House criteria. For these electoral democracies, party system stability had a significant effect on Rule of Law. The more stable the party system, the higher the RL.

Measuring fragmentation by the number of parties represented in parliament, we found no significant effects on Rule of Law. Other measures worked no better. (There was no correlation between our measures of fragmentation and competitiveness.) We suspect that Proposition 5 was not supported because it conflated two different theories of democratic government. The majoritarian model favors popular control of government through two rival groups struggling to gain control of government. The pluralist model (or better, the consociational model) favors having government shared by politically salient social groups.

The model—majoritarian or consociational—that operates in a given country depends on its governmental and social structure. Having multiple parties in parliament—which produces high party system fragmentation—works against the majoritarian model of government but tends to support the consociational model. Our test may have failed because it did not separate the countries according to the presumed operative model of democracy.

Notwithstanding the failure to support Proposition 5, we found support for all other proposed effects of party systems on country governance as measured by Rule of Law. Countries with party systems rate higher on RL than those without parties, excepting the few island nations that hold nonpartisan elections. More competitive party systems are significantly related to higher RL scores. In electoral democracies, more stable party systems are significantly related to higher RL scores. Although the percentages of explained variance increased only marginally, the party system coefficients were all statistically significant at the standard level.

Party System Properties: Cause or Effect?

To this point, we have not specified why greater party system competitiveness and stability should be related to higher Rule of Law scores for countries. Does the party system contribute to their higher scores—as assumed in the propositions we tested—or does a more competitive and stable party system merely reflect the extent to which countries enforce the governmental value, rule of law? One can argue that party system competitiveness and stability are simply the effects of rule of law as a generic value. When countries observe the rule of law, opposition parties are freer to compete with governmental parties for political power in multiple elections. Thus, positive properties of party systems become the effect, not the cause, of rule of law.

We argue the contrary: that party system competitiveness and stability cause countries to promote the rule of law. While non-competitive parties have little incentive to promote it, competitive parties do have an incentive. They promote it because voters prefer government by rule of law to government by the whim of the rulers. Promoting the rule of law meshes with competitive parties' strategic goals: to win votes and seats. Put more generally, a competitive party system has an incentive to promote country governance—of which the WGI variable, Rule of Law, is just one manifestation.

It is time to consider the other Worldwide Governance Indicators: Government Effectiveness, Control of Corruption, and Regulatory Quality. (We exclude Voice and Accountability because it includes party competition as a component.). Essentially, all our findings of party system effects hold for those indicators as well. The more competitive and stable the party system, the higher the Government Effectiveness, the Control of Corruption, and the Regulatory Quality.

The argument that rule of law causes party competitiveness by freeing parties to compete in elections does not apply to Government Effectiveness. How could one argue that effective government produces more competitive parties? How could one argue that

party competitiveness is a reasonable consequence of Control of Corruption—or of Regulatory Quality?

That a competitive party system is significantly related to all four indicators of country governance suggests that the nature of the party system is causal, not consequential. Recall our earlier definition of governance as the extent to which a state delivers to its citizens the desired benefits of government at acceptable costs. Competitive political parties propose government benefits in order to win votes and seats. Hence, they promote the Rule of Law, Government Effectiveness, Control of Corruption, and Regulatory Quality—all meta-values that voters favor. That argues for the positive effect of party systems on country governance.

Party Systems and Country Governance discusses the many limitations of this cross-national study of one set of governance indicators in 2007. While not a definitive study, it did produce mostly strong and consistent results that support the underlying assumption of those who fund programs to develop party systems abroad: party systems do matter.

CHAPTER 15

Revolution

KEY TERMS

Revolution
Robespierre
Napoleon
Edmund Burke
Iranian Revolution
The Arab Spring

Montesquieu
The Committee of Public Safety
Thomas Paine
The Shah of Iran
Ayatollah Khomeini
Muhammad Musaddiq

DISCUSSION QUESTIONS

1. Compare and contrast the American and French Revolutions. Address the similarities and differences.

2. What influence did Napoleon have on spreading the French Revolution and nationalism?

3. Address the policies of the shah of Iran.

4. Discuss the factors that contributed to the success of the Iranian Revolution.

5. Address the reasons why revolutionary movements were initially successful during the Arab Spring.

WHAT IS A REVOLUTION?

A **revolution** is a fundamental change in the rules, values, and institutions of a society that often involve violent conflict. Some examples include the American, French, Russian, Chinese, and Iranian Revolutions.

THE AMERICAN REVOLUTION

The American Revolution was a separation from Great Britain. British traditions were the basis for the colonies' legal and political traditions. However, they started developing different ideas of representation and economic goals. Locke had an appeal in the colonies, as well as the thoughts of Montesquieu and the Enlightenment in general. **Montesquieu** influenced the American Revolution through his ideas of separation of powers, which stated that there should be separate executive, legislative, and judicial authority to ensure that one person, or a small group, did not dominate the entire government.

THE FRENCH REVOLUTION

In France, there were problems with expenditures and budget deficits. The tax system was such that the nobility and the church were exempt from taxes. More and more of the burden fell on the middle and lower classes. The French king Louis XVI called a meeting of the Estates General to raise taxes. The middle class sought to make reforms in the system to ensure fairer taxation and more opportunities for the middle class. Because the monarchy was opposed, the movement became radicalized. After much frustration and disappointment, a crowd stormed the Bastille, which was a prison and a symbol of state authority. The storming of the Bastille forced Louis XVI to agree to a new constitution.

Radical Phase of the Revolution

The new constitution did not bring about stability. There was a great deal of political infighting between the king and parliament. This was exacerbated by war as other countries, led by conservative monarchs, were opposed to the reforms of the French revolution. Many of the revolutionaries felt that the king was conspiring with foreign powers. This was confirmed for many when the king and queen were caught in disguise attempting to leave the country. Louis XVI was eventually convicted of treason and executed.

Radicals (**the Committee of Public Safety**) took over the revolution and instituted the Reign of Terror, which sought to kill any perceived enemies of the revolution. Many of the victims were members of the aristocracy. Eventually, **Robespierre**, who led the committee, was executed by the revolution.

THE FRENCH AND AMERICAN REVOLUTIONS COMPARED

The American Revolution was more of a separation with Great Britain. It confirmed the dominant ideology and values that were emerging in the American colonies. The French revolution was a true revolution as the values of society and political institutions totally changed.

- The French Revolution had the modest goals of establishing a republican form of government.
- It would eventually become much more radical after dealing with the intransigence of the monarchy.
- It brought about new government institutions and introduced a new value system. The revolution became radicalized and eventually gave way to the dictatorship of Napoleon Bonaparte.

Napoleon was a product of the French Revolution. He was born on the island of Corsica to a minor noble family. The French Revolution gave Napoleon an opportunity to enter the French military academy. The revolution emphasized promotion by merit as opposed to family connections. Napoleon was able to rise rapidly through the ranks of the French Army. He distinguished himself in the campaigns in Italy. He returned to France and became active in politics. Napoleon became one of the members of the directorate and used his military support to claim sole power. In 1803, he arranged to crown himself emperor. He attempted to conquer most of Europe and almost succeeded. He could not beat Britain because of British control of the seas. Like many would-be conquerors, Napoleon overextended his forces and resources. His undoing was his attack on Russia in 1812. The horrible winter weather conditions and lack of supplies forced a French retreat after initially occupying Moscow. Napoleon lost most of his army, and those losses could not be made up. Eventually, he was defeated and forced into exile. He escaped to France and ruled again for 100 days but was defeated by a combined British and Prussian force at Waterloo. He was exiled to the island of St. Helena in the South Atlantic.

While Napoleon was a despot and sought to subjugate other peoples, he did spread the ideals of the French Revolution through his top-down reforms in the lands he conquered. These included limiting the powers of the church, a fairer system of taxation, and more rights for the middle class. He also unwittingly promoted the growth of nationalism, the passionate attachment to a nation-state. In the areas he conquered, such as Spain, parts of what would become Germany, and Russia, people rose up against the invaders.

THEORISTS ON REVOLUTION

- Edmund Burke: **Burke** believed that revolutions in general were not a good thing, as he valued traditional institutions. He did feel the American Revolution was beneficial because it further developed already established institutions. He hated the French Revolution because he viewed it as spreading disorder and chaos.
- Thomas Paine: **Paine**, the author of the pamphlet titled *Common Sense*, saw the French Revolution as just. He viewed monarchy as perpetuating injustice.
- John Locke: Locke believed people had the right to revolt when the government deprived them of their natural rights. He did caution against revolution on impulse.

SIGNIFICANT REVOLUTIONS

In the twentieth century, there have been many significant revolutions. The Russian and Chinese Revolutions were covered earlier in the text. The **Iranian Revolution** of 1978–1979 was extremely significant as it influenced/shaped the Middle East and the international system in the late twentieth and early twenty-first centuries.

The Pahlavi dynasty had come to power in Iran in 1925. The founder of the dynasty, Reza Khan, was an army officer who gained political power and eventually purged his rivals. He initially wanted to make Iran a republic like Turkey under Ataturk. However, the conservative religious authorities were opposed to this, so he arranged for the last Qajar monarch to be deposed and had himself installed as shah. His policies were to centralize the country and build up the military. He also sought to bring about Westernization in the society, as well as the economy and politics.

Reza Shah was deposed in 1941 by a joint British-Soviet invasion because of his support for Nazi Germany. His son Muhammad Reza Pahlavi was installed as shah. During World War II, the USSR and Britain, and later the United States, occupied Iran. Iran was an important conduit of lend-lease aid to the USSR during the first part of the war. After the war, the United States aided Iran in getting the Soviets to withdraw from the country. In the 1950s, a nationalist prime minister, **Muhammad Musaddiq**, nationalized the Anglo-Iranian Oil Company. This provoked a crisis with Great Britain and an international embargo of Iranian oil. Under the Truman administration, the United States sought to mediate the dispute. President Eisenhower, who became president in 1953, viewed Musaddiq as a threat and wanted American access to the Iranian oil industry. During his administration, the CIA conspired with British intelligence, Iranian military officers, and other conservatives in Iran to overthrow Musaddiq. This put the shah firmly back in power and helped to develop what would eventually become a royalist dictatorship.

The shah centered all power onto himself. He glorified ancient Iran and the pre-Islamic past. He changed the calendar to go back to the time of Cyrus the Great. He also shunned the traditional classes and tried to develop new economic elites. He attempted to weaken the power of the traditional merchants of the bazaar who supported religious leaders. He sought, for example, to encourage supermarkets and shopping malls at the expense of traditional merchants.

He also forged a political-military alliance with the United States. Under President Richard Nixon, the United States agreed to allow the shah to purchase any conventional weapons system he wished without a Defense Department review.

The shah seemed secure in power, and to many outsiders, Iran was a stable and prosperous country. However, this was a façade. There was growing tension in the country. More and more people were moving from the countryside in search of jobs. They congregated around the mosques and the religious leaders. Many religious leaders felt the shah was disrespecting Islam and giving the country over to foreigners. One of the leading clerics opposed to the shah was **Ayatollah Khomeini**. Khomeini had been deported from the country in response to leading protests against the Status of Forces Agreement the Shah concluded with the United States in the 1960s. He argued that this was an affront to Iranian sovereignty. The ayatollah had been living in Iraq. When protests escalated in Iran in 1978, the shah convinced the Iraqi government to force the ayatollah to leave. The rationale of the Iranian government was to get him out of the region, but this added to his credibility and allowed him to broadcast his message even more widely when he ended up in Paris. There he had access to the global media.

The revolution escalated throughout 1978, with the government alternating between cracking down on demonstrators and attempting to reform. Eventually, the shah left the country on January 16, 1979, for a "vacation." He never returned. The last government the shah put in place collapsed in February 1979. Ayatollah Khomeini named a government, and eventually an Islamic republic was established. This republic would serve as a model for other Muslim radicals. The new Iranian government had influence predominantly in areas where the Shia branch of Islam was in the majority. This would include parts of the Eastern Arabian Peninsula, Lebanon, and, eventually, once the Baathist government of Iraq had been swept away after the US-led invasion of 2003, Iraq.

The second round of revolutions took place in the Middle East with **the Arab Spring** of 2010–2011. The revolution began in response to unrest and protest started, first in Tunisia and then spreading across North Africa and into the Fertile Crescent. Eventually, the governments of Tunisia, Libya, and Egypt were swept away. The unrest spread to Syria, where there is currently a civil war raging, as well as Yemen. A factor that led to the toppling of these authoritarian governments was the effect of social media. Social media was not a factor during the Iranian Revolution. Instead, cassette tapes of Ayatollah Khomeini's sermons were smuggled into Iran and circulated among his followers. He also had access to the global media when, under pressure from Iran, the Iraqi government forced him to leave. He traveled to Paris where he had access to the global media. More recently, the political movements in the Arab world were credited to social media and cell phones. People were able to communicate and organize instantly. This made it very difficult for the government to stop or manipulate these protests.

Longtime authoritarian political leaders, such as Zine El Abidine Ben Ali of Tunisia and Hosni Mubarak of Egypt, were deposed. Muammar Gaddafi of Libya was killed in an uprising in 2011. Ali Abdullah Saleh of Yemen was killed in 2017. Yemen today is engulfed in a civil war in which regional powers Saudi Arabia and Iran are supporting rival factions. Currently, Bashar al-Assad is fighting a long civil war against several groups in Syria. He is hanging onto power with Russian and Iranian support against a coalition of different groups supported by the United States, Saudi Arabia, and other regional states. Unfortunately, the overthrowing of these authoritarian leaders did not bring about democracies for the most part. There has been some reform in Tunisia. However, Libya is being torn apart as different groups are fighting for control. In addition, the armament of the former Libyan Army has found its way to other conflict zones in Africa. In Egypt, the Muslim Brotherhood won an election but within about a year was overthrown by the military. The military has maintained its traditional control over the country. While the people at the top may have changed, the military is still the dominant institution.

UNDERSTANDING THE REVOLUTIONS OF 2011

Weakness and Resilience in Middle Eastern Autocracies
Jack A. Goldstone

The wave of revolutions sweeping the Middle East bears a striking resemblance to previous political earthquakes. As in Europe in 1848, rising food prices and high unemployment have fueled popular protests from Morocco to Oman. As in Eastern Europe and the Soviet Union in 1989, frustration with closed, corrupt, and unresponsive political systems has led to defections among elites and the fall of once powerful regimes in Tunisia, Egypt, and perhaps Libya. Yet 1848 and 1989 are not the right analogies for this past winter's events. The revolutions of 1848 sought to overturn traditional monarchies, and those in 1989 were aimed at toppling communist governments. The revolutions of 2011 are fighting something quite different: "sultanistic" dictatorships. Although such regimes often appear unshakable, they are actually highly vulnerable, because the very strategies they use to stay in power make them brittle, not resilient. It is no coincidence that although popular protests have shaken much of the Middle East, the only revolutions to succeed so far—those in Tunisia and Egypt—have been against modern sultans.

For a revolution to succeed, a number of factors have to come together. The government must appear so irremediably unjust or inept that it is widely viewed as a threat to the country's future; elites (especially in the military) must be alienated from the state and no longer willing to defend it; a broad-based section of the population, spanning ethnic and religious groups and socioeconomic classes, must mobilize; and international powers must either refuse to step in to defend the government or constrain it from using maximum force to defend itself.

Revolutions rarely triumph because these conditions rarely coincide. This is especially the case in traditional monarchies and one-party states, whose leaders often manage to maintain popular support by making appeals to respect for royal tradition or nationalism. Elites, who are often enriched by such governments, will only forsake them if their circumstances or the ideology of the rulers changes drastically. And in almost all cases, broad-based popular mobilization is difficult to achieve because it requires bridging the disparate interests of the urban and rural poor, the middle class, students, professionals, and different ethnic or religious groups. History is replete with student movements, workers' strikes, and peasant uprisings that were readily put down because they remained a revolt of one group, rather than of broad coalitions. Finally, other countries have often intervened to prop up embattled rulers in order to stabilize the international system.

Jack A. Goldstone, "Understanding the Revolutions of 2011: Weakness and Resilience in Middle Eastern Autocracies," Foreign Affairs, vol. 90, no. 3, pp. 8–16. Copyright © 2011 by Council on Foreign Relations, Inc. Reprinted with permission.

Yet there is another kind of dictatorship that often proves much more vulnerable, rarely retaining power for more than a generation: the sultanistic regime. Such governments arise when a national leader expands his personal power at the expense of formal institutions. Sultanistic dictators appeal to no ideology and have no purpose other than maintaining their personal authority. They may preserve some of the formal aspects of democracy—elections, political parties, a national assembly, or a constitution—but they rule above them by installing compliant supporters in key positions and sometimes by declaring states of emergency, which they justify by appealing to fears of external (or internal) enemies.

Behind the scenes, such dictators generally amass great wealth, which they use to buy the loyalty of supporters and punish opponents. Because they need resources to fuel their patronage machine, they typically promote economic development, through industrialization, commodity exports, and education. They also seek relationships with foreign countries, promising stability in exchange for aid and investment. However wealth comes into the country, most of it is funneled to the sultan and his cronies.

The new sultans control their countries' military elites by keeping them divided. Typically, the security forces are separated into several commands (army, air force, police, intelligence)—each of which reports directly to the leader. The leader monopolizes contact between the commands, between the military and civilians, and with foreign governments, a practice that makes sultans essential for both coordinating the security forces and channeling foreign aid and investment. To reinforce fears that foreign aid and political coordination would disappear in their absence, sultans typically avoid appointing possible successors.

To keep the masses depoliticized and unorganized, sultans control elections and political parties and pay their populations off with subsidies for key goods, such as electricity, gasoline, and foodstuffs. When combined with surveillance, media control, and intimidation, these efforts generally ensure that citizens stay disconnected and passive.

By following this pattern, politically adept sultans around the world have managed to accumulate vast wealth and high concentrations of power. Among the most famous in recent history were Mexico's Porfirio Díaz, Iran's Mohammad Reza Shah Pahlavi, Nicaragua's Somoza dynasty, Haiti's Duvalier dynasty, the Philippines' Ferdinand Marcos, and Indonesia's Suharto.

But as those sultans all learned, and as the new generation of sultans in the Middle East—including Bashar al-Assad in Syria, Omar al-Bashir in Sudan, Zine el-Abidine Ben Ali in Tunisia, Hosni Mubarak in Egypt, Muammar al-Qaddafi in Libya, and Ali Abdullah Saleh in Yemen—has discovered, power that is too concentrated can be difficult to hold on to.

Paper Tigers

For all their attempts to prop themselves up, sultanistic dictatorships have inherent vulnerabilities that only increase over time. Sultans must strike a careful balance between self-enrichment and rewarding the elite: if the ruler rewards himself and neglects the elite, a key incentive for the elite to support the regime is removed. But as sultans come to feel more entrenched and indispensable, their corruption frequently becomes more brazen and concentrated among a small inner circle. As the sultan monopolizes foreign aid and investment or gets too close to unpopular foreign governments, he may alienate elite and popular groups even further.

Meanwhile, as the economy grows and education expands under a sultanistic dictator, the number of people with higher aspirations and a keener sensitivity to the intrusions of police surveillance and abuse increases. And if the entire population grows rapidly while the lion's share of economic gains is hoarded by the elite, inequality and unemployment surge as well. As the costs of subsidies and other programs the regime uses to appease citizens rise, keeping the masses depoliticized places even more stress on the regime. If protests start, sultans may offer reforms or expand patronage benefits—as Marcos did in the Philippines in 1984 to head off escalating public anger. Yet as Marcos learned in 1986, these sops are generally ineffective once people have begun to clamor for ending the sultan's rule.

The weaknesses of sultanistic regimes are magnified as the leader ages and the question of succession becomes more acute. Sultanistic rulers have sometimes been able to hand over leadership to younger family members. This is only possible when the government has been operating effectively and has maintained elite support (as in Syria in 2000, when President Hafez al-Assad handed power to his son Bashar) or if another country backs the regime (as in Iran in 1941, when Western governments promoted the succession from Reza Shah to his son Mohammad Reza Pahlavi). If the regime's corruption has already alienated the country's elites, they may turn on it and try to block a dynastic succession, seeking to regain control of the state (which is what happened in Indonesia in the late 1990s, when the Asian financial crisis dealt a blow to Suharto's patronage machine).

The very indispensability of the sultan also works against a smooth transfer of power. Most of the ministers and other high officials are too deeply identified with the chief executive to survive his fall from power. For example, the shah's 1978 attempt to avoid revolution by substituting his prime minister, Shahpur Bakhtiar, for himself as head of government did not work; the entire regime fell the next year. Ultimately, such moves satisfy neither the demands of the mobilized masses seeking major economic and political change nor the aspirations of the urban and professional class that has taken to the streets to demand inclusion in the control of the state.

Then there are the security forces. By dividing their command structure, the sultan may reduce the threat they pose. But this strategy also makes the security forces more prone to defections in the event of mass protests. Lack of unity leads to splits within the security services; meanwhile, the fact that the regime is not backed by any appealing ideology or by independent institutions ensures that the military has less motivation to put down protests. Much of the military may decide that the country's interests are better served by regime change. If part of the armed forces defects—as happened under Díaz, the shah of Iran, Marcos, and Suharto—the government can unravel with astonishing rapidity. In the end, the befuddled ruler, still convinced of his indispensability

and invulnerability, suddenly finds himself isolated and powerless.

The degree of a sultan's weakness is often visible only in retrospect. Although it is easy to identify states with high levels of corruption, unemployment, and personalist rule, the extent to which elites oppose the regime and the likelihood that the military will defect often become apparent only once large-scale protests have begun. After all, the elite and military officers have every reason to hide their true feelings until a crucial moment arises, and it is impossible to know which provocation will lead to mass, rather than local, mobilization. The rapid unraveling of sultanistic regimes thus often comes as a shock.

In some cases, of course, the military does not immediately defect in the face of rebellion. In Nicaragua in the early 1970s, for example, Anastasio Somoza Debayle was able to use loyal troops in Nicaragua's National Guard to put down the rebellion against him. But even when the regime can draw on loyal sectors of the military, it rarely manages to survive. It simply breaks down at a slower pace, with significant bloodshed or even civil war resulting along the way. Somoza's success in 1975 was short-lived; his increasing brutality and corruption brought about an even larger rebellion in the years that followed. After some pitched battles, even formerly loyal troops began to desert, and Somoza fled the country in 1979.

International pressure can also turn the tide. The final blow to Marcos' rule was the complete withdrawal of U.S. support after Marcos dubiously claimed victory in the presidential election held in 1986. When the United States turned away from the regime, his remaining supporters folded, and the nonviolent People Power Revolution forced him into exile.

Rock the Casbah

The revolutions unfolding across the Middle East represent the breakdown of increasingly corrupt sultanistic regimes. Although economies across the region have grown in recent years, the gains have bypassed the majority of the population, being amassed instead by a wealthy few. Mubarak and his family reportedly built up a fortune of between $40 billion and $70 billion, and 39 officials and businessmen close to Mubarak's son Gamal are alleged to have made fortunes averaging more than $1 billion each. In Tunisia, a 2008 U.S. diplomatic cable released by the whistleblower Web site WikiLeaks noted a spike in corruption, warning that Ben Ali's family was becoming so predatory that new investment and job creation were being stifled and that his family's ostentation was provoking widespread outrage.

Fast-growing and urbanizing populations in the Middle East have been hurt by low wages and by food prices that rose by 32 percent in the last year alone, according to the United Nations' Food and Agriculture Organization. But it is not simply such rising prices, or a lack of growth, that fuels revolutions; it is the persistence of widespread and unrelieved poverty amid increasingly extravagant wealth.

Discontent has also been stoked by high unemployment, which has stemmed in part from the surge in the Arab world's young population. The percentage of young adults—those aged 15–29 as a fraction of all those over 15—ranges from 38 percent in Bahrain and Tunisia to over 50 percent in Yemen (compared to 26 percent in the United States). Not only is the proportion of young people in the Middle East extraordinarily high, but their numbers have grown quickly over a short period of time. Since 1990, youth population aged 15–29 has grown by 50 percent in Libya and Tunisia, 65 percent in Egypt, and 125 percent in Yemen.

Thanks to the modernization policies of their sultanistic governments, many of these young people have been able to go to university, especially in recent years. Indeed, college enrollment has soared across the region in recent decades, more than tripling in Tunisia, quadrupling in Egypt, and expanding tenfold in Libya.

It would be difficult, if not impossible, for any government to create enough jobs to keep pace. For the sultanistic regimes, the problem has been especially difficult to manage. As part of their patronage strategies, Ben Ali and Mubarak had long provided state subsidies to workers and families through such programs as Tunisia's National Employment Fund—which trained workers, created jobs, and issued loans—and Egypt's policy of guaranteeing job placement for college graduates. But these safety nets were phased out in the last decade to reduce expenditures. Vocational training, moreover, was weak, and access to public and many private jobs was tightly controlled by those connected to the regime. This led to incredibly high youth unemployment across the Middle East: the figure for the region hit 23 percent, or twice the global average, in 2009. Unemployment among the educated, moreover, has been even worse: in Egypt, college graduates are ten times as likely to have no job as those with only an elementary school education.

In many developing economies, the informal sector provides an outlet for the unemployed. Yet the sultans in the Middle East made even those activities difficult. After all, the protests were sparked by the self-immolation of Mohamed Bouazizi, a 26-year-old Tunisian man who was unable to find formal work and whose fruit cart was confiscated by the police. Educated youth and workers in Tunisia and Egypt have been carrying out local protests and strikes for years to call attention to high unemployment, low wages, police harassment, and state corruption. This time, their protests combined and spread to other demographics.

These regimes' concentration of wealth and brazen corruption increasingly offended their militaries. Ben Ali and Mubarak both came from the professional military; indeed, Egypt had been ruled by former officers since 1952. Yet in both countries, the military had seen its status eclipsed. Egypt's military leaders controlled some local businesses, but they fiercely resented Gamal Mubarak, who was Hosni Mubarak's heir apparent. As a banker, he preferred to build his influence through business and political cronies rather than through the military, and those connected to him gained huge profits from government monopolies and deals with foreign investors. In Tunisia, Ben Ali kept the military at arm's length to ensure that it would not harbor political ambitions. Yet he let his wife and her relatives shake down Tunisian businessmen and build seaside mansions. In both countries, military resentments made the military less likely to crack down on mass protests; officers and soldiers would not kill their countrymen just to keep the Ben Ali and Mubarak families and their favorites in power.

A similar defection among factions of the Libyan military led to Qaddafi's rapid loss of large territories. As of this writing, however, Qaddafi's use of mercenaries and exploitation of tribal loyalties have prevented his fall. And in Yemen, Saleh has been kept afloat, if barely, by U.S. aid given in support of his opposition to Islamist terrorists and by the tribal and regional divisions among his opponents. Still, if the opposition unites, as it seems to be doing, and the United States becomes reluctant to back his increasingly repressive regime, Saleh could be the next sultan to topple.

The Revolutions' Limits

As of this writing, Sudan and Syria, the other sultanistic regions in the region, have not seen major popular protests. Yet Bashir's corruption and the concentration of wealth in Khartoum have become brazen. One of the historic rationales for his regime—keeping the whole of Sudan under northern control—recently disappeared with southern Sudan's January 2011 vote in favor of independence. In Syria, Assad has so far retained nationalist support because of his hard-line policies toward Israel and Lebanon. He still maintains the massive state employment programs that have kept Syrians passive for decades, but he has no mass base of support and is dependent on a tiny elite, whose corruption is increasingly notorious. Although it is hard to say how staunch the elite and military support for Bashir and Assad is, both regimes are probably even weaker than they appear and could quickly crumble in the face of broad-based protests.

The region's monarchies are more likely to retain power. This is not because they face no calls for change. In fact, Morocco, Jordan, Oman, and the Persian Gulf kingdoms face the same demographic, educational, and economic challenges that the sultanistic regimes do, and they must reform to meet them. But the monarchies have one big advantage: their political structures are flexible. Modern monarchies can retain considerable executive power while ceding legislative power to elected parliaments. In times of unrest, crowds are more likely to protest for legislative change than for abandonment of the monarchy. This gives monarchs more room to maneuver to pacify the people. Facing protests in 1848, the monarchies in Germany and Italy, for example, extended their constitutions, reduced the absolute power of the king, and accepted elected legislatures as the price of avoiding further efforts at revolution.

In monarchies, moreover, succession can result in change and reform, rather than the destruction of the entire system. A dynastic succession is legitimate and may thus be welcomed rather than feared, as in a typical sultanistic state. For example, in Morocco in 1999, the public greeted King Mohammed VI's ascension to the throne with great hopes for change. And in fact, Mohammed VI has investigated some of the regime's previous legal abuses and worked to somewhat strengthen women's rights. He has calmed recent protests in Morocco by promising major constitutional reforms. In Bahrain, Jordan, Kuwait, Morocco, Oman, and Saudi Arabia, rulers will likely to be able to stay in office if they are willing to share their power with elected officials or hand the reins to a younger family member who heralds significant reforms.

The regime most likely to avoid significant change in the near term is Iran. Although Iran has been called a sultanistic regime, it is different in several respects: unlike any other regime in the region, the ayatollahs espouse an ideology of anti-Western Shiism and Persian nationalism that draws considerable support from ordinary people. This makes it more like a party-state with a mass base of support. Iran is also led by a combination of several strong leaders, not just one: Supreme Leader Ali Khamenei, President Mahmoud Ahmadinejad, and Parliamentary Chair Ali Larijani. So there is no one corrupt or inefficient sultan on which to focus dissent. Finally, the Iranian regime enjoys the support of the Basij, an ideologically committed militia, and the Revolutionary Guards, which are deeply intertwined with the government. There is little chance that these forces will defect in the face of mass protests.

After the Revolutions

Those hoping for Tunisia and Egypt to make the transition to stable democracy quickly will likely be disappointed. Revolutions are just the beginning of a long process. Even after a peaceful revolution, it generally takes half a decade for any type of stable regime to consolidate. If a civil war or a counterrevolution arises (as appears to be happening in Libya), the reconstruction of the state takes still longer.

In general, after the post-revolutionary honeymoon period ends, divisions within the opposition start to surface. Although holding new elections is a straightforward step, election campaigns and then decisions taken by new legislatures will open debates over taxation and state spending, corruption, foreign policy, the role of the military, the powers of the president, official policy on religious law and practice, minority rights, and so on. As conservatives, populists, Islamists, and modernizing reformers fiercely vie for power in Tunisia, Egypt, and perhaps Libya, those countries will likely face lengthy periods of abrupt government turnovers and policy reversals—similar to what occurred in the Philippines and many Eastern European countries after their revolutions.

Some Western governments, having long supported Ben Ali and Mubarak as bulwarks against a rising tide of radical Islam, now fear that Islamist groups are poised to take over. The Muslim Brotherhood in Egypt is the best organized of the opposition groups there, and so stands to gain in open elections, particularly if elections are held soon, before other parties are organized. Yet the historical record of revolutions in sultanistic regimes should somewhat alleviate such concerns. Not a single sultan overthrown in the last 30 years—including in Haiti, the Philippines, Romania, Zaire, Indonesia, Georgia, and Kyrgyzstan—has been succeeded by an ideologically driven or radical government. Rather, in every case, the end product has been a flawed democracy—often corrupt and prone to authoritarian tendencies, but not aggressive or extremist.

This marks a significant shift in world history. Between 1949 and 1979, every revolution against a sultanistic regime—in China, Cuba, Vietnam, Cambodia, Iran, and Nicaragua—resulted in a communist or an Islamist government. At the time, most intellectuals in the developing world favored the communist model of revolution against capitalist states. And in Iran, the desire to avoid both capitalism and communism and the increasing popularity of traditional Shiite clerical authority resulted in a push for an Islamist government. Yet since the 1980s, neither the communist nor the Islamist model has had much appeal. Both are widely perceived as failures at producing economic growth and popular accountability—the two chief goals of all recent anti-sultanistic revolutions.

Noting that high unemployment spurred regime change, some in the United States have called for a Marshall Plan for the Middle East to stabilize the region. But in 1945, Europe had a history of prior democratic regimes and a devastated physical infrastructure that needed rebuilding. Tunisia and Egypt have intact economies with excellent recent growth records, but they need to build new democratic institutions. Pouring money into these countries before they have created accountable governments would only fuel corruption and undermine their progress toward democracy.

What is more, the United States and other Western nations have little credibility in the Middle East given their long support for sultanistic dictators. Any efforts to use aid to back certain groups or influence electoral outcomes are likely to arouse suspicion. What the revolutionaries need from outsiders is vocal support for the process of democracy, a willingness to accept all groups that play by democratic rules, and a positive response to any requests for technical assistance in institution building.

The greatest risk that Tunisia and Egypt now face is an attempt at counterrevolution by military conservatives, a group that has often sought to claim power after a sultan has been removed. This occurred in Mexico after Díaz was overthrown, in Haiti after Jean-Claude Duvalier's departure, and in the Philippines after Marcos' fall. And after Suharto was forced from power in Indonesia, the military exerted its strength by cracking down on independence movements in East Timor, which Indonesia had occupied since 1975.

In the last few decades, attempted counterrevolutions (such as those in the Philippines in 1987–88 and Haiti in 2004) have largely fizzled out. They have not reversed democratic gains or driven post-sultanistic regimes into the arms of extremists—religious or otherwise.

However, such attempts weaken new democracies and distract them from undertaking much-needed reforms. They can also provoke a radical reaction. If Tunisia's or Egypt's military attempts to claim power or block Islamists from participating in the new regime, or the region's monarchies seek to keep their regimes closed through repression rather than open them up via reforms, radical forces will only be strengthened. As one example, the opposition in Bahrain, which had been seeking constitutional reforms, has reacted to Saudi action to repress its protests by calling for the overthrow of Bahrain's monarchy instead of its reform. Inclusiveness should be the order of the day.

The other main threat to democracies in the Middle East is war. Historically, revolutionary regimes have hardened and become more radical in response to international conflict. It was not the fall of the Bastille but war with Austria that gave the radical Jacobins power during the French Revolution. Similarly, it was Iran's war with Iraq that gave Ayotallah Ruhollah Khomeini the opportunity to drive out Iran's secular moderates. In fact, the one event that may cause radicals to hijack the Middle Eastern revolutions is if Israeli anxiety or Palestinian provocations escalate hostility between Egypt and Israel, leading to renewed war.

That said, there is still reason for optimism. Prior to 2011, the Middle East stood out on the map as the sole remaining region in the world virtually devoid of democracy. The Jasmine and Nile Revolutions look set to change all that. Whatever the final outcome, this much can be said: the rule of the sultans is coming to an end.